338.477902

*Down the Programmed
Rabbit Hole*

Anthony Haden-Guest

Down the Programmed
Rabbit Hole

Travels through Muzak, Hilton, Coca-Cola, Walt Disney and
other world empires

Hart-Davis, MacGibbon · London

Granada Publishing Limited
First published in Great Britain 1972 by Hart-Davis, MacGibbon Ltd
3 Upper James Street London WIR 4BP

Copyright © 1972 by Anthony Haden-Guest

ISBN 0 246 10598 4

Printed in Great Britain by
Northumberland Press Limited, Gateshead

Contents

Introduction

Comedy is the result of imposing something mechanical upon the living.

Henri Bergson

If there were dreams to sell
What would you buy?
Thomas Lovell Beddoes

The emblem of the Walt Disney World, that ample terrain in the Florida scrublands, portrays the planet Earth with Mickey Mouse ears. A telling enough device, and I had thought of beginning with my account of that magic (and now entirely computerised) kingdom.

But, no. It is a journal, and should begin at the beginning. Not quite at the beginning perhaps because it began on the periphery, and with details. Marshal Tito's Diner's Club card. A *Playboy* centre-fold tacked up among the oleographs of Krishna in a Malaysian kampong. A girl in Leningrad, whose Western collection included two volumes of the *Reader's Digest* Condensed Books. A Paramount Chief in Sierra Leone, one of whose ceremonial robes anticipated a couture motif of 1972, by featuring a design of Coca-Cola bottles on a poly-chrome ground.

All just oddments in themselves, of course, flotsam from the jetsell world of Hilton, Hertz and American Express. Dream fall-out.

These are not further studies of the muscle of the multi-nationals. Corporate gigantism and global sprawl are much to the point, but not all-important. Coca-Cola is quite a little fellow compared with, say, IT&T and is relatively rarely the subject of political ire. But it is the Coke sign that is more widely known than the Cross. For that matter, Pan-Am own more hotels than TWA, but TWA control Hilton International, and it is the Hiltons which have become an image and a myth.

I am interested in the myths, the global imagery which has inevitably been created by the business empires. It has as much to do with landscaping the future as the political wheeling-and-dealing or the wielding of economic strength. *Tarzan versus IBM* was Jean-Luc Godard's original title for *Alphaville* and I had thought of purloining it (one other desperate suggestion: *Future Schlock*) but Tarzan and IBM are both on the same side. Winning the hearts and minds.

My drive is curiosity. There does seem a certain inevitability about the process, or at least a logic. Given a free choice, people seem quite as likely to plump for the products of the chairman of Procter & Gamble as the thoughts of any competitive chairman.

These are journals, so this is journalism. I have not, at any rate, tried for one more critique of the Business Culture, nor even a pop/mandarin celebration. I just wanted to poke around the myth factories, to see where and how it was done, to talk to the people responsible.

They turn out to be high-minded, mostly, and gifted with terrible innocence. There are impressive quantities of bonhomie amongst the landscape gardeners of the new reality, and more than a touch of old-time boosterism. There is a concern for issues, the environmental pieties, oddly mixed with a quite inordinate respect for the rituals of technology. The Space Programme, in this context, has acquired the validating and tedious role of a state religion.

On the other hand, they tend to be sublimely incurious as to effect. There is nothing that cannot be controlled and merchandised. 'The only thing we can't make is something we can't think about,' said Sorenson of Ford's, joyously. 'The perfect Caribbean island didn't exist,' say the ads for Paradise Island (a property of Resorts International Inc.), 'so we created it.'

It has been a journey through an occasionally unnerving terrain, but fertile in spots of dark fun. Monkeys imported for Tarzan movies infest Florida, and super-computers are built half in positive, half in negative. The Muzak satellite is to wing through the heavens no doubt in convenient proximity to the Orbital Hilton. The surreal becomes banal. The chances are that if the world grows Mickey Mouse ears, nobody will notice.

▩ A Trip
to
Tarzana

In which the writer visits Edgar Rice Burroughs Inc. in Tarzana, Los Angeles, and discovers the Apeman's plans for global conquest.

It seemed only proper that the administrative headquarters of Edgar Rice Burroughs Inc. should be located in Tarzana, Los Angeles. However, Tarzana (pop. 20,000 or thereabouts) lies out in the San Fernando Valley and like most of the Valley townships it is, frankly, a pretty torpid place. Not even its name—adopted with the novelist's permission in 1928—can lend it much by way of exotic allure. Neither as Apeman nor as lost Lord Greystoke would Tarzan have found much to recommend it. At least he grunted *Stone jungle!* on glimpsing New York in the last of the MGM Weissmuller dramas. It is doubtful if he would have been moved to even this perverse tribute by Tarzana.

At least, the Burroughs Inc. office has a nice rural feel to it. Trees surround it. Black beams are scarred with real chisel marks. Fleetingly I remember the forest hut so graphically described in *Tarzan of the Apes.*

Inside it is wall-to-wall Apeman. Shelves full of Tarzan first editions and other Burroughsiana. Pictures of the jungle lord in striking postures. 'These paintings were used for the original illustrations,' Bob Hodes says, 'and they've become *priceless.*'

Hodes, who is Vice-President of Edgar Rice Burroughs Inc., and Hulbert—'Hully'—Burroughs, who is the dead maestro's son, are sitting in an executive office. Hodes occupies the desk.

1

He has a forceful manner and a black beard of trimly rakish Beverly Hills cut. His feet are stuck into blue-and-white sneakers with the nonchalance that is quasi-formal in Los Angeles.

Hully Burroughs is sitting in a chair in the corner. He is mildly spoken and inclined to deflect questions of import in the direction of Hodes. Nor does Bob Hodes, a sometime legal whizkid, shrink from his role as Tarzan's mouthpiece.

'I just got back from Europe,' he says with energy, 'and Tarzan is enjoying a fantastic revival. I made deals—*good* deals—in England, France, Holland, Germany, Italy ... All because publishers are taking another look, and saying— *Hey! This is today!*'

Because it isn't just the older generation to whom Tarzan is a hero figure. The young, too, recognise the noble jungle drop-out for what he is. An ecological folk hero! *Sure.* 'He really is. He's done everything. And the issue here is if you have both generations looking on Tarzan as a hero—where's the generation gap?'

It is the authentic note of enlightened mercantilism, and eminently appropriate to Edgar Rice Burroughs Inc. Tarzan is both image and industry. As an image he belongs to an exclusive twentieth-century pantheon, a club of super-heroes who demand recognition over immense areas of the Earth's surface. As such he jostles on the altar with an odd *mélange* of idols, and is surpassed by—not Superman, nor Sherlock Holmes, nor Frankenstein's Monster. Even Mickey Mouse is more or less symbolic nowadays: a trademark. When did you last hear Mickey talk?

Nor is the Tarzan industry negligible, though it's hardly on a par with Walt Disney Inc. Even so, Tarzan imagery has spread into every form of art, life and merchandise. Tarzan exists in twenty-six novels, now in his sixtieth year re-issued for the umpteenth time in the UK by Flamingo books. The arboreal demigod still swings in a dozen languages through the comic strips.

Tarzan has, of course appeared on a billion dollarsworth of celluloid and video. There have been fourteen movie-actor/

apemen, and Ron Ely, on the television. Inevitably there are plans for more, and a season of Tarzan oldies are planned for London's National Film Theatre.

The Apeman has, of course, been widely franchised. Tarzan has sold, and sells, a welter of virile goods including petrol, sweatshirts and infants' bow-and-arrow sets. There is Tarzan bread and Tarzan bubblegum. Small vans pushing Tarzan soft ice-cream trundle around the London streets at the appropriate season.

Tarzan has inspired the sincere, if unwanted, compliment of numberless imitations including *Bomba, the Jungle Boy*; *Tam, Son of the Tiger*; *Kaspa, the Lion Man*; *Kioga, Hawk of the Wilderness*; and, but of course, *Sheena, the Jungle Queen*. In other unsolicited borrowings of a higher, or occasionally lower, sort Tarzan has been made sport of in comedy routines, contemporary paintings and movies.

Recent plans for a Tarzan musical have apparently been shelved. This is a pity. It was to have been designed by Salvador Dali and produced by certain of the producers of *Hair*. Rights were being peddled, Bob Hodes says with zeal, for half of one per cent more than the George Bernard Shaw Estate got for *My Fair Lady*—'because I wanted the richest deal that's ever been made on behalf of an author!'

The plans will doubtless be resumed some day or other. Tarzan the Invulnerable. Just as with the Disney menagerie there is some sort of intrinsic magic which (so far) not even the crassest of merchandising seems able to destroy. Failure is not in Tarzan's make-up.

Which is not inexplicable. Tarzan and Edgar Rice Burroughs Inc. grew out of a classic Failure-Success Story. 'I was born in Peking at the time that my father was military adviser to the Empress of China and lived there, in the Forbidden City, until I was ten years old.' So Burroughs once began a short autobiography accurately entitled, *Edgar Rice Burroughs, Fiction Writer*.

Actually, Burroughs was born in Chicago, 1875, and his father was a distiller of fluids for car batteries. He was thrown out of school, failed to get into West Point for an army commission, so joined up as a US Cavalry trooper, but was in-

3

valided out a year later with a dickey heart. He went gold-prospecting in Idaho—now being married—but lost his stash over the card-table, and the venture collapsed. At twenty-nine, he donned the blue serge uniform of a railway police-man in Salt Lake City, which he abandoned for the marginally greater freedom of travelling, at one time or another in light-bulbs, confectionery, pencil sharpeners, and a patent cure for alcoholism. All failed. The Burroughs family, back home now in Chicago, had to be supported by his parents.

But ERB had begun to write. His first product was in a science-fictive vein, ultimately called *The Princess of Mars*. The author was so upset by his own feverish imaginings that he submitted it to *All-Story Magazine* under the pseudonym of 'Normal Bean', this being British argot for Ordinary Chap. Too British, evidently. The mag purchased the work for $400 but printed the author's name as 'Norman Bean'.

Tarzan of the Apes was ERB's third foray into fiction, and was published by the same organ in 1912, on this occasion at a fee of $700, and embellished with a pic by Clinton Pettee in which the ape-man for the first time, but distinctly not the last, is shown plunging a blade into Numa the Lion. No fewer than fourteen publishers declined to show interest in Tarzan's hardback rights, until rumours of the intensive demand began filtering through and one of them re-con-sidered.

Tarzan of the Apes was published by A. C. McClurg in 1914. The movie rights were turned down by the American Film Co., which is now quite understandably defunct, and were taken up by the National Film Corporation of America. In 1916 the production was put under way, starring a chunky ukelele player, Winslow Winston, who, however, left the set, and history, to join the army, and was replaced by the some-time circus strongman, Elmo Lincoln. The Apes, by the way, were played by the mesomorphs of the New Orleans Athletic Club stitched into skins.

The movie grossed more than a million dollars, one of the very first to do so, and the Tarzan industry was under way. Less than a decade after his failure pushing candy, ERB

4

acquired the palazzo of a newspaper magnate, plus a 540-acre estate into which he plunked five pools.

This is now Tarzana, though unfortunately no longer company property, having been sold off, Hully Burroughs says ruefully, some time in the early '30s.

'If Mr Burroughs had held on to the property he owned here,' says Hodes, with a chortle, 'we wouldn't have to be doing very much else. It's probably worth close to a billion dollars!'

Foresight of this sort, though, being as rare out of the jungle as in, the company's fortunes still must depend not on such accidental acquisitions, but on the initial assets, the Edgar Rice Burroughs product itself. And despite the flawed and frankly undistinguished nature of much of this (not to mention such by-products as the movies), such is the radiant energy of the ERB wishdream that these remain very considerable assets indeed. Like the Disney branded products, these are assets—Edgar Rice Burroughs Inc. feel—which are capable of being merchandised to within an inch of their mythic life.

The books remain the steadiest line, popping into print worldwide without too much prompting from ERB Inc. A certain amount of updating is permitted, Hodes says, especially with regard to such sensitive matters as race.

'A man writing in middle-class white America in 1911 did have, at best, a patronising attitude ... One curious thing, Mr Burroughs used the word "blacks" to describe Negroes, so in 1962 our American publisher asked for permission to change that word because they thought it would be offensive. And it's curious because that's the word now that is the vogue. So you can see what we're up against.'

There has also been a German problem. Understandably, one might feel, since the Burroughs treatment of the Germans was so unfeeling that in 1933 his works were consigned to the bonfire along with those of Einstein and Sigmund Freud. But, no, this isn't the point.

'I just got back from Germany and the publisher there insisted on—*softening* some things. The Germans are very sensitive about giving offence to any nationality.

'Curiously enough,' Hodes says, 'they want to change passages where *other* nationalities were badly treated. They never said a *word* about the treatment of Germans.'

There is also the matter of the Russians. Old ERB himself had been fairly hard-line about this, even including an unflattering vignette of the then Soviet leader in one romance.

'There's a letter from his publisher,' Hodes says, with a gleaming grin. "They said, "See here, you can't use Joe Stalin like this. He's our *ally*" ... and your dad replied "I can use the name any damn way I feel like until he pays me royalties!"'

Right now, though, the company has been pursuing an active *détente* with the Soviet Union.

'I made three trips there, trying to make a deal. But it's so difficult,' observes Hodes. 'I had a very interesting arrangement set up. I found a publisher in Finland who does the overflow work for the Russians. He's got Cyrillic characters and so forth, so we would not be selling *rights* to the Russians, we would be selling *books* to the Russians. And they will pay for books ...

'Also we would take payment in Russian guitars so that they would not have to give away any hard currency. And we had a guitar distributor in Finland who was willing to receive the guitars and pay Finmarks to the Finnish publisher, who would then pay *me* my royalties.'

'I wish that deal had gone through,' says Hully Burroughs. 'It would have been so exciting.'

'The problem with doing business with the Russians,' Hodes explains resignedly: 'They have such a bureaucratic society. They loved the idea, they wanted to do it. But I could see it was like talking to a wet paper bag ...'

Nor, apparently, have dealings with the movie-makers been much better. They have, of course, been financially more fruitful, but equally frustrating. As a matter of fact, ERB Inc. seems inclined to write off just about the entire celluloid Tarzan *œuvre* to date *en bloc*.

'Very few of the films are up to the standard of the original stories,' Hully Burroughs says: 'It's just short-sightedness, in my opinion, on the part of the producers. You remember the

6

Johnny Weissmuller version? This *Me Tarzan—You Jane* stupid inarticulate dialogue? Well, that to me contradicted the idea my dad had of a very articulate, intelligent, well-educated man ...'

But the times they are a-changing, and there are more producers in the offing, Hodes says. More deals. There is that whole little exploited chunk of Burroughs which is set on the planets, for one thing, in which John Carter, a figure of Tarzanic *noblesse*, has interesting adventures on Mars and Venus.

'We'd like to see a Mars picture,' says Hodes.

They will, one feels, they will.

Meantime, back here on Earth, Edgar Rice Burroughs Inc. isn't letting the jungle grass grow under its feet. It isn't enough, they feel, just to sit back and rake in the royalties which are anyway lamentably small. 'For instance, we're doing well if we get six per cent from a paperback,' Hodes says. 'In the movies we get, say, twenty-five to forty per cent. After everybody's finished stealing from us ...'

Larger possibilities are in the air, Bob Hodes says. 'One project that we have that's getting a lot of *my* attention is ... You know the Club Méditerranée? Well, what we are trying to do is what the Club Méditerranée *says* it's trying to do. It doesn't quite go all the way ...

'It's our thought to start a vacation club of Tarzan villages. And the idea is, of course, the African motif ... back-to-nature ... and the complete personal freedom to do anything at all!'

Bob Hodes becomes rhapsodic as he goes into the personal freedoms involved, and it is no surprise to discover that the idea germinated during brainstorming sessions with the talents of *Hair*. Peter Blake once painted Tarzan, Jane and Boy as the sleeky radiant California Family, with the coppery glow rare in Africa, though common in Malibu, and the encompassing jungle somehow an extension of the sanitised foliage around the pool. The conceptual Tarzan villages also begin to sound like one more extension of the Golden State.

'And our people located an island in the Caribbean that's

for sale, and we may conceivably take an option on it,' Hodes says.

An island?

'Of course, the key to this whole thing, we must—we *must* —find a place where there will be no law-enforcement whatsoever. But,' he adds, gloomily, 'somehow governments have a way of ... exerting control ...'

What about a State of Tarzana, I suggest idly, with your own coinage and stamps?

'Don't laugh!' Bob Hodes says. 'Don't laugh! This is not just pie in the sky. We've been talking to the Rothschild Bank in Paris about this. There are a number of very, very small African countries that have *absolutely nothing*. No economy, no nothing!

'All they have is their independence and their UN ambassador, and the thought is to merchandise the whole country ... Take it over! Change the name, and just take this resort idea on a national scale, so the entire country is run as a ... *beautiful place*.'

Gambia, for instance, is under active consideration, Hodes says. This is a small, attractive country on the West Coast, north of Sierra Leone, and not far distant from the area where Tarzan's noble parents were originally marooned. (Scholars have pinpointed Angola, but since ERB never set actual foot in Africa the point is academic.) Fortuitously, I had visited Gambia recently, and found it full of Swedes.

Hodes and Hully Burroughs listen to my on-site report, and ask about the bug problem.

It seemed pretty clean, I say, but mention that theoretically Gambia remains part of the British Empire.

Bob Hodes doesn't seem to think that this would necessarily be a problem, and unveils a model aeroplane for my inspection. He holds it up with enormous panache.

'That's another project,' Hully Burroughs says.

The aeroplane is lettered TARZAN AIR. It has a zebra-striped tail.

'None of this is secret in any way,' Hodes assures me: 'But the difficulty of writing about things like that is I never like to say that we're going to do this, and we're going to do that. And nothing ever happens ...

'Because obviously all these projects are pretty immense, and they're not easily put together.'

To what extent is AIR TARZAN actually, well, serious?

'It depends on the resorts,' Hodes says, sensibly. 'We would run our own charter air-line. Well, we've already investigated that, and the McDonnell-Douglas Aircraft Corporation is willing to assist us in building runways, and airports, and whatever ...

'And there are ways to run our own charter aircraft to these resorts, and then lay off the aeroplanes somewhere else. There are people around the world who know exactly how to do this, how to keep that aeroplane moving, and still it would appear as if it's our air-line.'

How much cash would be necessary for these ambitious schemes?

Not as much as one might think, Hodes says. The aeroplane would be leased. 'And the island?' He broods, momentarily. 'Probably ten million dollars would start it off. And there's a lot of investment capital *just waiting* for projects like this. We have two offers now from companies who want to *manage* this for us ...'

Suddenly, I recall one persistent theme in the Burroughs saga. Not only is the Africa of his mind overrun by apes, and lions, and unruly tribes, criss-crossed by safaris, and plagued by evil explorers intent on stealing the sacred idol's jewel eye, but there are also the beautiful girls in the various Lost, Hidden and Forbidden Cities ... the barely attainable Utopia once only reached by arduous swinging through the unspoilt jungle, but in the conceptual future a few hours away by TARZAN AIR. An available dream. Carefully, Bob Hodes puts his dummy air-liner away.

✖ *We Shall Have Muzak*
(Wherever We Go)

In which the writer encounters Muzak Inc. in Manhattan, and discusses the techniques of human engineering with the Muzak makers. He attends a Muzak recording session, and later visits Muzak's outlying stations, such as that in London.

MUZAK: A Human Engineering Concept
                    (sign in the Muzak Inc. lobby)

'That's one problem that we face today,' says Dr William Wokoun, intently, '... *noise*. We are going to have to protect people against noise pollution.' Dr William (Bill) Wokoun has the precision-trimmed hair, and a suit apparently cut from a Boeing fuselage of the Technocrat, but his face is pallid, *illuminated*: the Scholar. Wokoun works for the Muzak Corporation as Director of Human Engineering.

One pet project, for example—'*Experimental*, you understand?'—has just been tried out in a New York bank. Even banks, it seems, have this noise problem, a sonic overload of ... chairs scraping/coughing/machines spluttering/high heels tittupping over vinyl. 'It is becoming very evident that you've got to protect people who are working,' Wokoun says.

'They will have to wear ear-plugs or ear-muffs. But people don't *like* to do this' (Wokoun explains) 'because it makes them feel ... isolated.

'So we've been experimenting with a way of making it more comfortable to wear the headsets ... by piping in Muzak.'

He pauses. Wokoun has an unusual voice, level, barely inflected, mechanical almost, except for touches of dry humour, and underneath one senses the current of controlled passion.

I have heard this Voice before. It is the voice of NASA man. In fact, before moving to Muzak, Bill Wokoun did work for the US Army, in the Human Engineering Laboratories at the Aberdeen Proving Grounds, Maryland.

Bill Wokoun is ... well, Wokoun; and Jane Jarvis, and Don O'Neill, and Umberto Muscio, are the Muzak makers, and this is big time in Muzak's history. As a concept, it is almost fifty years old. Most importantly though right now *the entire operation is being computerised.* From now on the thinking behind the arrangement of those uniquely woozy medleys will be done not by some cranky programmer but by totally unprejudiced electronic circuitry.

The Muzak Corporation was early in the promising field of landscape-gardening the future. Efficient/Prosperous/Productive. What Muzak calls, with a propriety air, the Programmed Environment.

As my meeting with Muzak approached, my sensitivity to their product heightened. Muzak flowed through my inner ear in department stores, and in hotel lobbies it stippled the air with mascara colours. Muzak stimulated the appetite in expense-account eateries and Muzak assuaged the bruised ego in cocktail-bars. Amongst the tarnish-proof horse-brasses and olde-oak-beamery of London pubs, Muzak plinked inconsolably of new, unhappy, near-by things, and in airliners, just as the neon demanded that belts be buckled and cigarettes scrunched, the Muzak would come welling in, possibly reassuring some, but filling me with alarm.

I had primed myself with brochures. Muzak is an amiable company, and lavish with brochures. *The raw material of Muzak is music,* explains one, succinctly. *Muzak serves 43 of the top 50 largest industrial companies,* observes another. Likewise 22 of the top 25 insurance companies, and 43 of the 50 biggie banks.

Names are invoked. General Motors, Standard Oil, Ford, GE, IBM, Chrysler, IT&T, Texaco, Gulf Oil, US Steel, Westinghouse, EI du Pont de Nemours, RCA, Goodyear, Swift, Procter & Gamble, Eastman Kodak, Greyhound, Atlantic Richfield, International Harvester, Lockheed, Litton, Firestone, General Dynamic and General Foods ... Bank America, the First National City, J. P. Morgan, Wells Fargo ... Sears Roebuck, J. C. Penney, Macy, Gimbel Bros, F. W. Woolworth and Great Atlantic & Pacific Tea.

A Homeric catalogue of the American Epic, in fact, and overseas Muzak has become, if anything, still more of a by-word. *'Today Muzak programming',* another pamphlet points out, *'is available in Argentina, Australia, Belgium, Brazil, Canada, Colombia, Denmark, Finland, France, Germany, Great Britain, Israel, Japan, Mexico, New Zealand, Norway, Peru, Philippines, Spain, Switzerland, United States and Uruguay.'*

The University of Alabama play football to Muzak, as do the Los Angeles Rams. Muzak comforts the afflicted in the Dog & Cat Hospital, Garden City, and in Baltimore you can get an earful in a swimming-pool *underwater* showing that they can teach the legendary Sirens a thing or two. Muzak can be heard on the Laurel race track, a Turkish bath in San Francisco, the Houston Astrodome, and (somewhat to my surprise) amongst the plush modernismus of the upper storeys of the Los Angeles Music Centre.

Muzak is to mourn the dead in a scheduled 39-storey 21,000 tomb high-rise cemetery in Rio de Janeiro. George E. Smith, an Illinois agronomist, piped Muzak to his cornfields and reported a triple yield. *'In ice-bound radar stations,'* a further pamphlet says, with a note of lyricism, *'it stimulates the men who man the DEW-line, the Distant Early Warning Cordon.'* Not, one hopes, too much.

There is Muzak in the Pentagon. Both Johnson and Nixon had it in the White House. Nixon has the facility at Key Biscayne, while LBJ uses it down on the ranch, where speakers are individually wired to the trees.

Muzak will attend your birth in (for instance) the Mercy Hospital, Carolina; and in (for instance) the Nelson Funeral Home, Arkansas, or a crematorium in Birmingham, England, Muzak will lament your passing. Up on the hem of Outer Space, is was not *Also spracht Zarathustra* but Muzak that was piped up to Neil Armstrong and Buzz Aldrin as they prepared to annexe the moon.

The Muzak of the Spheres . . . and what was this first galactic programme? No answer. *'Maybe'*, Umberto Muscio, Chairman of Muzak hazarded, *'NASA don't want that disclosed.'*

Muzak turns over four hundred million dollars a year. It is heard by eighty million people *every day*. Which in terms of (admittedly captive) audiences leaves other music makers from Bach to the Beatles pretty much nowhere.

The next sound you hear may probably be the sound of:

Spinning Wheel, in an expertly processed version of that Blood, Sweat and Tears hit, was playing in the lobby of my corporation's Manhattan HQ on my first visit. The new uptown offices in the lee of the Pan-Am Building are being got together, and these are the old executive offices downtown on Park, on top of what are still the Muzak works. There are warm, nutritious tints everywhere, orange, peach, and fudge, and the chairman's office has those artless bits of bric-à-brac that executives like to give each other, awards for public speaking, and for flying a million miles; the business culture equivalents of the heads of buffalo and the stuffed bluefish. Also, framed repros of old broadsheets including—a deft touch —*The Beggar's Opera.*

Umberto Muscio greets me *con brio*. He is (he explains) an unreconstructed JFK Liberal 'like Tom Watson at IBM'. This is a (fair) intimation that he is informed/articulate/aware of the humane issues of the time. Muscio—'Bing' to his friends —is wearing a superbly-cut pinstripe suit, and his manner is at once animated and languid. His face is not unlike the young Stravinsky's, mobile and sensitive, with the in-depth tan of an expensive shoe.

Zippily, Muscio gives me a résumé of Muzak thinking. 'Muzak isn't music to *listen to*,' he emphasises: 'It is music to *hear*. Muzak is *functional music.*' There are three main Muzak programmes, for Heavy Industry, Light Industry, and the Basic or Office Programme. In each of these, fifteen minutes of music, or 'sound-in-motion' as Muscio likes to call it, is followed by fifteen minutes of silence.

'We once had a sales manager,' Muscio recalls, 'who took

the line that we should say we are selling the *silence* as much as the Muzak.'

Upon reflection, this line of sales-talk was dropped.

Muzak, says Muscio, is truly international. Manila, Melbourne and Miami enjoy precisely the same programming, with a disregard of so-called cultural differences lamentably rare elswhere. (Later I discover, with a twinge of pride, that only Great Britain has the mixture of cussedness and financial muscle to demand its own mixes. A bit more rock.)

And Moscow? Well, yes. Muscio recalls having lunched with a correspondent from *Izvestia* who was most interested. Music is, it seems, currently being tried on the Soviet working man, but not yet Muzak. Oh well, the company probably wouldn't get their royalties anyway.

Other international oddities are discussed. As of this moment, for instance, neither Holland nor Italy are favourable. Governments are *sensitive* about the air. 'They think we might send coded messages ... or some guy might seize the whole multiplex, and start broadcasting *Arise! Ye wretches of the Earth!* or something ...

'Greece? Yes, I think we're going into Greece. The *ironical* thing is that we have no trouble in totalitarian countries. We have no problem in Spain.'

The global spread is being accomplished by means of a franchise system, which Muscio expounds *andante*. Now Muzak franchises are not easily to be had. Like titles of the Holy Roman Empire or taxi-driver medallions in Manhattan they must be inherited, purchased or somehow conned from the present lucky owners, and the going-rate is forty times the monthly billing—'which depends on whether we are talking about Los Angeles or Muskego, Oklahoma'.

The Muskego statistics don't come to mind, but the privilege of wiring the Angelenos in might change hands, Muscio believes, at roughly two million dollars.

Franchises have included Dr Frank Stanton, of CBS, who has sold Cincinnati to Danny Kaye, but retains Columbus and Lexington. The chairman of Loft's Candy has a franchise, as does the man who bought the Detroit Tigers. The *Philadelphia Bulletin* and the *Baltimore Sun* are just two franchisees better known in other media, as—by an imaginative extension of their own turf—are the publishers of *Better Homes and Gardens.*

The Copenhagen franchisee, Muscio says joyfully, is a famous musician, namely Bent Fabricius, composer of *Alley Cat,* who also has designs on Norway. The Austin, Texas, franchisee is that loyal consumer, Lyndon Baines Johnson.

What of Muscio himself before his connection with Muzak?

He was, he says, with an air-conditioning firm.

An air-conditioning firm.

Muscio grins, understandingly. 'There *is* some sort of co-relation ... I mean, both Muzak and air-conditioning are part of the *Environment.*'

This is, of course, a voodoo word nowadays. It is capitalised with the same reverential emphasis that used to be allowed to 'Free World', say. And the Muzak Corporation is very big on the Environment. Hell, even their house magazine is called *Environs.* But the thing is that the attitude of Muzak to the Environment is essentially *dynamic.* It is not (as so many other corporations see it) some great, circumambient passive glob, which gets fouled up, and causes an expensive fuss. The Environment according to Muzak is something to be *created.* And, appropriately for a firm whose interest in it is almost paternal, their vision of things to come is one of shining optimism.

Glowingly, Umberto Muscio talks of piping Muzak to the housewife, thereby (somehow) enhancing the privacy of the home. Outdoors, Muzak will wing across the open spaces. The potential in mood-control and in crowd-control has hardly been *scratched.* 'All this is part of the work of our Human Factors Division ...'

But what of that awkward squad who don't actually *want* Muzak as part of their Environment? Now or ever?

'Oh *those,*' Muscio says, infinitely weary. He contemplates the Culture Klan. 'You know I was at this meeting the other day, and I was approached, and they said, you know, with this *wonderful opportunity* why is it that you don't improve the cultural taste of people?

'Now we obviously can't play Beethoven's Fifth. It would

be almost sacrilegious, because we have to play in these ... segments. What can you do? A one minute segment? Two minutes? The answer is that we're not a cultural medium. Muzak is part of the Environment and we've got to be Contemporary' (another voodoo word) 'but, beyond that, we can't cater to ... *tastes*.'

Muscio *furioso*. He mentions an article he has enjoyed. It makes a telling point about the Eastern Liberal Establishment. 'They are an *ethnic group*. They all think the same. And one of the things they think is that they don't like Muzak.

'You know why? *They don't like it because it's too popular, that's why!*'

No, the business of Muzak is business, and not with the intelligentsia, but in the great world out there. Even in the great world, though, are there not some grouchy citizens less than grateful for the service?

Yes, and this is what Muzak calls the *irreducible minority*. 'But in an office some people might not like the air-conditioning. Or the colour of the walls. The *good* thing about a democracy is that minorities get their say, but a minority cannot *run* a majority. You know Orwell's *1984*?' Muscio glances at me, shrewdly: '*Everybody is equal but some are more equal than others*.'

The quote, or rather slight misquote, comes in fact from *Animal Farm*, but I take the point, and allusion to either of Orwell's works seems courageous, under the circumstances. The Orwell *œuvre*, does rather seem to spring to the collective Muzak subconscious though. One headline in the *Muzak Bulletin* (put out by the British franchisee, Associated Television) reads: '*A Muzak transmission studio is a dream of 1984 automation*.'

'If Muzak makes people happy ... and contented in their environment,' Muscio asks, commonsensically, just a touch plaintively, '*like* air-conditioning or a colour-scheme—*How can it not be good?*'

A Brief History. The Muzak Story begins in 1922, which was when Major General Squier, then Chief Signal Officer in the US Army, but not above a spot of business on the side, took out a historic patent. This was for transmission into the home of 'news, instructions, music, local advertising etc.'.

Company histories often have rather a biblical ring. Antique tales of power, glory and cunning, wars of attrition, expansion and succession are lent a determinist, genealogical flavour. The Book of Muzak is no exception.

The Squier Patent was acquired by the North American Company. The North American Company begat Wired Radio Inc. and Associated Music Publishers Inc.

And in the Year 1934 Wired Radio Inc. begat the Muzak Corporation.

And in the Year 1936 the Muzak Corporation got it together and said *Let there be Sound!*

And in the Year 1941 an interest leading to complete control was acquired by Mr William Benton, later to become Senator Benton, and—later yet—to control the *Encyclopedia Britannica*, which processes and disseminates fact rather as Muzak does sound.

And most recently, Muzak became part of the Wrather Corporation, which is run by Jack Wrather who likewise controls Lassie, the Lone Ranger, and the Disneyland Hotel.

And, right now, Muzak either is, or is not, about to be taken over by TelePrompTer, whose fortune was made from the idiot-cards that help out TV performers. The only problem here was a small hassle in which TelePrompTer and Mr Irving Kahn, its chairman, were variously accused of bribery, conspiracy and perjury in attempting to get an exclusive cablevision franchise for Johnstown, Pa. Well, the Johnstown mayor resigned. All will, no doubt, sort itself out.

As to the *inner history* of Muzak, however, the metamorphosis came in the mid-forties. Until then the service had been canned Background Music, pure and simple, a cheap and compact substitute for those seedy string ensembles whose greeny-black dress-clothes were all too visible through the potted palms.

The programmes of the time are menu-like in format, and wanly evocative.

In 1939, for instance, the schedule began at six p.m. with *Wai O Mine Haha*, an early example of Hawaian kitsch, followed by *Rosemarie* (Rudolf Friml). At 6.45 *Tears from my Inkwell* was moistly succeeded by *April Showers*—'Bombo'. Also *I'm in a Dancing Mood*, Victor Herbert's *Debutante Waltzes* and—that touch of class—Tchaikowski's *Mélodie Opus 42, No. 3*. The fun concluded with Sigmund Romberg's *You are all I've wanted* at nine sharp. Heartstring-tweaking stuff all of it, but a far cry from the standards of today, as pithily expressed in the slogan—'*Muzak—Specialists in the Physiological and Psychological Applications of Music*'.

'It was Don who first started Muzak on its new line,' Wokoun says. Don is Don O'Neill, Muzak's senior programme controller and ranking egghead. He has a baggy grey suit, and his manner is professorial, reserved, with unexpected quirks of humour. O'Neill joined Muzak in 1936, and within a decade his vision of the New Muzak was beginning to emerge. 'It was 1946 . . . I decided on the rhythms fairly early.'

These are the rhythms of the Ascending Curve, and they are fundamental to a theory that is complicated without being particularly complex. An initial observation was that production in factory and office, just about anywhere, I daresay, is inclined to *slump* during the day's work. Closer study revealed a double slump. In the middle of the morning, and the afternoon.

Plentiful work has gone into buttressing these interesting findings. The pioneer research of Wyatt & Langon, for example, establishes no fewer than four main work-curves, ranging from the collapse of utter fatigue to the subtler decline that occurs '*when the work is distasteful and the operative is severely bored*'.

Don O'Neill's specific creative flash was that productivity might be stimulated if the monotony was relieved by *music*. Not any old music. This would defeat the object by grabbing the attention itself. No, *functional music*. Thus the New Muzak was founded on a perception which is, in its way, not unlike the luminous paradoxes of Zen.

Boring work is made less boring by boring music.

Further work, understandably, has gone into amplifying this cheering insight. Weighty reports have weightier titles. EFFECTS OF MUZAK ON INDUSTRIAL EFFICIENCY,

18

EFFECTS OF MUZAK ON OFFICE PERSONNEL, and, yet more austerely confident, APPLICATION OF FUNCTIONAL MUSIC TO WORKER EFFICIENCY.

They are chock-a-block with graphs/charts/lists. The daily ups-and-downs of the Severely Bored are plotted, numbered and gridded into what look like slices of an Alpine *massif*. The tone is clinical, even modest, laced headily with para-scientific verbiage. We are, for instance, warned agains the 'Hawthorne Effect', an old chestnut which means, '*A change in employee productivity caused by an awareness that reactions to environmental changes are being observed.*' Oh, yes. Quite so.

Other basics are brought to light by RESEARCH FINDINGS ON THE PHYSIOLOGICAL AND PSYCHOLOGICAL EFFECTS OF MUSIC AND MUZAK. Music, it explains, is not just the magic force it was to the 'Primitives', nor the moral force it was to the Greeks. Music has scientific properties also.

Just to enumerate a handful: It increases the metabolism; spreads up breathing, typing, writing; increases (or, sometimes, *decreases*) muscular energy; reduces suggestibility; delays fatigue; facilitates attention; and produces marked, if rather variable, effects on blood pressure and pulse.

By 1956, making use of all these foibles of the flesh, Don O'Neill finally had workable *Muzak Programming and Stimulus Charts*. Patterns with upward scoops of sonic stimulus which *exactly* compensate for those dark quarter-hours of the soul when '*employee's residual energy is lowest*'. Sonic splints and bandages for the ailing psyche.

The music, O'Neill explains, should embody a 'constant progression of brightness'. This is done by analysing the separate segments into their constituent chunks, namely Tempo, Rhythm, Instrumentation, and Tonal Mass (this last meaning the 'difference between, say, a violin, a quartet, and a full string section'. All these properties arc assessed in the *Muzak Mood Rating* in which the bit of music, scores from a sombre Minus Three to an ecstatic Plus Eight.

The fifteen-minute silences in between the fifteen minutes of sound are, O'Neill adds, because other studies have shown

19

that, 'The maximum you should play in any working area is about half the time the employee is there.'

Not unnaturally, a properly got together Mood Stimulus Progression Chart looks like the group electro-encephalogram of the Addams Family. But even analyses as sophisticated as these do not satisfy the Muzak men. 'We are now looking at some of the more physiological things again,' confides O'Neill.

Recent scrutiny has apparently nailed down two big variables in music: the Melody and the Rhythm. 'In one study we found a *second* melodic factor but'—sadly—'It didn't hold up. It may be a Will o' the Wisp ...

'Now we are hypothesising—no more than that right now— from observations we have made of hospital patients that these may be related to the activity of the nervous system. So that rhythmic music may stimulate the *sympathetic* system and melodic music may stimulate the *para-sympathetic* system.'

I suppose I look puzzled, because Bill Wokoun explains: 'We've been finding something with our patients at St Joseph's.' This is the Yonkers hospital where Muzak is wired into the wards: 'The cardiac cases seem to respond better to melodic music, while the peptic ulcer patients seem to respond better to rhythmic music.'

And this, it is intimated, is just a beginning. Muzak is getting closer, ever closer, into transforming this elementary tinkering into an exact science ... *the Total Programme* ... Which will (I suggest) be able to pep people up or quieten them down?

O'Neill ruminates.

'You're simplifying rather grossly, but that is basically the point of it. Yes.'

'We are not so much interested in what music we use,' O'Neill sums up, crisply. 'It is with the *sequence* that you achieve results.'

And the results have been gratifying for just about all concerned. One Muzak report details the results of '*studies of attitudes of thousands of employees towards Muzak in 105 companies*'. The emphasis is on the effects upon productivity, of course.'*The relationship between such results whether or not an employee "likes" Muzak is, however, tenuous so we have omitted it, even though replies are consistently over 90% favourable,'* says the report, adding quaintly: *'Customers don't buy Muzak to entertain their employees.'*

Satisfied respondents to the questionnaire seem a convincing cross-section of the national life, running from the Aerosonic Corporation and Atlas Underwear down to the US Property & Fiscal Office. Of the 105 companies, 86.4% agreed that Muzak 'helped them in their work'. Admittedly only 48.1% of the toilers at the Austen Riggs Mental Hospital found that 'It makes my work more enjoyable', but the City of Hamilton, Ohio, came up with a 100% response to the same question. (The process of establishing these figures is not always made crystal clear.)

An Alabama knitting mill revealed that production improved by 9.11% after Muzak was installed, and the typists at Lever Bros made 38.8% fewer mistakes. Employee turnover dropped 53.3% said Eastern Airlines who also reported that spot-checks on the switchboard girls at their New York reservations desk (marked over a series of calls on a points system) showed that Muzak had improved *General Conversation Control* from 3.43 to 3.64, *Friendliness of Tone* from 3.28 to 3.40, and *Tact* from 3.34 to 3.66.

At the Prentice Hall direct operation, Muzak diminished lateness by 36% and absenteeism by 12%. *'Older workers',* they noted, *'improved more than did younger workers.'* At the Toledo Scale Company there was a useful 16.8% improvement in 'reading comprehension'.

The University of Illinois, Dept of Mechanical and Industrial Engineering, found a 17-18% improvement reflecting *'The effect of background music on productivity of different monotonous tasks'.* (Well, *somebody* has to do them.) In the West Delaware High School, Iowa, *'More than 70% of the students who responded believed that the music helped them in school.'* In the Long Branch High School, New Jersey, eighteen out of twenty-five teachers advised the use of Muzak. Six found it helped with discipline.

I telephone to arrange another meeting. Muscio is on another call, and I am put on hold. A muted click and the instrument is glutinous with, of all things. *Greensleeves*. I press it to my ear, transfixed, a Ray Bradbury sound addict, until Muscio comes on, full of vim.

'What do you think? It's a new experiment, completely new. Reservation desks, complaints departments in stores, they want something to listen to. Just *waiting* makes it kind of worse.'

He switches me back for a taste of Merrie-England, but inadvertently cuts me off.

My next meeting with Wokoun and O'Neill. Also present is Muscio, between spurts of office activity; and Jane Jarvis, an amiable and efficient lady, who is currently engaged in codifying, storing—yes, computerising—this entire inventory.

The inventory is crucial. There are thirty thousand compositions in store: say, five weeks, six days, and eighteen hours of non-stop listening pleasure, without ever hearing the same bit twice. Much of the inventory has been pretty much put to sleep, but even so Muzak is a treasure-trove for the determined archaeologist, with magic moments constantly reappearing from composers and works long since elsewhere lost in oblivion. In a Muzak speaker (to quote William Burroughs, sprig of the computer family, in another context) *Dead Fingers Talk*. How else can one catch Satin Slippers and Scarf Dance? Czibulka, Franz Drdla, Cyril Scott, and Eurovision's Beautiful Losers of Yesteryear? Snatches from neglected virtuosi like Chaminade and from all-too-shortlived musicals like *Twang*?

Muzak does not, however, spend much time wading across the marshmallow-lands of its past. Every year some three hundred new selections are recorded. 'Take something we did ten years ago and something we do now. We have strengthened the rhythms,' O'Neill says. 'Mr Muscio has been leading us in this path.'

'My theory is very simple,' Muscio says: 'Although Muzak is *heard* rather than listened to, I still maintain it has to be done in Contemporary Style, because—although you may not be conscious of it—it will still *affect* you. So we make the music as much contemporary idiom as we possibly can.'

A demonstration-track is played. Pre-Muscio.

'Can you hear the difference?' says Jane Jarvis. Yes, it is sort of soupy.

'You can *hear* that orchestra,' chuckles O'Neill.

'Hungarian uniforms,' says Muscio, *'with epaulettes.'*

Now we get the Muscio Sound. It is bouncier, incontestably, but still no threat to Tamla-Motown. 'We don't play Hard Rock because it's a little too ... obvious,' Muscio agrees, but he adds that what used to be the Mantovani audience is now the Bert Kaempfert audience. Well, yes, I say, but is that change quite revolutionary *enough*?

'You just took one of the points that I think is damned important,' says Muscio, 'and that is that a whole generation has grown up since Elvis Presley. We live in a world of accelerated change, and the one facet of our culture which probably manifests that change more than any other is the music. If you've got a whole new generation since Elvis Presley which has grown up ... with that, you know, we've got to change the music *to* that.

'And this is one of the changes we've been doing. It's *evolutionary*. Obviously, you can't just—*voom!*' (finger click) 'go from old-type Mantovani to ... you know, *juxtapose* the two. But we've done an evolutionary change. We're very conscious of the young audience, and we have done music with them in mind, and recognising that they are going to be the people listening ten, fifteen years from now, and they are the people who are working in offices *now*.'

I examine the Muzak shopping lists. Tearsheets of the Top 100 from *Cash Box* and *Billboard*'s Hot 100, with the possibles ticked. Yes, the ticks have been accumulated by the showtunes and by slush balladry, but not altogether. I have just been treated to a processed *Woodstock* and Muscio is talking knowingly of Frank Zappa: 'He's very clever. I think we've used a couple of his things ...'

Later I ask Jane Jarvis if any group has ever refused rights for his material to be used.

'Well, yes. That *has* happened. But it's only because they don't realise how *wonderful* the exposure is. They generally come around ...

'You know, we actually have rekindled interest in a lot of things by our exposure. As a matter of fact, we've had people say—Gee! I forgot I wrote that tune.' (She laughs, happily.) 'We did a tune which was written by Charles Tobias, who had a string of probably two hundred hits ... *Misused* ... and one was *One Dozen Roses*, which was a big hit during World War Two. At any rate we did a tune of his called *Little Curly Hair In The High Chair*, and he had actually forgotten that he had written that song!'

Yes, but who has refused permission? Protest Groups?

'No, no, no. It's never that. It's always a new publishing company that simply doesn't know anything about the business, and it's generally a new group that suddenly comes to fame, and for some reason or other don't know how important a thing like this is ...

'Oh, it happens very rarely. Generally all we do is refer them to the big publishing companies, and it's: *Gee! I hope I didn't give you the wrong impression!*'

Why then have neither the Beatles nor the Stones yet had their material used?

'That's only because their lyrics are so vital to their tunes ... we thought we would actually not do justice to them. We *did* once do a Beatles number. However it was never released in this country for some reason or other. I don't know why. It was before I was in charge here.'

Never the Stones?

'We've *never* done any of those. They simply don't lend themselves to the Muzak concept. They're very attractive, I mean, I have several Stones albums, but they're not ... *melodious*. Of course, that's just my opinion and we may change our minds about it.'

So nobody has yet priced themselves out of the Muzak market?

'Oh *Good Lord* no. You know we've had Ted Heath do many arrangements for us ...'

As to Muzak-Rock, Jane Jarvis explains that Muzak takes the *music*, not the groups.

'Those groups, you know, charge astronomical fees and, furthermore, their rendition wouldn't fit in ... In other words the rock groups that you refer to are actually slanted to *public performance* as much as to anything. They think of the way they look in person, and the way they appeal in person ... and as young people listen to the albums they recreate in their minds the actual playing of these things.

'Whereas we are only interested in the *sound*. So in order to have the ... *complete ear appeal* we hire musicians who are very adept at rock.' Jane Jarvis pauses. Have I finally got it?

'We do,' she amplifies, 'what we call *Professional Rock*.'

All the merchandise that Muzak acquires is re-recorded, processed into the correct consistency. The human voice being notoriously distracting, vocals are removed. Good arrangers are vital, and there are about forty-five on file. 'We keep looking for new people,' says O'Neill. 'We get reports ... and we have various men who are shall we say in the *contemporary* vein? Last year, for instance, we used Nick Perito, who is the arranger for ... *Perry Como*. And Galt McDermot, who wrote the score for *Hair*.'

What did McDermot do?

'Well, we just picked out three or four songs. *Good Morning, Starshine,* and *Hair*, and ... I forget what the name of the song is. And'—chuckle—'he just made 'em a little less *wild*.

'And we select the top musicians in the City of New York. Men that can walk into a studio, and you can throw a piece of music at them. And they run this thing down, maybe once or twice, if that much, and then they'll play the number as though they've been playing it all the while.

'And we'll do, you see, the equivalent of an LP in two and a half hours.'

There was, for instance, one recording session in which Nick Perito and a seventeen-man orchestra polished off twelve numbers, including the theme from *Love Story*. A Muzak brochure (almost inevitably) celebrates the event. A still from the movie is speckled pink and silver, and the wording does, perhaps, give an idea of Muzak's unearthly expertise.

The original screenplay arrangement of Love Story *was designed to set a scene, to describe a situation and to identify with leads. Emphasis is on guitar and piano, with orchestra in subordinate role.*

The Muzak interpretation, created by Nick Perito to specification, is arranged to produce a desired effect. While we feature piano and guitar they are employed as part of a broad orchestra feature. By design the Muzak version of Love Story *is flowing and beautifully interpretive, all the while keeping an almost mystical tempo, both in fact and by implication. The Muzak version is full sound at all times regardless of the number of musicians actually playing.*

The recordings are graded in terms of stimulus potential. Which partly depends, naturally, on which of the three Muzak programmes is being considered. 'If you've got a lot of machines around and then you put in violins,' O'Neill points out, 'the machine noise is going to *mask* the violins.'

So the Heavy Industry programme requires something 'stronger ... more compulsive'. Not *too compulsive*, of course, Productivity isn't boosted when inattentive hands are lopped off by lathes. 'For the Office Programme the rhythms would tend to be a little ... *sweeter*.' Like *Love Story*, in fact.

All these vital statistics are recorded. The Group; the Artist; the Playing Time; the Rhythm, Tempo, Instrumentation. Everything that can help the programmer, to marshal the music together into quarter-hour stretches of Ascending Curve. And to put all *those* together to create the Muzak Stimulus Curve.

'What we call', Muscio says, 'the Ultimate Print-Out.'

We are the Muzak Makers
We are the Dreamers of Dreams

A stroll around the Muzak plant is a formidable experience. All that hi-precision hardware, a zillion iggly bits smoothly packaged in *Star Trek*-Bauhaus, soundlessly disgorging sound into the aether. This is the NASA aesthetic, with the same sensation that what is going on is either urgently necessary or desperately trivial.

I am accompanied by Muscio, and by a Senior Vice-President, JRH (Hank) Wilson, who carefully makes it plain that he is not the man to explain the abstruser reaches of Muzak Theory. 'I'm just Vice-President of Products. Under that comes all engineering. It is my responsibility to see that Muzak sounds right from its inception here to its ultimate use.'

What is going on right here, for instance, is the actual taping of a Muzak programme. Tapes spool unstoppably through the banked machines, while overseers sit in small cubicles. I am introduced to Milly, a sedate blonde. Does she ever get tired of Muzak?

'I love Muzak,' she says.

'I never asked her if she liked Muzak before,' Muscio says, shaking his head with wonderment, and beaming.

'I *love* Muzak,' she repeats, stoutly.

Wilson indicates Milly's dashboard. 'You'll note here the lever labelled compression.' Yes. 'The reason is that ... well, this is not what the *composer* of the selection would like aesthetically, or the *orchestra leader*, but if we're heard in noisy areas it is essential that we narrow the dynamic range.

'Otherwise, in a noise situation, the soft notes will fall *under* the noise, you see? In essence, what we're doing is bringing up the level, like you'd bring up volume control, which brings up the soft patches too ...'

Wilson pauses, seeks *le mot juste*.

'Then we ... *squash* the ones that are too loud.'

Ordinarily Muzak compresses up to fifteen decibels, but will on occasion go to twenty-five. And isn't this likely to have quite a pronounced effect?

'Well, yes. Like I say aesthetically we certainly aren't perfect. But'—genially—'we are respectful about it.

'Designing and building our own equipment is extremely important. Muzak cannot accomplish what it was designed to do unless we approach the *natural sound*. We try and control the quality as it is played back all over the world. True we don't *get* it all over the world, because of importation problems.' (Ruefully.) 'Therefore we don't have total standardisation of equipment.'

And how much does this great intestinal tract actually cost?

'Good Lord! I never added it up. I guess ... half a million at least.'

Further on is the Special Studio, whose programmes other than the three main ones are got together. With technic joy Wilson fiddles with the gizmos. 'Are you a stereo fan? If you'll kindly stand there, you'll hear some *beautiful* separation ...'

I stand there. *The Exodus Theme* is followed by *California, Here I Come,* and, yes, the separation is beautiful.

Special Programmes include Travel Muzak, for planes and things. 'That's just straight background music. There's no programming curve to it at all.' And also more exotic delights. There is the machine that is forever waiting to drop a helping of Irish jigs in the aural broth on St Patrick's Day.

What better way to add to a restaurant's motif than to have a selection of ethnic music? demands a writer in *Environs,* sensibly. *From German tunes to Irish and Jewish favourites. You can have music from any country.*

Hard rock is a must in any boutique to help create a mod mood. Muzak has programmes of hard rock, soft rock ... even soul music.

There is even a selection of non-denominational music appropriate to the solemnity of a funeral home. Anything at all—from show tunes to country-western to melodies from the gay nineties. Just ask for it and Muzak has it—for all types of businesses.

Then there are those historic programmes in which the Muzak people take a special pride, like the one which choired Pope Paul as he moved through the heavens by Avianca flight to Columbia. This was an assemblage of light classical and such, with a diplomatically Italianate touch. *Allegretto in G Major, Cavalleria Rusticana* and *La Traviata,* in properly rewrought chunks, were among the secular delights which accompanied His Holiness in the sky. Also—and but for the profound earnestness of Muzak Inc. one might have suspected a merry prankster—a snatch of Brahms' *Cradle Song.*

La Traviata also figured in the programme that was hurriedly taped after the assassination of President Kennedy.

Agonised thought went into this. The intention was to steer a course between the outright frivolous and the intolerably gloomy. A note, in fact, of sombre uplift but carefully skirting the religious sound. 'We are played in *bars* and places,' explains Don O'Neill. The day began with Beethoven and concluded with Tschaikovsky. In between—well, I can't do better than reproduce some characteristic segments of programming.

Romance of Nadir
Song of Songs
Our Love
Andante Cantabile
Lamp is Low
A Dream
My Own
When Shadows Fall
Tales of Hoffmann
Story of a Starry Night
Night
Long the Night Without You
Tender Thoughts
When Day is Done

Yes, we get the message. Dreamy and nocturnal, right? Then, a couple of Ascending Curves later:

Swedish Rhapsody
Serenade
A Dream (a popular number this)
Through the Years
Barcarolle
Autumn Song
Midsummer Mood
Intermezzo
Devotion
Largo
Reverie
Angels' Serenade

29

Serenade D'Amore
Autumn Gold
At Parting
Street of Tears
Theme from 'Tenderloin'
Beau Soir

And so on, and on, and moistly, yet merrily on, following the Westerly path of the declining day, while that huge audience —no, not *listens*, but (in the slightly processed lines of the Poet Wordsworth)

> *—hearing often-times*
> *The still, sad Muzak of humanity,*
> *Nor harsh, nor grating, though of ample power*
> *To chasten and subdue.*

Oh, one more thing, remembers O'Neill with a rueful chuckle, what with things getting so emotional in the Dallas aftermath. 'We took *Yellow Rose of Texas* off the air.'

The special programme devised for the cardiac ward in St Joseph's, Yonkers, demanded other skills. This was got together for the severe heart cases who have, evidently, a pronounced tendency to gloom.

'They are thinking—Me! Me!' Muscio explains.

The programme was supposed to induce 'a gentle mood of Euphoria ... nothing too drastic'. Oddly enough, it was later found that the programme wasn't nearly drastic enough The patients actually preferred the red-blooded jollity of the ordinary Cocktail-Lounge-type programme.

It had occurred to me that some of the song *titles* in the first programme might have seemed unfortunate to the more incorrigibly pessimistic of the cardiac patients. *I've Got You Under My Skin* is followed by *When a Maid Comes Knocking At Your Heart*, and *I Couldn't Sleep a Wink Last Night* is soon succeeded by *Please Catch Me, I'm Falling*. But who cares about song titles anyway?

Some, apparently, do.

'We've had ... problems with a couple of songs,' reminisces O'Neill. 'On one of our planes there was a passenger who

30

happened to remember the *second* line of a song. Either her husband was staying, or he was going on another plane, and the second line was, 'We shall never meet again.'

O'Neill and Wokoun chuckle at the memory. Muzak hath power!

'So she had *hysterics*. They had to bring the plane back to let her off. We caught it in the neck for that one.'

Past the Special Programme sector are the Muzak transmitters themselves, oddly megalithic in appearance, an electronic Stonehenge. Here, for instance, and individually labelled, are the machines that service Zum-Zum, the Brasserie, and a special Latinate hotpot for the diners at Mama Leone's. Here are the private *mélanges* for the Sherry Netherlands, the Regency Park; plangent Polynesian stuff for the Hawaii and Trader Vic's, and mixes for the Trattoria Enrico and the Fonda del Sol.

'*Muzak,*' as another glossy hand-out remarks, '*emphasises the quality of good food, drink, and surroundings. It banishes the cold silence that inhibits conversation, replacing it with a blanket of friendly privacy.*'

Friendly privacy ... No wonder the thoughtful restaurateur can expect some return for his attentions. '*Muzak encourages people to linger—to stay for another drink, to take that dessert or other profitable extra.*'

Other transmitters are putting out the three basic programmes, and Muscio becomes lyrical as he describes how— *at this very moment*—a great, lukewarm river of sound is washing through every telephone exchange in New York, and how it is being transmitted further by radio from the top of the Empire State Building, and how it is being picked up by another station halfway out on Long Island, which is—after all—*long*, one hundred and fifty miles: 'From the top of the Empire State Building, between our telephone networks and our repeater, we're covering ... most of New Jersey ... all of Westchester County ... all of New York City ... Long Island ... and Southern Connecticut up as far as New Haven ...'

Muscio gestures. At New York out there, and the East

Coast, spread like a monster ear. Orwell (yes, again) had a vision of the future which was a human boot forever crushing a human face. Umberto Muscio's vision is a kindlier one. A human ear forever plugged with Muzak.

What, by the way, is the actual content of the programme with which this half-millionsworth of hi-grade electronics is— *at this very moment*—inundating the locale?

'We can tell you what is playing *anywhere ... at any time,*' Muscio says, and listens. None of us recognise the tune. He consults a schedule, and his watch.

'It should be the *Nish Waltz,*' he says. 'Then *Begin the Beguine ...*'

The Nish Waltz? We wait a few moments. Yes, *Begin the Beguine* begins.

'*Any* time,' Muscio says, happily.

After the Muzak programme has been beamed over this particular New York turf, it will be sent in to do the rounds. The tape is canned in a metal discoid, and transported to St Louis, first, or Memphis—'Memphis is the most usual'—and they will transmit and send it on to the next centre. There are ninety transmission bases on the Muzak circuit and they will transmit at intervals of a week to give the tape time to be moved.

Finally—after the entire United States has enjoyed the programme—it will be sent around the various Muzak markets abroad. It isn't bad as a global plan really, and if there's a touch of the ox-cart about the way the tapes are transported (planes, trains, boats and such), well, even this is under creative consideration.

'You might be interested,' Muscio wonders, 'in looking into *the future?*'

Yes, I say.

'We are thinking ultimately of *satellites.*'

A Muzak satellite?

Muscio glows. Prophetically.

'When they will be available,' he says.

At which time Muzak will be poised on the brink of eternity, so to speak, but back here on Earth a sign reminds that moth and rust continue to corrupt.

32

In The Event Of Failure Of Basic Programme Do Not Panic, it reads, reassuringly. *Muzak Has An Automatic Sensing Unit Which Will Trigger A Standby M4R Machine Into Operation After Four Minutes Of Basic Programme Failure No Audio. The Sensing Unit Will Automatically Turn On The Bottom Number Three M4R Machine Which Is Taped In A pre-Set Condition.*

The reason being not just commercial. Muzak has *responsibilities*.

'There are people who have become accustomed to listening to us,' Muscio explains, paternally. 'They get up'—Muscio clicks a finger like a metronome—'and they start work —*when* the music starts. And they know it's exactly on the quarter hour.

'So we have to keep going ... We'd have the wrong music for that particular moment in the day, until somebody could get here. But it would still be cycling in the proper'—double finger click—'Fifteen-minute cycles ...'

Just suppose. A multiple blow-out. The main machine *and* all the back-ups. What is the risk of Absolute Silence descending?

Muscio considers. Barring Acts of God or War, he feels, the risk is marginal to the point of invisibility.

'If all three quit, the most we'd be out is ... fifteen minutes.'

I have been looking forward to sitting-in on a recording session. This is to be the New Muzak. 'Not Rock and Roll,' says O'Neill, 'but something a bit ... *jazzy*.' The session is at the Capitol Studio on West 46th, and the group is called 'The Greatest Jazz Band in the World'.

A sound-proof, see-through partition divides the Muzak personnel from the players. We are a small cadre of musicologists and engineers, headed by Jane Jarvis and Dr Wokoun and we are surrounded by that familiar functional gunge, bleary omelette paintwork, and samsonite chairs on spotty lino, empty cigarette packs and styrofoam cups, viscous at the bottom. Also the hardware, knobbed, and dialled, and the crazy green light of the oscilloscope.

The Greatest Jazz Band in the World number eight and

are lined up opposite us, as if waiting for the cyanide pellet, except they are grinning perkily at each other, and at us. They have the Jazzman Look, which is ultra-sharp or ultra-sloppy. There is one serious youth, but mainly they are upwards from middle-aged, and the image is over-familiar, a smudged xerox, from the one with pale, shiny hair slicked back from a ravaged matinée idol profile to the only black, sleepy-eyed, in a narrow-brimmed hat. Middle-Sinatra.

A little banter over the intercom, and off they go.

They are terrific. Revving through, clean and sweet, coasting through the whole programme with hardly one crash of gears. Poor bastards! I think. Old jazzmen never die, they just play away. And for Muzak Inc. this band does include some pretty formidable talent. The balding tenor sax is Bud Freeman, who has worked with Tommy Dorsey, Benny Goodman, Paul Whiteman. Billy Butterfield, on the trumpet, played with Artie Shaw, and also with Benny Goodman. Vic Dickenson, the trombonist in the Sinatra hat, used to play with Basie.

Afterwards, the band has a Coke and a smoke. We go into the studio.

'Congratulations, boys,' says Jane Jarvis, delighted.

'Is this your first Muzak session?' I ask.

'No-o-o-o,' Bud Freeman says, amiably, 'we've done several.'

Have they actually ever heard their product?

'No-o-o-o.'

'I heard it once,' Vic Dickenson disagrees, 'On a lift in San Juan.'

Soon, they say, they are going to London. Will they play in (what is left of) the clubs? They might play in Ronnie's, Freeman says. Just one night. For old times' sake.

This means Ronnie Scott's Club in Soho. Thelonious Monk, Miles Davis and Stan Getz have all done week-long gigs there fairly recently.

Why is the Greatest Jazz Band in the World only contemplating a one-night stand?

Well, Freeman explains apologetically, their fee is sort of ... high. But they'll do one night, just for old times' sake.

They begin to get their instruments organised. Other gigs

have included Nixon's Inauguration, the Lincoln Center, and a private golf singding for Bing Crosby. Also, naturally, the steady work from Muzak.

So much for the easier ironies.

Muzak when soft voices die
Vibrates in the memory

Meanwhile, back in the Human Factors division, Bill Wokoun and, indeed, O'Neill and Jane Jarvis, are just as zealous about the future as Umberto Muscio, plus being a bit more primed with detail.

'The possibilities for crowd control are *extremely* interesting,' Wokoun says. 'There was a police station that was going to install Muzak. That could have been interesting ... No, not the cells. The interrogation area. But a few days before we were going in, a new police chief was appointed.

'As to public places, we really need more experimentation. Of course, it's already in use in several open shopping-areas, but as to streets ... parks ... there are problems of *transmission*.

'We had Muzak in the streets during the Inauguration of President Nixon, from *speakers*. But there's a whole lot more experimentation needed.

'Also we are going to have it in the *home*. We look on the kitchen as a Work Area. There are transmission problems, but we'll do it sometime,' Wokoun assures me, adding with superb intensity: 'Perhaps the Muzak will be co-ordinated with *walls* ... changing colour through the day.'

Jane Jarvis talks about a learning programme she has worked on. Children like to work with the music on nowadays she says, and Wokoun adds that it has been installed in school mathematics classes. He admits, though, that Muzak's help towards mental productivity has been so far beyond their statistical analysis.

'We do not really have any good valuation on this, and I'll tell you why. Whenever you do an experiment, you look for some criterion, and it's very hard, virtually impossible—although we keep trying to chip away at it—to find a way of measuring this.

35

'Let me give you an example.' Bill casts around for an example of mental productivity. 'Suppose you have two men sitting side by side in an advertising agency. One man has one idea in a week, but it's a *very good* idea. The other man has fifty ideas, which are all of them bad. Who of these two men has done better? You need some way, you see, of evaluating the output.

'But there is no way that you can quantify *idea* output at the moment ... Of course, we'd like to be able to do this.'

Measure brainpower? From the outside?

'Yes, the people out at the University of Utah have been very interested in this. But it's difficult to pin down right now.'

Unfolding horizons, indeed. And the Muzak Inc. personnel are tetchy at implied critiques of Muzak's social role.

'I don't think you can call it Big Brotherism,' O'Neill says. 'Is it Big Brotherism to install air-conditioning?' (That recurrent image. Muzak has, after all, been called sound you inhale.) 'Obviously it's good if your workers are happier. They work harder. But is this Big Brotherism?'

It is a reprise on my first briefing and what, I ask, perservering, of the determined dissenters?

'There aren't very many,' says O'Neill.

'Only about three per cent *actively* dislike Muzak,' says Wokoun, scientifically.

'You know,' says O'Neill. That sudden, quirky grin. 'The Classicists ... of Purest Ray Serene.'

But even the Muzak Corporation has had its setbacks. The classicists of purest ray serene have included, for instance, Grand Central Station, in which venue it used to be played over the sound system until it was removed by an unexpectedly vituperative consumer rebellion, and also the Time-Life Building. 'You know ... somebody high up doesn't like it,' Muscio says, wearily tolerant of freakish execs.

Elsewhere, the story is amplified.

'Harry Luce would be *thinking*,' says a Timesman, 'and he'd get into a lift, and he'd be thinking, and suddenly he would hear that ... *stuff*.

'He just said—*Get rid of it!*'

36

The Three Percenters!
Hell's Angels in the Muzak World.
Muzak smiles that tolerant, pitying smile.

Muzak that kindlier on the spirit lies
Than tir'd eyelids upon tir'd eyes

'We're in a slaughterhouse,' Wokoun says, with zeal. 'Apparently they were having problems. The animals' blood would *clot*. They say the blood flows more freely now.' He explains. 'The Muzak relaxes them. And we're in this *cemetery* in California ...'

Muzak Inc. is proud of the imaginative uses to which the service is put. At my request Bill Wokoun has dug out some of the more experimental.

'We served the first submarine that was underwater ninety days in a row ... USS *Skipjack*. As for a zoo, we serve, right now, the Bronx Zoo. And a Dog Hotel, if you like to look at it that way, over in New Jersey.

'They call it the quote Greatest Dog Kennel in the World unquote. We are', Wokoun says, with glee, 'dealing with *superlatives* here.

'And we have farmers that say Muzak makes hens lay more eggs and cows give more milk. Some people say that if you play Muzak to corn it will yield better. There is a franchisee in Florida who is playing Muzak to a grove of mango plants ...'

Mango plants.

'This is not as far-fetched as it may sound. Bugs or birds could be stimulated. After all, they have *colour* preferences. But I would say that these are still only ... interesting possibilities.

'As to open-air areas, there is a park with Muzak in my own home-town, Chicago. And there is a garbage-dump that has Muzak in Minneapolis.

'I imagine that this would be for the *workers*,' adds Wokoun, with sunny humour, 'but if it works on plants, who knows, garbage may be next.'

* * *

Well, not absolutely *next*. Upcoming on the agenda is a more demanding role than the greening of Florida or pollution control in Minneapolis. Vigilance. Human vigilance.

The motorist, for instance. There are experiments at the University of New South Wales testing Muzak *vis-à-vis* driving alertness. Muscio cites Nader approvingly, and adds that the automobile makers have said that the human equipment *behind* the wheel is the real problem.

'Now, if that be so, they have, at least to *my* mind, aggravated the problem. Evidently stereo is the hottest optional item in a car. But entertainment music is meant to be *listened to* where functional music is meant to be *heard*.'

And that late-night radio stuff is the worst thing possible. 'It tends to make you relax, and want to go to sleep.' Which is not, of course, the effect of Muzak.

'I'm not saying, you know, it's the Alpha and Omega to solve all traffic problems. But if vigilance is a factor in automobile driving, then the Ascending Curve makes you more vigilant. And it should be desirable in a car.'

And what could be plainer than that? Nor is traffic hazardry the only field in which Muzak can do its bit for life and limb. Not for nothing is Muzak now listed as *Optional Equipment* with the US Armed Forces.

Bill Wokoun, after all, has been working on the relationship between music and vigilance ever since his old days as a training officer in the Human Engineering labs. In an interesting paper in the *Science Journal* (November 1969) he alludes to important work in related fields. Like the inquiry that D. O. Hebb of McGill made into the effects of monotony.

This revealed that, '*After a period of lying quietly on a soft bed, looking through a translucent visor, with arms encased in padded cotton tubes, the subjects began losing contact with reality and started hallucinating.*'

The monkey tricks of H. G. Harlow at the University of Wisconsin are perhaps even more mindblowing. Harlow was able to establish, clinically, that monkeys would '*learn to dissassemble rather elaborate puzzles for no more reward than the sheer joy of taking them apart*'.

Quite a step beyond the simplistic view of drives in the

Animal Kingdom, as Wokoun emphasises. 'Even *parakeets*, in a study I did one time, will work just to get variety. There's something new in psychology here.'

H. G. Harlow went on to record even more bizarre behaviour patterns among his simian subjects. *'When confined in a closed, darkened box, they pressed a bar to earn glimpses of what was going on in the laboratory outside ... Clearly even animals will work to get a variety of stimulation in their environment.'*

The message comes out loud and clear.

Life confined in a box is boring.

Not even monkeys (or parakeets) like being bored.

Life is less boring with Muzak.

Monkeys confined in closed, darkened boxes will be happier monkeys to the Sound of Muzak.

It was neither Hebb nor Harlow who was to make the most innovative use of these data, but Bill Wokoun. I suppose the most thought-provoking of his experiments was the one that, with admirable thoroughness, he set up twice, a primitive version in 1963, and a more elaborate affair in 1968.

The intention was to check what effect the installation of Muzak would have on the personnel who man the nation's missile sites.

The discovery that human observers, searching for targets on radar scopes, could not perform their jobs effectively for more than half an hour was a momentous one, Wokoun says in the 1968 report (AMCMS Code 5026.11.81900) and who would argue with that? How *did* they find out, by the way? *Despite the importance of these functions, it often proves impractical or impossible to have machines take them over completely.*

Guide-lines had been established in 1963. *'Your buddy's life is in your hands,'* the missile finger-men had been reminded. And while the canned music played, those hands were demonstrably steadier. In this 1968 test *'the subjects were 41 male students from the author's classes at the Human Engineering Laboratories.*

'Each subject was tested while seated alone in one of four

*Industrial Acoustics Co. model 402-A audiometric booths ...
Inside the booths were approximately 6 feet square by 6½ feet
high. A vigilance stimulus box was on the table in front of
the subject. To his left, on the floor, there was a seven-inch
loudspeaker in a closed baffle.'*

The 'Vigilance Stimulus Box', by the way, looks strikingly
like the famous 'Black Boxes' used for telepathic healing, and
other exploits of pseudo-science. Each box was set with four
'magic eyes' mounted 1½ inches apart. The 'magic eyes' were
circular mini-screens, and running from the centre of each
circle to the bottom was an arc of shadow sizeable as a gener-
ous slice of cake.

Periodically, one of these arcs would narrow to a slit. This
was a 'stimulus', and supposedly equivalent to, say, the radar
sighting of a Soviet nuke.

Below each 'magic eye' there was a push-button.

When the subject saw a stimulus, he pushed the push-
button.

The subjects were not told that the background music was
anything to do with the test. Instead, a loudspeaker told them
that *'Modern missile systems are becoming more and more
automated. Once a target has been detected, the system practically runs by itself. It can track the target automatically, compute its course, and fire at it until it has been destroyed. But
soldiers still have to keep watch on radar scopes to detect
targets in the first place, and to decide which targets to fire
at. This experiment will measure how well you can detect
target signals.'*

It had already been shown in 1963 that the men were more
watchful with canned music than without it. The idea here
was to sharpen it up a bit, so as to get the Muzak just right,
and not have the chaps snoozing on the job.

'Natural' Wide Range music and filtered music were
played, alternatively. 'Filtered' means that the music just has
pitch. The harmonics have been filtered out, under which
circumstances, Wokoun notes with interest: *'One Bell Laboratories demonstration shows that a soprano, a piano, and a
factory whistle sound alike.'*

So, the Muzak played.

The Stimulus Boxes, intermittently, stimulated.

The subjects observed.

Other observers, unobservable thanks to a clever system of one-way windows, observed the subjects.

The results of the test were entirely gratifying. Several recommendations were made regarding the Defence of the West. Briefly, it was found that 'natural' sound gave more dependable results than filtered sound. Also, the vigilance of the missile men would be affected by the *instrumentation*. Strings being a touch soporific, what this particular military situation required (observers said, without apparent irony) was a reliance on Brass.

Observers through the booth's one-way windows, sums up the report, contentedly, *showed that the subjects virtually never pressed buttons unless there was a stimulus.*

Which is virtually splendid.

One nagging disquiet remained, though in my mind, not the report.

Afterwards, the subjects had been asked what they thought of it all. Everybody (well, virtually) liked the Muzak. The 1963 subjects even completed a questionnaire in which they enthused that *The Music was Really Great, The Music helped me to Relax and do a Good Job,* and so on, and so forth, except that there was this—*irreducible minority,* and they didn't like the music one bit.

The Music is Sometimes Disconcerting, they complained. Or *The Music Kept Me From Concentrating.* Or (trucently) *I Didn't Like The Tunes.*

Now it is a fact that anywhere except in the Human Engineering Laboratories the tunes might have been chosen by somebody with a rococo sense of fun. There is *Born Free* and *Please Wait* which is followed, none-the-less, by that stimulating Fifth Dimension hit, *Up, Up and Away!*

The last number but one on the programme is *If You'll Just Come Back To Me.*

I just hope that none of that surly three per cent gets *too* mad.

The United Kingdom Muzak franchise is, I discovered, and

not without a complex patriotic twinge, the fourth largest in the world. It is owned by yet another media operation, Associated Television, which is run by cigar-chomping Lew Grade, also a pioneer in giving the public what they wanted. Muzak UK has an annual turnover of half a million pounds, and some three thousand outlets.

These include such synonyms for the British Way of Life as the Abbey National Building Society; the Automobile Association; Bass Charrington; Birmingham City Council; Brooke Bond/Oxo Limited; British European Airways; British Oxygen; British Steel Corporation; Co-operative Wholesale Society; *Daily Mirror*; East Midlands Electricity Board; Ever Ready; Greater London Council; Green Shield Trading Stamp Company; Hill Samuel; Hong Kong and Shanghai Banking Corporation; Hoover; ICI; Lloyd's Bank; Mars Ltd; Westminster Bank; North Thames Gas Board; Prudential Assurance; Raleigh Industries; Reckitt & Coleman's; Sainsbury's; Save & Prosper; Shroder Wagg; Scottish Amicable Life Assurance; Solicitors' Law Stationery Society; South Wales Electricity Board; United Dominions Trust; Unilever Limited.

Other venues, which must be all the more pleasing for being less predictable, include, Interflora, the well-known flower service, Penguin Books, the Oxford University Press, and those crusaders for the quality of life, the Department of the Environment.

Muzak maintain five studios in the British Isles, but the headquarters are in ATV House, which is a muscular stones-throw from where Oxford Street meets Park Lane. Muzak is on the third floor, just two floors down from Pye Records, which is the source of a certain amount of mordant humour in that other sector of the music biz. ('Some guys tried to have it taken out,' one of the rock cognoscenti tells me. 'They said what a *terrible* impression it made, people going up to a hip record company, and listening to ... that stuff. But the executives wouldn't hear of it. It'll make an even worse impression if we don't even have it in our own lifts, they said.')

Three eminences from the British management are waiting in the Managing Director's office, which is glossily panelled and hung with sensitive Oriental artworks, plus a few modern oils. The Managing Director is LS—'Bill'—Michael. With him are Peter Williams, who is the General Manager, and the Sales Director, Stan Lea.

Bill Michael is crisp, amiable, confident. Sales in Britain are, he says, positively spiralling. 'We have *never* had so many enquiries per week'—and the boundaries themselves of the Muzak province are being pushed back. An operation is being put under way for bringing Muzak to the citizens of Southern Ireland (under some pressure, it seems, from the Eire authorities, who have been delicately hinting that it is time the franchisee got moving). True, no subscribers to the service have yet been turned up in the Ould Sod, but Muzak Inc. is quietly confident.

All over Europe things are moving, reports Michael, just back from a visit to the German franchisee (which is thirty-five per cent owned by the parent company in the US). Even in France prospects are getting rosier.

'It was difficult,' says Michael, 'as long as de Gaulle was in power ...'

Michael has been with the company for a decade. Before that, he was an executive in the woollens trade. Britain, he explains, is by virtue of the success of the franchise in an incredibly strong position *vis-à-vis* New York. Concessions include, uniquely, some special programming. Not special, of course, in the sense of containing material not available in the ordinary repertoire, but special *arrangements*.

There seem to be two main reasons for this. The New York version is that there are copyright problems peculiar to the British Isles which is true enough, and another reason, omitted in New York but emphasised in London, is that the British are rather *avant garde* in their preferences in the canned music field.

'That stuff with a lot of strings is still enormously popular over there,' Bill Michael says. 'We like up-to-date sounds ...

'And we are big enough to make these demands. If *Oslo* said they weren't happy with the programmes ... Well, with a country of three million people and a Muzak audience *that* big'—Michael grins comfortably, and makes a squinching

gesture with forefinger and thumb—'Muzak would just say
... take the programmes, or lump it!'

So our own programmes we get, a rare example of the
Special Relationship in action. 'They even have Union Jacks
on them,' says Bill Michael.

I mention that I have seen our machines in New York and
the flag, unfortunately, was nowhere to be seen.

'Oh well ... they probably put them on specially for our
visits.'

'Do you have one of our cue sheets?' asks Peter Williams,
meaning the programmes. He is young, with the pinkish
bonhomie of a rugby forward, and gets me one of the British
specials.

'That's rather unfortunate,' he says with a jolly laugh. 'This
one begins with *The End of the World*.'

There is good-natured laughter, and I scrutinise this
souped-up British schedule. The stepped-up rock content is
evident here and there (*A Whiter Shade of Pale*), but for the
most part these listings of song sequences, whose titles are
only marginally familiar, if that, read best as a sort of surreal
verse. 2.15 p.m., for instance, on an undisclosed date offered
the following:

> *Sherry*
> *Habanera*
> *Thwomp*
> *Cherry*

which was succeeded, in the wee small hours of the following
morning, by:

> *What Can I Say After I Say*
> *Maybe*
> *Ay Cosista Linda*
> *Change Of Heart*
> *More*
> *We Fell In Love To Muzak*
> *My Sin*
> *What Is There To Say*

The Muzak master-tapes arrive in the British Isles by sea, in three-months' helpings at a time. They are packed in metal discs the size of a superior pizza, and they arrive well in advance so that even if the tapes were to be involved in some conceptual *Titanic* catastrophe of the future, the risk of silence falling on the English station is negligible. (A further insurance is that replicas of the entire Muzak library are maintained in London. I mention this as a positive re-assurance that not even, say, a nuclear first strike against Manhattan would necessarily gag Muzak.)

There is, the British Muzak men concede, an element of consumer resistance in Europe unknown in the United States. This manifests itself in several ways. There are, for instance, those adolescents of all ages who prefer to listen to rock on the radio (thereby, according to Dr Joan FitzHerbert, 'seeking a return to a pre-natal Nirvana').

'Radio One is a chief competitor of ours,' Michael says, adding that Muzak never repeats itself, which admittedly could not always be said of the dire and babbling DJs.

But other of the Muzak antis are of somewhat less simple mettle.

'Most of the people who disapprove of Muzak have intellectual pretensions,' Michael says, tolerantly. 'They say I don't want to be got at. I don't want people manipulating my subconscious ...

'Yes, we say, We *are* manipulating your subconscious. *But we are doing it for your own good!*'

He pauses briefly, and adds, 'But mostly the people who complain aren't really in our market anyway.'

One further problem with the Muzak image (if the visual allusion is not too out of place in this context) arises, ironically enough, from the corporation's very success, namely from the circumstance that in Britain and Europe, probably more that even the United States, *all* canned and piped music tends to get called Muzak, occasionally with a small M. An outsider might assume that it would be a matter of some satisfaction to have become, like Cellophane, say, and Durex, one of those prestigious brand-names that have acquired quasi-dictionary status. There are, it seems, disadvantages.

Like, for instance, the inferior rivals.

'The trouble is,' Bill Michael says, sombrely, 'when people ask me What do you do? And I say I'm with Muzak ... and they say, Oh, Do you mean that rubbish I hear in the pub?'

This unsympathetic reaction, Michael knows, is seldom a reaction to the Muzak product itself, but to its cutprice and unscientific competitors. Stan Lea agrees, seriously. Stan Lea has crinkly hair and an obliging smile, and—as sales boss—it is he who is directly faced with outselling these other systems. It is, he explains, *easy* to produce a substandard product.

'You can have a shortfall *technically*. Or you can neglect the artistic side.'

We go out to lunch, descending in the disputed lift.

The Muzak is at such a pitch of inaudibility that we have to listen for a moment or two to establish that it is, in fact, playing. 'Well, the thing is,' Bill Michael says, 'we have to rely on other people's power.'

Over in the restaurant, oddly, the Muzak is only a few degrees louder, sounding a bit like a radio under a blanket, but this, Lea says, is the restaurateur's own choice.

Truly, Michael, Lea and Williams are to be respected for carving out such a formidable satrapy if all their audience is as wayward as this.

Over lunch, Bill Michael talks about modern painting a bit (he prefers Vasarely to Bridget Riley) before the conversation glides back to Muzak.

'They had music in the streets during the Siege of Leningrad,' says Stan Lea: 'From speakers ... to keep up morale.'

'At home,' Bill Michael tells me, 'I have Mozart in my study. My wife has Radio One in the kitchen.

'And we have Muzak in the living room ...'

He grins. 'There's a dreadful din when all the doors are open.'

After lunch, we return, and I hear a portion of the new Muzak LP. The sleeve-notes are gluey with that now familiar phraseology. *Stimulus progression produces a psychological and physiological effect,* etc., and there are the usual resonant allusions to the '*Muzak Board of Scientific Advisers*'. The

46

Side A music goes *It's Impossible* (arranged by Mel Davis); *Lolita* (arranged by Frank Hunter); *I Think I Love You* (arranged by Dick Hyman); *Rose Garden* (arranged by Al Caiola): *Temptation Eyes* (Frank Hunter, again); *Black Magic Woman* (Phil Bodner). Side B consists of six numbers, from *Love Story* to *Keep It Happy*, all arranged by Nick Perito, who is, I recall, Perry Como's arranger.

The main psychological and physiological effect on me is a sharp and inexplicable stab of nostalgia.

Afterwards, I accompany Williams into the General Managerial office. Beside the door, there are a number of machines, the size of a hi-fi unit. These are the devices which are sold or rented to those areas which are still out of reach of Muzak proper. Like certain dubious areas in Wales and the Far North, namely North of Newcastle. The barbaric Scots can only take imperfect advantage of Muzak programming by acquiring one of these machines, renting the short-time tapes, and playing the stuff themselves—a practice, I hasten to add, which is rather frowned on back in the USA. But back in the USA, of course, disseminating Muzak over telephone wires presents little problem. Over here, what with out tetchy government monopolies, things are trickier, and Planned Music Ltd., another ATV subsidiary, is doing good business with the machines anyway.

The difficulty *vis-à-vis* the Scots, the Irish and, indeed, the Welsh is probably more apparent than real. It would seem sentimental to suppose a specific cultural imperviousness to Muzak Inc., and certainly no Celtic programming is envisaged. Bill Michael speaks of the whole mistaken concept of Ethnic Muzak with weary tolerance. He recalls those early days when Muzak tried (and failed) to soup their product up with fandangos and stuff for Latin America.

'Or the Indians ... the Chinese ... the Hawaians ... It's *foreground* music. Neither background nor entertainment. They just don't have the repertoire that Muzak has ...'

Yes, the day of Muzak is just beginning to dawn. Especially in Europe. Here the market is on the verge of its biggest expansion ever. That whole old-fashioned generation of crustily narrow-minded executives is dying off. So far they

47

have the work areas which is, as Michael points out, a captive market, but what next? Department stores are one huge, relatively untapped market. The strait-laced prejudices which have kept customers from being supplied with the service in the Harrod's Food Hall, the Fortnum's Fountain and the Rainbow Room at Derry & Toms will succumb to commercial realism.

Williams jabs a forceful finger at a map on his wall. It shows the British Isles, burgeoning with coloured circles, red and blue, convoluted and fungoid shapes—Muzak, in its oddly vegetable growth.

'It may sound ... *corny*,' Williams says. He speaks with an endearingly halting sincerity which is *exactly right*. 'But with us Muzak isn't just a product ... It's almost a *religion*.'

> *Was it a vision, or a waking dream?*
> *Fled is that Muzak: Do I wake or sleep?*

The new HQ of Muzak Inc. is at 100, Park Avenue. You take the elevator to the nineteenth floor, and go through these smokily bluish see-through doors, and ... where are the pastel tints? The several varieties of plastic foliage? The photo of the Vietnamese orphan being raised by the Corporation?

A girl sits at a hemispherical desk of aluminium. Overhead, there is blue neon, cerulean squiggles glimmer and dissolve on the perforated metal ceiling, the metal slab walls, the polished granite underfoot. I sit in front of a circular steel table on a circular chair, chrome and a rubbery black seat, and just above my head hangs this metal cylinder, punctured with holes, an ineffable cheese grater, and dribbling Muzak ... strains of a more liquid version of The Whos' *Tommy* weave the metallic shimmer into a—Total Environmental Concept ... that marvellous Barbarella panache of mid-sixties futurismo. The Cosmic Boutique Look.

Ebullient as ever, Umberto Muscio conducts me on tour. He bangs with the flat of his hand on the slab-metal doors of the boardroom, and they swing open. 'That's the thing about the Functional Look,' he says with, perhaps, the merest tinge of ambivalence: 'They don't like doorknobs.' Here

48

there is more metal, and sky-blue neon. Also a screen for movies, and some sort of installation marked MUZAK—CONTROLLED TIME, which, however, refers to nothing more ominous than yet another of these indefatigable schemes —using Muzak circuitry to synchronise the world's clocks.

Muscio's office is also sunk in this continuum, what with whiteness, and chrome, and polished metals, and this round white marble table, which is 'conducive to freer and more stimulating exchange of ideas' than the boring, familiar oblong. (Hugh Hefner had a similar insight, but applied it to beds.)

Muscio switches on the lights. This is a ceilingful of perspex rods, of varying lengths, and the effect is indeed spectacular, like a crystal cancer, but he quickly switches them off, explaining, 'They made a bit of a ... booboo. When the lights are on, it gets hot quicker than the air-conditioning can handle it.'

The trouble with the Functional Look (as, not for the first time, I observe) is that rather often it doesn't actually *work*.

Bing Muscio talks about the New Image. The Contemporary Environment. 'This does definitely symbolise what we are doing now,' he says. 'The Age of Mantovani and Strings is behind us. Instead of panelling, we have ...' He gestures at a large abstract painting ... 'It is a creative way of saying *visually* what Muzak is doing *acoustically*.'

All Art Aspires to the Condition of Muzak ... The abstract in question was commissioned by Muscio from Raymond D. Harrow, Creative Director of Muzak Inc. Harrow is youngish, Manhattan-sallow, with short dark hair, and a neat suit and tie. He had already worked at the corporation for some years, but they had never asked him to do them a painting before. Abstracts (he says) weren't quite in his line anyway. The job of the Creative Department is providing goodies to promote Muzak which are sold to the franchisees at cost.

As a matter of fact, Muscio's first idea when he asked Ray to do an Original Oil Painting was just to have something to put on the sleeve of a Muzak album. (Yes, there are Muzak albums. And so much for my schemes of bootleg-Muzak.)

Muscio's only guide-lines were that somehow the painting should tell the New Muzak story.

Harrow went to work. 'With an abstract painting,' he explains, 'what you have in your mind or what you have in front of you is not what you are going actually to put on canvas. So it's not really like what I call a *tracer*.

'Of course, I'm not saying that the famous painters throughout history were actually *tracing* something. But what they did with a brush, you could do just as easily, and *better*, with a camera. Which is why abstract painting came about to begin with. You know, they were tired of trying to copy what a camera can do ...'

The problem was an intriguing one. Setting forth the Spirit of Muzak in another medium. At first things didn't go too well. Ray Harrow worked and worked, but everything was too ... *tight*.

'Finally, after a few attempts, I put everything away, and waited, because everything I did just turned out—absolutely, completely *wrong*.

'I waited one more day, then I went back with a different attitude ... a freer attitude really ... and the first one that I tried came out just as I wanted.

'And—fortunately—that's what everyone else wanted too.'

The mode of the painting is abstract-expressionist, done with the deft supercool of the later practitioners of that unhappily defunct movement. It is, in some respects, the last of the Bigbiz Abstracts, the ones that used to decorate corporation lobbies, and now survive only when durably executed in mosaic or enamel.

The paint is applied in an energetic diagonal, the more muted colours, suggesting 'calm, serene moods' are at the bottom left, then 'as the stimulus is built up, the strokes become more definite ... there's a contrast of colours. It's *brighter*.'

Harrow entitled the work *Stimulus Progression*, and it's an omnipresent image, the corporation Mickey Mouse. It decorates coffee-mugs, pencil caddies, Zippo lighters and cufflinks. Trimmed into a circle, it has been transformed into cocktail-glass coasters, and chopped into tiny sections it adorns

50

stationery and business-cards. One franchisee from Texas has had it put on golf balls.

Goods of this sort, by the way, are carefully tailored to differing markets, from the snazzy gold lighters for the high-rolling clients to the throwaway freebies that are pushed through direct mail. Other differences must be considered too ... 'Whereas they might be quite sophisticated here in New York, the market mightn't be quite the same in, say, Tennessee ... or Arkansas.'

I look around the office. Art materials as neat as a display, a pile of games ... board-games called *Ecology*, *Dirty Water*, *Smog*, and a figurine of Rodin's Thinker.

(This is a favourite artwork of the corporate culture. At some echelons of IBM it is used instead of the gnomic THINK. I sometimes wonder if this classic of business décor would preserve its popularity if it was more widely known that it supposedly represents Despair at the Gates of Hell.)

Yes, Ray says, they are considering some sort of game. Something to do with the Environment. Also there is some jewellery being designed. And the Muzak Christmas Card, which shows ... well, they explain it better themselves.

This unique and dramatic Christmas card is a photographic interpretation of Christmas in contemporary idiom.
Framed by three glistening stars, the impressionistic Christmas tree is a study in kinetics: exciting cartwheels of color, suspended in space by stabs of strobe light.

We hope this specially designed Christmas Card will enhance your holiday happiness, just as MUZAK fosters a pleasant and productive environment throughout the rest of the year.

Just down the spanking new corridor in spanking new offices are Jane Jarvis and Wokoun. Wokoun's Human Factors Division is still plugging away, unstoppably. More studies on Noise Pollution, and a look at the growth-area of Feminism.

Women as a Workforce, one paper reads, noting that

women tire easily, having a faster heartbeat than men and '30% fewer red cells'. They are also, luckily, particularly susceptible to Muzak.

But the most stimulating new development, in my view, is broached in a recent issue of *Environs* under the clarion headline 'S.O.S. ... *The '70's A Decade of Emergency.'* The study commences *'A recent brazen bombing attack on New York City's Police Headquarters proved with stark finality that the "reddest-hot button" in the '70's is SECURITY. Previous bombing attacks on the office headquarters of some of our giant corporations already had produced a substantial degree of sudden urban anxiety.'*

But all is not lost. And Muzak Inc. has acquired another trenchant slogan.

The 'New Muzak'—a System of Security for the '70's

And another.

Muzak is a Total Communications System

What this means is that, fifty years after, Muzak Inc. has begun to appreciate some of the possibilities latent in Major-General Squier's initial patent, including the transmission not merely of music, but of 'instructions'.

Technically, the thing is simplicity itself, as Bill Wokoun points out. All you need is a double circuit, so that you can flip off the music, and flip on whatever it's necessary to flip—'Warnings of a fire, or a bomb-scare, or any emergency like that.

'It gives the capability of getting messages to people— *wherever* they are.'

The first Muzak Total Communications System has already been installed in an industrial plant in Baltimore. 'They had a couple of bomb-scares, and they were quite ready for it.'

Meanwhile, Jane Jarvis is computerising the operation.

This is, in fact, a double job.

It means, firstly, turning the whole usable library over to the computer memory. Every detail of every tune must be recorded, every idiosyncrasy. Like the *minus*, which tells the computer that 'the performance is getting to be rather old.

Or, if it isn't old, it *sounds* old. A little dated.'

Or the 'P' which says that the tune may only be played at Peak periods—'so one of these very bright, very punchy affairs can no longer appear accidentally in the wrong time of day which we have had happen in the past when simply ... the mind quit working'.

But this is paperwork. The real agony lies not in familiarising the Tin Brain with the respective qualities of *Hula Blues* ('H' for Hawaian Only) and *Tenderly* (anytime), but with the—*creative process*, arranging Muzak Programming entire, reproducing every kink and wobble in the Ascending Curves, Stimulus Progressions and Mood Controls, the peaks and slumps of the Muzak of Time, so that this extraordinary and novel advance in the Man:Machine Interface *is actually seen to work.*

'I'll tell you what this really represents,' Jane Jarvis says, with a soft pride: 'I actually sat down and analysed everything I thought, as I was doing the programming. *Why do I do this?*

'And I wrote a series of notes to myself ... *Why* I did it. And then I took programme after programme, and analysed why it was that certain programmes were so much better than others ... What really represented the best musical thinking.'

Just one obvious pitfall was avoided. The computer must be prevented from repetition, from sticking to the One Perfect Programme.

'Pretty soon even an untrained ear, or somebody who wasn't even *listening*, would catch on to that ... They'd say— *Okay! It's five after nine, it's time for a harpsichord!*

'You know—It wouldn't take long. So every group is slightly different ...' She prods at the abstruse notations which somehow prevent the machine from brainlessly whistling the same few tunes.

So, essentially, I say, the computer memory will be a map of your own experience?

'*It really is!* This is what it amounts to ...

'But only by trial and error. I am not programming this to suit my individual taste ... But, you see, I had to make the best possible use of the material that is available to me in the library. Mind you, had I been the musical director from the inception of Muzak, it might have come out quite differently, because then there *would* have been subjective thinking.

'This is the first time in the history of music—*or* of computers—that such a thing has ever been attempted, or *thought of* ... Many people thought it couldn't be done, but it *can* be done, and it *has* been done.

'And it's better than what we were doing before.'

I pause. This is modesty carried almost to a fault. In what way is the computer actually *better*?

'Because everything has been pre-thought-out! This information'—stab of the hand—'represents the best possible thinking ... the best possible consideration ...

'You know, there were some days the programmes wouldn't be as good as other days—because we were so inundated with the tedium. It became stultifying, you see. There were days when I literally had to psych myself to do a good job, because it became a *visual* problem—just this business of looking at yellow cards and trying to remember what it *sounded* like.

'But mainly the reason is ...' Jane Jarvis meditates, brow gently furrowing. 'You know, those of us who have to programme music on a daily basis cannot *help* but have personal feelings about it.

'There are certain things you just like better!'

She smiles, helplessly. 'But there are tunes which *should* be used, because their *rendition* is valid. And now they will have their place in the sun, simply because they are entered in *here*, and the computer doesn't give a damn whether it likes piano better than it does the ... trombone.

'But there are certain artists I happen to enjoy more than others, and I naturally gravitate towards them—I just can't help it!

'That is where human frailty comes in.'

I leave, walking with Umberto Muscio down the corridors, the shelves of crisp new brochures. Past midget outcrops of computerware, wires spilling from the top like platefuls of coloured vermicelli.

Into the marvellous lobby, steely-blue, and the muted shine of granite/glass/metal, and the hanging cylinder from which Muzak ebbs and flows like the sea.

'People who visit us', Muscio says, 'say it is like stepping into the Space Age!'

✖ *Coca-Cola!*
The First Part

*In which the writer visits Atlanta, Georgia, home-town
of the world's greatest soft drink, and contemplates the
past, present, and especially the future of Coca-Cola.*

In the bright, confident morning of the Space Age, the Coca-
Cola Company was as affected as the rest of Western culture.
In fact, letters began to trickle through to the corporate
headquarters in Atlanta, Georgia. They were from parties
interested in the franchise for the moon.

This has still not been disposed of. When the last batch
of astronauts returned—astronauts are pretty big on Coke—
they were greeted by a sign, reading:

WELCOME BACK TO EARTH
HOME OF COCA-COLA

A claim it would be fruitless to deny. A company brochure
shows Coke being consumed on camels in Cairo, in gondolas
in Venice, and beside waterfalls in Bogota. *The sun never sets
on the world of Coca-Cola,* it justifiably crows, appropriating
the slogan from another empire of which this is no longer precisely true. On the West Coast of Africa I had an audience
with a Paramount Chief, a man of great dignity, whose ceremonial robe portrayed Coca-Cola bottles on a pink ground.
In Biafra, during the siege, I paid two pounds for a bottle of
Coke, and happily, considering the alternatives.

Nor is it just a matter of ubiquity. There is the sheer cultural permeation of the stuff. While working on this I would
sometimes check the rate with which I found references to the

beverage. They are practically impossible to count, or avoid. Within the same ten days Christopher Isherwood is interviewed while quaffing a Coke, and meatballs-and-Coke are served at a diplomatic reception by the new state of Bangla Desh. 'Coke Freaks' are photographed in Athens and a photographic reportage on Vietnam shows Coke cans transformed into impromptu torches. A British fashion-glossy drapes its marvellous deathmask-aesthetic models around various exotic locales and in the background of each lurks a Coca-Cola sign. Coca-Cola is as embedded in the culture as Simon Rodia physically embedded the bottles in Watts Towers.

Nor is the company about to complain. Their promotional vigour is a by-word. The director of *Diamonds Are Forever*, that James Bond bofforama, has testified to his difficulties in this respect. Whenever his back was turned he would find that somebody had stuck up a Coca-Cola sign.

And what music-lover will forget the turn of 1971/72 when the charts in a great many countries—including the US and Britain—were dominated by the New Seekers, a group with the crisp bite of a stale meringue, singing *I'd like to buy the world a home. And furnish it with love.*

Irreproachable sentiments which had already become familiar in a commercial featuring a group of kids (devoutly multiracial, but with an identical clean gleam). This had been shot, we were told, on a Hillside-in-Italy. Where the New Seekers' hit differed from the original lay mainly in what was *omitted*. Namely:

> *I'd like to teach the world to sing*
> *In perfect harmony*
> *I'd like to buy the world a Coke*
> *And keep it company*
> (refrain)
> *It's the Real Thing!*

This is the first jingle to have made the transition (so far), and it couldn't have happened to a nicer multi-national corporation. The Coke slice of the proceeds went straight to charity—'We aren't in showbiz,' as an executive told me, winningly—so that the only thing that the company will get out of it is another free millionsworth of exposure for what is, I suppose, the most exposed product in the world.

Also they are left with one cheering reflection.

'Operation Arden' can hardly fail.

'Operation Arden' was code-named after the cosmetics queen, aptly, because it is an organic part of just about the most strenuous corporate face-lift ever. The thing is that Coke has (or had) been having a few stressful years. Not, that is, *financially* stressful. Quite the reverse. Since it beat off an uppity challenge by Pepsi in the mid-50s, Coke has fizzed from strength to strength. For fifteen years straight it has had earnings gains, and now controls 42% of the US soft drink market—more than its next six rivals put together. Coca-Cola controls the world's largest army of retail salesmen and—after the US Post Office—the second largest fleet of trucks. Globally it sells 110 million Cokes a day.

The problems have been in other areas, no less sensitive. More than most products, *Coca-Cola is its image,* and it is here that the storms have blown up. Like the promotional bingo scandal, and the federal suit that alleged false advertising claims, and—most wounding of all—the media brouhaha about 'callous' working conditions for migrants in Florida.

Radical sniping was, perhaps, to be expected. 'We are part of the American Way, along with the Flag,' an executive says, stoically, knowing where people wear the flag nowadays. 'Coca-Colonisation' became a term much bandied about, and cartoonists showed bottles being put to unusual purposes in Vietnam.

None of that was particularly convincing. When all's said and done, Coca-Cola is just soda pop, and pretty cheap at that. Of greater and continuing urgency is the eco-consumerist commotion. One hundred and ten million Cokes a day is, after all, one hundred and ten million Cokes a day, or a hell of a welter of metal and glass. On Earth Day in Kings Road, London, a young lady paraded wearing, most notably, Coke cans. Striking, but non-returnable.

The Coca-Cola Company took things in hand. Op Arden cleaned up the (loyal old word) Image. Coke became *'The*

Real Thing', and *'Things go better with a Coke'*—always good for a raunchy snigger—joined the tarnished treasury of some seventy-five obsolete trumpet calls including *'The Pause that Refreshes'* and such less-remembered pearls as *'Enjoy a Glass of Liquid Laughter'*.

Visually, things were standardised. There used to be hundreds of different logotypes, but the standard one was that rotund, red device. This has been replaced by an oblong, and the red has less Dracula-appeal, being brighter, less arterial. It is bisected by a graphic flourish in white.

The familiar circle will survive for decades yet, peeling and flaking off the world's bar walls, in a babel of enticement and command, but the new look is already dominant. The new look is modern, thrustful, concerned.

Coca-Cola is a very, very concerned corporation indeed.

The birthplace and spiritual base of Coca-Cola is Atlanta, Georgia. The Old South. 'We have two great traditions,' I am told by a slurry-voiced air stewardess, herself an Atlanta girl, *'Gone With The Wind* and Coca-Cola.'

A young PR man from the corporation meets me at the airport. He sizzles with enthusiasm, as we drive through the mellow sub-tropic twilight, and the first sight of Atlanta is, yes, a startler. I only had the vaguest preconceptions, but they certainly didn't include this display set-piece, an eyeful of skyscrapers. Flash-Gordonville!

This is the Peachtree Center, and it is dominated by my hotel, the Regency Hyatt. The Regency Hyatt has a revolving mushroom dome in screaming aquamarine plastic. This is a famous sight, and so is the lobby which swoops straight up for fourteen floors. Creepers dangle from the different internal storeys and a lift of glassy Fortnums flamboyance zips up and down. A bar of grimly spiked black metal is suspended from the roof, and on the lobby floor—where the locals walk and gawk in their Southland excesses of strawberry jackets, chartreuse trousers and two-tone shoes—there is a fountain got together from chromed metal and glass tubing which pulses with internal haemorrhages of water. It must be fifty foot high, and is uniquely ugly.

This hotel is Los-Angeles-Insurance-Company-Rococo pushed about as far as it will go, and is (I am to discover) one of the rare works found inspirational by the architects of the Disney World. It is symbolic of the New Atlanta, which has become the capital of the New South, a city in which the Coca-Cola Corporation takes a discreet, but justifiable, paternal pride.

Atlanta typifies Coke around the world remarks a bumper issue of *The Refresher*, a company magazine. Pleasant pictures show how Coke drenches the local scene. School-kids are shown working with pencils and paper supplied by the local bottler, and at play riding ponies derived from the same friendly source. The Mayor of Atlanta is seen in front of his seal of office hospitably offering a bottle of Coke to a visitor while the black-tie set are observed during an operatic interval quaffing it, with more delicacy, out of paper cups. The police are discovered guzzling it both in a prowl car and in a helicopter, likewise part-donated by the bottler. In one stunning picture fifteen Southern Belles are presenting a ballet. Their headpieces are facsimiles of the Coke bottle cap, and they are wearing bottle-green bodystockings which make it abundantly plain why the bottle used to be called a 'Mae West'. Also large replicas of bottles hang from bosom to crotch.

The headquarters are impressive. The older building is neo-palladian red brick, and the new one, opened in 1967, has a pale gridded exterior. Inside—well, 'the conceptual presentation by Associated Space Design Inc.' paints the picture.

Coca-Cola has come to belong to Everyman, the boys at Space Design point out. *To him it means fun, refreshment, a sense of tradition and pride, and a steadiness in a not-so-steady world. It is with this identity in mind that we intend to create the interiors of the new Coca-Cola USA building.*

What Everyman gets is glossy great lobbies, caviar-crepuscular in marble, and offices with black plastic fitments, and long Godardiste corridors, which are pale, or silver, that peccary-stippled silver vinyl which ought to recall a space station, but looks a bit too much like the stuff that is made into cheap handbags or showgirls' G-strings.

The Coca-Cola secretaries are Southern girls, for the most

part. They have ribbons in their hair and smiles of sultry innocence. In the morning they coo like doves: 'How are *you* this morning?' 'Jes' fine.'

Actually they seem a degree ambivalent about the New Image. 'It's sort of sterile,' complains one, and it doesn't necessarily all *work*. She alludes to the president's telephone, which was put in a drawer. The problem being that the drawer has to be opened, and somebody falls over it.

Everyman (or Everywoman) also gets plentiful art. Moving from executive to executive I pass a corporate collection which includes Henry Moore, Sonya Delaunay, Kenneth Noland, Alexander Calder, not to mention Samoan bark paintings, Punjabi textiles, Micronesian wood carvings, Bobo masks from the Upper Volta, and gravestone rubbings from Cape Cod.

Everyman is not, frankly, always impressed. 'I like a picture that *looks* like a picture,' admits a junior exec, covertly —but what does perpetually rejoice his heart is the omnipresence of Coca-Cola.

This includes that gorgeous old artwork, the originals of calendar girls from the '40s and '50s that hang in lobbies, and the rash of memorabilia and iconography in every office: Coke cufflinks, Coke ashtrays. Coke paperweights, golden Coke bottles, Coke cartoons, and Coke plaques—and (of course) the Real Thing itself. There are Coca-Cola dispensers in niches in the corridors, and on every desk Cokes appear in bottles, cans, tumblers and paper cups and are glugged and replenished with stupefying speed. A huge gush of the stuff seems to effervesce through the entire building, like blood surging to and from the heart, the systole and diastole of a world of Coca-Cola.

Brief History. Coca-Cola was born in 1886 to an Atlanta pharmacist, John S. Pemberton. The event is celebrated in a leaflet called *The American Way of Business—An Economics Unit About The Free Enterprise System Presented by The Coca-Cola Company,* which displays a Coke bottle on the cover, centred on a Confederate flag. The story opens so.

It was a warm May day in Atlanta, Georgia, in 1886. Too warm to be cooped up in the big brick house on Marietta

*Street. Out in the back yard it was pleasant. A gentle breeze
kept the glowing coals alive under the big three-legged pot
and the syrup in it bubbled gently. 'Doc' Pemberton stirred
the reddish-brown mixture carefully, dipped up a small
portion and tasted it. It looked good, smelled good, and what's
more, it tasted good.*

*He took a sample of the syrup to Willis Venable who ran
Atlanta's biggest soda fountain in Jacob's Drug Store. Venable
put an ounce of the syrup in a glass, filled it with water and
ice and tasted it. He smacked his lips and drank the whole
glassful. That was the first drink of Coca-Cola.*

This being in the days before the Pursuit of Happiness
was recognised as the most important constitutional right,
'Doc' Pemberton initially was pushing the stuff for its medicinal properties, namely as a relief for hangovers, headaches,
menstrual stress, and much besides. As such it supplanted
his earlier mix, French Wine Coca—Ideal Nerve and Tonic
Stimulant, and joined an array of patent medicines which
included Indian Queen Hair Dye, Extract of Styllinger (which
did wonders for the blood), and Globe of Flower Cough Syrup.

All four directors of the Pemberton Chemical Company
were asked to suggest a name for the infant. It was Frank
Robinson, the book-keeper, who inches into history by not
only suggesting the name 'Coca-Cola', but writing it out in
the chunkily flowing Spenserian script of the time.

A couple of years later, Coca-Cola is already thriving, and
Asa Griggs Candler comes onstage. He had arrived in town
some years previously as a hopeful apprentice. A company biog
strikes the proper note: *He wore home-made clothes and had
exactly $1.75 in his pocket when he began to walk the city
streets looking for work.*

Yes, he got a job, duly became a druggist of substance, and
began buying into Coca-Cola. By 1891 he had complete control at a cost, it is said, of $2,000. The following year a Georgia
Corporation was formed with a capital of $100,000. Candler
called it 'The Coca-Cola Company'.

Subsequently, the chronology becomes a sequence of milestones. Coke was first bottled, for example, by Joe Biedenharn
in 1894. Biedenharn was a confectioner in Vicksburg, Missis-

sippi, but not just your ordinary confectioner. *Tall and lithe of stature, he held himself straight as a ramrod,* recalls another biography. *The years rested lightly upon his shoulders. His snow-white hair, bushy eyebrows, and blue-grey eyes, twinkling with good humour, were strongly reminiscent of Mark Twain.*

In 1899 a further contract assured the sale of bottled Coke throughout the USA. This was one of the most bizarre contracts in history. Candler sold all rights for just one dollar to a couple of live-wire Chattanooga lawyers, Benjamin Franklin Thomas and Joseph Brown Whitehead. They split the country between them. Capital of $5,000 was advanced by a young Chattanooga businessman, J. T. Lupton.

None of these men suffered. Lupton's son was later said to be worth two hundred million dollars.

In 1901, Coke spent $100,000 on advertising, and in 1911 a round million.

1915 was a very good year. Alexander Samuelson, an employee of the Root Glass Company of Terre Haute, Indiana, designed the classic Coke bottle. It was a bit more bosomy then, and the second bottle ever to be patented, the first being the squinched-in Dimple Haig. The Roots, who patented it, didn't do so badly either.

In 1916, Candler retired to become Mayor of Atlanta, and in 1919 the board sold out to a syndicate. Candler was furious. It changed hands for twenty-five million dollars, and soon was turning over that amount a year.

In 1920, there was a lawsuit against the Koke Co., which went all the way to the Supreme Court, where Justice Oliver Wendell Holmes saved the Coca-Cola bacon with a judgment that most of the company men know by heart: *'It means a single thing coming from a single source, and well-known to the community.'*

In 1924, the Coca-Cola Co. of Canada was created. And global conquest began.

In 1929, with things gloomy elsewhere, Archie Lee of the D'Arcy Advertising Agency coined the phrase, *'The Pause that Refreshes'*. Also the first large electric sign was installed. In Times Square.

In 1932 research started on automatic vendors. In 1941, the president of Coke promised to 'see that every man in uniform gets a bottle of Coca-Cola for 5c wherever he is and whatever it costs'.

In 1940 a coke bottle was placed in the Crypt of Civilisation, Oglethorpe, Atlanta, for the benefit of future generations.

In 1948 the advertising budget went past twenty million and in 1953 beyond thirty. This coincided with an unexpected challenge. All this time, the Coca-Cola Company had been selling one product in one size bottle, the nubby six-and-a-half ouncer, while Pepsi and the rest were beginning to advance into the Supermarket Era, with 'economic family-sizes' and what have you. They boomed.

Prodded into action, Coke too began experimenting with shapes and sizes—devotees may recall the two-gallon fridge-sized drum—and, finally, diversified. Fanta was purchased, and Sprite. Then Minute Maid, which had burgeoned from an army contract, enabling them to perfect a mode of powdering oranges. Along with Minute Maid came the spiffing health drink, Hi-C.

Hi-C and Minute Maid have been a source of profit, but also of grief, to Coca-Cola.

The next hassle came in the early '60s when Pepsi and Royal Crown launched their successful dietetic colas. Coke reacted, if hardly as fast as a speeding bullet, and launched Tab. Tab never got to better than third place and, anyway, then came the cyclamates ban in 1969, and the diet market toppled. So much so that Coke's Fresca which hadn't even been *marketed* as a diet drink plunged 25%.

Currently, Coca-Cola own or handle products including Maryland Club, which is an instant decaffeinated coffee, and Butter-Nut instant tea. Also a Japanese sherbet called Magic Ice, any number of juices, ades and mixes, including a potion called Simba, with no reference intended to the Leopard Men of Africa, whose policy of disembowelling outsiders would probably not commend them to the Coca-Cola Company.

The experimentation never stops. Outside a first-floor room

a sign reads PRODUCT EVALUATION. Inside is a long black counter, partitioned into glass-walled cubicles, like confessionals done to laboratory specifications.

I sit down, and two dixie cups appear. Brimful of reddish fluid. One is coded 'B' and one 'T'. Roneographed sheets suggest my possible comments. For instance.

Give your opinion of the FLAVOUR of each sample on the scale.

> I LIKE IT EXTREMELY
> I LIKE IT VERY MUCH
> I LIKE IT MODERATELY
> I LIKE IT SLIGHTLY
> I NEITHER LIKE/DISLIKE IT
> I DISLIKE IT SLIGHTLY
> I DISLIKE IT MODERATELY
> I DISLIKE IT VERY MUCH
> I DISLIKE IT EXTREMELY

For the record, I disliked 'T' moderately and liked 'B' slightly. So if the world is soon awash with 'B', you'll know who to blame.

Coca-Cola, explains J. Lucian—'Luke'—Smith, is divided into five parts. There is Coca-Cola USA, the parent company, of which he is president, and which is quartered down here in Georgia, together with the corporate superstructure that oversees the whole Imperium.

The Export Corporation is up in New York, and in Toronto, Canada, there is Coca-Cola Ltd., or Ltée, as *le cas* may be. The two new boys are Tenco and the Coca-Cola Foods Division, which handle the diversification, and which are located, respectively, in New Jersey and Houston, Texas.

Nor is this all. Where Coke is unique, stresses Smith, is in its army of franchised *bottlers*. The net worth of Coca-Cola is said to be above four thousand million dollars, but even this figure includes only twenty-two of the 1,687 bottling plants around the world. Taken together, Coca-Cola is among the very largest privately-owned corporations in existence.

Slightly more than half the franchises are in the United States. Often they are held by the descendants of the first lucky bottlers whose family holdings have spread out into trees of positively Bourbon-Habsburg complexity. One unusual feature is that the franchises can neither be revoked nor bought back without the owner's consent, which gives the franchisees considerable punch. The twenty real biggies clump together into something called the President's Advisory Council which chews the fat with Luke Smith about once a quarter.

'The Coca-Cola Bottler is a big man in his community,' says Smith. There is a story that Coke has created more millionaires and multi-millionaires than any other one product. This is not contradicted by Coca-Cola.

The bottlers depend on the corporation for the essential syrup, which can be had from a couple of dozen plants. The UK plant in Ruislip, Middlesex, is one of the biggest, and exports three million pounds worth annually. The formula for the syrup is A Secret, and is guarded with a rigour all too rare at the Pentagon.

There are fifteen substances in Coca-Cola, and fourteen of them are known: sugar, caramel, caffeine, lime, nutmeg, and so on. The fifteenth is called 7X, and is only known to a tiny élite, never more than three or less than two. 'We do not travel together,' says one, sombrely.

Naturally this leaves plenty of room for guess-work. Mostly this hinges around the Coke/coke ambiguity, namely the Cocaine or other narcotic possibilities of Coca-Cola. *Hélas!* A writer using the nom-de-plume Black Shadow tells it like it is in a letter to the underground mag, *Rags* (unhappily defunct).

Not to bring you down, says the Shadow, *but the Coca-Cola scam on page eight of the January issue (let it evaporate and get off by sniffing the residue) is naught but a pipe dream. There are a lot of street myths about different ways to get off with Coca-Cola—precipitate with aspirin, soak a cigarette (or joint) and smoke it, etc, all stemming from the long-gone time when Coca-Cola actually contained a small amount of cocaine.*

The long-gone time was prior to 1901, when Candler had his merchandise analysed by a research chemist who found that the amount of cocaine deriving from the untreated coca leaves was so minuscule that anybody desiring the remotest effect would have to put away five and a half quarts. Anyone willing to risk their stomach walls for a buzz should note that even this trifling narcotic content was eliminated in the most Stalinist fashion.

Other matters in which the bottlers depend to some considerable extent on Coke know-how are the various promotional gimmickries. They are a whizz at these. Coke sponsors a formidable global array of sports programmes, community events and municipal helping-out. In Britain, for example, Coca-Cola Export has involved itself in swimming, where it doles out trophies like nobody's business, and now the British Alpine Junior Ski Tests.

Tens of thousands of sporting/educational films are circulated free. (One recent cricketing special stars Lindwall, Ritchie Benaud, Keith Miller, and Sir Donald Bradman.) Naturally, Coca-Cola tends to be swigged during the course of events. It's thirsty work, doing good.

Celebrities have been plugging Coke since the days of Lillian Russell and Mme Nordica. Joan Crawford did an early stint for Coke, frostily ignored by both parties since she joined the board of Pepsico. More recently those who have done a (well-paid) bit include Aretha Franklin (who sang radio jingles), the Who, Sugar Ray Robinson, the Harlem Globetrotters and Paul Newman. Newman, by the way, was appearing in, and narrating, a TV show called *Once Upon A Wheel*. He was wearing this Dupont Nylon jacket which was sewn with patches lettered Heuer, Goodyear, the Chevrolet Sports Department, Fram, Watkins Glen, Purolator Filters, and—dominating the entire left breast—Coca-Cola.

The enthusiasm of everyone concerned with this show (including Paul Newman himself) is electrifying, the bottlers were told. *Be prepared. You'll be selling more Coke than ever as 'Once Upon A Wheel' comes rolling around.*

This info appeared in *The Coca-Cola Bottler*, a magazine with an uncanny surface resemblance to the Rad/Lib/ Rock Paper, *Rolling Stone*, but with dissimilar contents. (There is a charming Jennifer's Diary/Suzy Knickerbocker component which tends to show innumerable bespectacled executives presenting each other with plaques.) This magazine used to be independent, but has now been taken over by the corporation. There were, apparently, a few mutterings among the bottlers about this. But, mostly, all is harmony. And with the business going the way it is, why not?

Smith explains the finance of promotion. 'The number of dollars put in are always more the bottlers' than ours. So the bottler profit aggregate is a good deal more than *our* profit aggregate. Meaning that the money stays in local communities.'

He leans back expansively. A girl comes in with another trayful of Cokes.

It is notable that the classic bottle was not produced for reasons of aesthetics, but at the urging of the company's then chief legal counsel, Harold Hirsch. Coke's awareness of the need for legal safeguards goes back even further. As early as 1896 a motion was taken during a general meeting which reads as follows.

The President was requested to consult an attorney in reference to the advisability of bringing a suit or suits against other parties who are selling substitutes for, or imitations of, Coca-Cola and to commence proceedings if so advised.

Coca-Cola, like liberty, can only be preserved through eternal vigilance. Vigilante-in-chief and head of Coca-Cola's massive legal department is Julius R. Lunsford Jr a former naval lawyer, and expert in court martial. I meet Lunsford in his office, which is in the older building, and austerely legal, shelved with legal tracts all pale greens and browns, and panelled with wood the colour of peanut-butter. Lunsford has a sensitive proboscis, and the air of jungly alertness of one of the heftier antelopes. The sanctity of the Coca-Cola trademark is his Territorial Imperative.

Mr Justice Frankfurter's observation that 'If it is true we live by symbols it is no less true that we purchase goods by them' is a favourite. And one of Lunsford's innumerable papers (*Trademarks: Prestige, Practice and Protection*) has as good an opening paragraph as I have come across recently anywhere.

68

Americans are trademark conscious people, Lunsford notes, *Trademarks influence our daily lives and symbolise our American system of free and competitive enterprise. We encounter them not only in the market place, but also in our work, in our play, in our reading, at the banks, at the theatre, on the highways, in every mode of transportation and in church. For example, after a refreshing sleep on his 'Beautyrest' mattress, the average American male is awakened by the alarm of a 'Westclox' clock. He arises and walks on the 'Callaway' or 'Barwick' carpet to the bathroom. He brushes his teeth with 'Ipana' toothpaste on a 'Dr Wes' toothbrush and applies 'Foamy' shaving cream to be removed by a 'Gillette' or 'Schick' razor. After a stimulating shower with 'Ivory' soap and while listening to the newscast from an 'RCA' or 'Philco' radio, he hurries into his 'BVD' underwear, dons an 'Arrow' or 'Gant' shirt freshly laundered with 'Duz' from the 'Laundromat', puts on his 'Elgin' watch and rushes downstairs to breakfast. In the kitchen, where the linoleum is bright with 'Johnson's' wax, he snatches two slices of 'Southern' bread from the 'Toastmaster' toaster and consumes a cup of 'Maryland Club' coffee and a glass of 'Minute Maid' orange juice* [these two preceding being, fortuitously, Coke products] *taken from the 'Frigidaire' or 'Coldspot' refrigerator. After breakfast he enjoys a 'Lucky Strike' or 'Winston' cigarette. Should he cut or burn his finger* [no doubt with the 'Gillette' razor or on the 'Toastmaster' toaster] *he would apply 'Vaseline' petroleum jelly or a 'Band-Aid' bandage. He dons his 'Stetson' hat and drives his 'Ford' automobile to work. On the way he will be reminded by his 'Motorola' radio that 'things go better with a Coke'.*

It's a Vision of the Good Life, in fact, especially for the brand names in question, which is just where Jules R. Lunsford comes in. Because even the above stretch of prose contains one gloomy might-have-been, namely linoleum, or Linoleum as it used to be. Just one company that let its guard down.

'It's a paradox,' says Lunsford. 'The better-known a name becomes, the harder it is to protect.' He reels off a roll-call of the fallen, whose names have slid into the public domain. 'There's cellophane. And you have vanilla, escalator, yo-yo

... You know the yo-yo was formerly a registered trademark? ... And there's aspirin. Aspirin is *very* interesting. In the United States aspirin is a generic designation, just a white tablet of no particular individual origin. But in the South, and in Canada to the North, Aspirin is still a trademark, and the exclusive property of the Bayer Company.'

Another *histoire* fresh in the corporate memory is the unhappy story of the Thermos, or thermos, as the (upper or lower) case may be. Thermos was a brand-name once upon a time, and the property of the King-Seeley Co., but so popular did the word become that other makers of vacuum-insulated bottles went to court, claiming an unfair handicap.

Aladdin, one competitor, appeared with a poll in which three out of four adults were unaware that Thermos was a trade name. They also lugged along bundles of clippings in which the item was spelt with a small 't'.

The Solomonesque judgment was that when spelt with a big 'T' Thermos applied to the King-Seeley product, but when spelt with a small letter it was anybody's.

Coca-Cola are not forgetting this decision in a hurry.

They have a battery of devices to protect their rights. One good wheeze was a magazine competition. The corporation published a limerick, and offered a prize to anybody who could improve on it. The limerick they were so proud of ran thus.

THE RULES THAT WE WRITE BY ARE THREE
WE ABHOR THE DIMINUTIVE 'C'
AND 'S' PRECEDED BY 'E' OR 'A'
IS NO BETTER THAN APOSTROPHE

If Atlanta was not immediately overwhelmed with limerick writers it might conceivably have been because of the offered prize, which was dinner with the lawyer.

More conventionally, the Coca-Cola legal staff emit a barrage of letters. A clippings service keeps them up to date, and whenever Coca-Cola or Coke is referred to with a small 'c' a letter wings its way to the sloppy editor, or whoever. The Letter is primly courteous in tone. Lunsford scans his correspondence with, for instance, the *New York Times.*

'We wrote them June 16th 1949. They wrote back, agreeable to respect our rights. We wrote again on December 2nd 1949.' He shuffles through the card index. 'Nothing else happened till September 23rd 1968. We wrote them again on August 1st 1969. I don't know what happened ...

'Now here's the *New York Daily News,* which is a tabloid. Gosh! We've written them '49, '49, '54, '62, '66, three times in '67, '68, '69 ...'

They seem a bit more resistant than the *Times,* I remark. 'And no acknowledgements,' agrees Lunsford. 'But you see what we've done. If we're charged with an act of omission, we say we've done everything we can ...'

Nor is it just the Press who are harried into grammatical rectitude. One crisp document called CONVERSATIONAL GUIDELINES is 'For the confidential use of radio announcers, disc jockeys and other programme personnel'.

Guideline 1, for instance, goes: *Coca-Cola and its companion trade-mark, Coke, identify a particular brand of refreshment. These trade-marks may be used at any time you wish to talk about a situation in which something good to drink is appropriate, such as 'Man, having an icy cold bottle of Coke is right on!'*

Guideline 3 explains that *Like deer and elk and a host of other words, Coke and Coca-Cola are both singular and plural.* It follows that *Never say 'All the people had Cokes'. Instead say 'All the people had bottles—or glasses—or drinks—of Coke!'*

Guideline 4 is that the company is upset if Coke gets personalised. The jocks are requested not to say *'Coca-Cola's The Great Pumpkin Show'* but *'The Great Pumpkin'* brought to you by your friendly neighbour who bottles Coca-Cola.

None-the-less, in spite of the sweet reasonableness of The Letter, some persons, editors, whoever, have been known to be unhelpful, even truculent at the touch of this helping hand. Especially in the outer reaches of the culture, where some areas are not so easy to police.

Coca-Cola, for instance, has enjoyed innumerable references in the highways and by-ways of literature. Mainly just as detail work, but occasionally something a bit more wounding creeps in. 'We have to depend on our personnel and our patrons and consumers to bring this to our attention,' Lunsford says, indicating that the clippings service is unequal to the task.

One imbroglio which still smarts involved the novelist John Steinbeck who, in *The Wayward Bus*, not only failed to capitalise Coke, but *did* capitalise Pepsi-Cola, and—the final straw—alleged that there was *no difference between the two beverages.*

It's no surprise that The Letter was soon winging its way towards the errant author. With true Deep South gentility, Coca-Cola merely complained about the small 'c'.

Steinbeck wrote back, a bit loftily.

'In English when a word is spelled with a small 'c' and is still acceptable, it has become a great word. Only the small need to capitalise.'

'Mr Steinbeck', says Lunsford, acidly, 'should have tried telling that to the former owners of Cellophane.'

Even more slighting is Pierre Salinger in a novel revolving around a diplomatic *crise* Somewhere in South America. No sooner is there a whiff of trouble than the hero is met by his military attaché.

'*Ambassador, we have Coca-Cola, American Cash Register and Campbell Soups waiting inside. They want to evacuate now.*'

What! Quitting? And worse is to come. As the Ambassador strides (grimly) into the residence *The Coca-Cola man stood up abruptly, blocking the ambassador* ...

'*I warn you, Hood. I have a complete inventory of the plant. When I come back, if there's as much as one typewriter missing, I'll file a claim against—*'

'*You won't be back,*' *said the ambassador* ...

Not be back! That alone, as any Coke man will tell you, is enough to damage the scene's credibility. After all, even Fidel Castro was seen glugging a Coke recently though, admittedly, with a fair amount of clowning. But Coca-Cola is used (if not resigned) to being exploited by what they tend to call eggheads and other such types down Georgia way.

In James Dickey's *Deliverance* one of the four sporty

businessmen is a Coca-Cola man, as is Jimmy Cagney in Wilder's *One Two Three*. The ad for *Move* showed Elliot Gould not only inside a Coke bottle, but looking pretty damned unhappy about it. In *On the Beach*, one of the great nuclear weepies, Gregory Peck abandons Ava Gardner in Australia and sails all the way to the US West Coast because morse signals suggest that maybe somebody is alive there after all.

The moment that we (and Peck) see that the message is being tapped out on the transmitter by a Coca-Cola bottle trapped in a Venetian blind is one of unforgettable eerie pathos.

Also, it makes sense.

A Coke bottle sending the last American message.

Other forms of exploitation are less benign. There is the straight commercial rip-off, like making the Coca-Cola tumbler into a candle container. Lighters and other gee-gaws have been modelled after Coke bottles, and Coke bottles have been halved and transformed to ashtrays. Yet more deplorably Coke tumblers have been filled with imitation ice-cream and sold on the 'Bad Taste' stall at the Chelsea Antique Market, London.

Even the Coca-Cola device itself has been profaned. Posters and T-shirts would carry that weightily undulant script, except that on closer scrutiny it would read COCAINE or COSA-NOSTRA. To some this might seem a perverse tribute, but not to the company.

'It was the *opposition* in this country,' says Lunsford, meaningfully, 'and they would *want* us to object, and it would increase the sale. We didn't want to do that no matter how scurrilous they might be. We didn't know whether it would fade ...

'We thought it would die out, but it hasn't. We're going to have to take some action. As to the T-shirts, we have got one manufacturer to discontinue. And we're going to take action, some kind of action, against the posters.'

He pauses, a bit helplessly. 'What action I don't know. Because unfortunately in New York a similar situation arose when a Girl Scout was pictured as being pregnant.'

I remember the poster: a pre-teen fat-tummied, and the slogan BE PREPARED.

'They lost the case,' Lunsford says, unhappily.

Another misuse of the script was (in intention) entirely friendly. Michael Chow, a London restaurateur, is a longtime devotee of Coke imagery, so much so that the matchbook of his newest eating-place in Queensway carries a near facsimile of the post-Op Arden Coke device on the cover. It reads:

IT'S THE REAL THING
ENJOY
CHOW-TWO

Most people rather assumed that Mr Chow must be getting a free supply of liquid laughter or something, for the publicity, but not at all. *Coke was livid*. Chow got one of Those Letters. The matchbooks (one hears) will be discontinued.

But it is the visual artists who have got the most fun out of Coke imagery. Most pop painters have alluded to it. Warhol has a silkscreen which is a rendition of a great many bottles, variously full, partially full, and empty. A sculptor, whose name escapes me, cast a bottle in bronze, adding ripely nippled boobs. Mel Ramos has an even more unusual image which I saw much later on La Cieniga Boulevard, Los Angeles, in which a Coca-Cola bottle is apparently emerging from the lower quarters of rather a pretty girl.

'Was there any come-back from the company?'

'Oh, no. But we did have trouble with one Ramos. It showed Virna Lisi sitting on a hamburger.'

'From the hamburger people?'

'No. From Virna Lisi's Press Agent . . .'

The Coca-Cola Company, though, is far from happy about Coke Culture. Warhol? Mel Ramos? It seems just one more instance of undesirables jumping their wholesome bandwagon. They went as far as sending one of The Letters to Jasper Johns when he too turned his talents on to the imagery. The company politely regretted his use of their registered trademark.

Jasper Johns wrote back offering in restitution the unrestricted use of the trade name 'Jasper Johns'.

There the matter, at the moment, rests.

On the other hand when Michael English, the British designer, mounted an exhibition called 'RUBBISH', a Coca-Cola cap, dented, was among the five genres of garbage that he depicted in stunning *trompe l'œil*.

A Coke spokesman said: *'The crown of our bottles is shown and we are naturally pleased. The artist is to be congratulated on his creativity by showing how everyday objects can be portrayed as things of beauty.'*

It is, I suppose, just possible that the alternative title of the RUBBISH exhibition might have had something to do with this rare forbearance. This was CELEBRITIES OF OUR AGE.

Other problems left to the legal heads are Substitution and Imitation. Substitution is when somebody goes into a soda fountain and demands Coke, but is given a foaming glassful of, er, the Enemy. Fountain-trade accounts for a third of US sales, so this is nothing to be sneezed at, and the company has ways of dealing with this misdemeanour.

'This is unique with the Coca-Cola Company and we're very proud of it,' says Lunsford, effervescently. 'We have what we call a Trade Research Department, which consists of between twenty-five and thirty males—*college graduates*—who constantly go through the United States and place orders for Coca-Cola and Coke at retail level.'

The commandoes work in already doubtful terrain. 'We get complaints from irate customers and from stockholders, that I went into this place last week and the Coca-Cola they served me tasted *terrible.*' They are on the road fifty weeks a year, moving from one suspect establishment to another. They tend to be flunked lawyers or something, and the average sojourn in the job is two years. 'But,' says Lunsford, 'we have three or four in Miami that really like it. They've never married, and they've been with us as long as ten or twelve years ...'

The *modus operandi* is as follows.

'They take a sample surreptitiously—*hopefully* surreptitiously—and they pour it into concealed containers. Then they place it in a clean prescription bottle, which has a screw-cap on it, and they identify it with a label saying it came from XYZ—the address, the date, the name of the man. If they don't have the name, they put a *description*. A man that appeared to be thirty-eight years old, five feet ten inches tall, and so on.

'They seal the closure, the screw-cap, with hot sealing-wax, in which they press the metallic seal that bears our embedded initials. And they send *that* down to our chemist, who has to break the seal to, get the contents of the bottle.'

Lunsford pauses, impressively. He seems not unaware of a touch of the James Bonds about all this.

'He analyses the bottle. If it analyses as Coca-Cola within the tolerances of Coca-Cola, he throws it away. If it's something other than Coca-Cola ... additional endeavours are pursued.'

The tolerances of Coca-Cola are great, and the additional endeavours are polite. Three samples are taken from the doubtful place, and if all are found wanting a courteous visit is paid. After all, it would make no sense alienating a potential customer. 'Approximately eighty per cent of these interviews are effective,' says Lunsford. 'The substitution is discontinued.'

With the recalcitrants, something firmer seems called for.

'In 1970 we filed fifty-four suits, which was the most number that we ever filed in a single year and we had, I think, forty-five successful completions.'

'What happened to the *rest*?' I ask.

'They carried over into '71.'

'Have you had any *failures*?'

Lunsford gleams, discreetly jubilant.

'We haven't yet, we haven't yet.'

Imitation is, in a way, a global form of substitution, and it may be the sincerest form of flattery but the Coca-Cola Company can happily do without it. A tragic error was way back when they lost control of the word 'Cola'. The list of international cola drinks is as long as your arm—I have myself drunk Appia-Cola in a Roman bar and a creepy stuff called Inca-Cola somewhere not too far from Tehuantpec—and many of them sound, or look, suspiciously like Coca-Cola.

The company resolutely tries to stamp out as many of these as it can, but it's only through the extremest of legal niceties that one can establish that Pepsi-Cola (say) is admissible whereas Cleo-Cola was not. The most recent tussle was with the third largest grocery chain in the States, whose own soft drink, Chek, had an artfully designed label not instantly distinguishable from Coke. Also a tobacco company which wanted to use the name 'Sprites'.

Is a cigar competitive?

'Well,' Lunsford expounds, 'a cigar is an impulse item, *bought* on the spur of the moment, *sold* in the same type of outlet as soft drinks, *consumed* with alcoholic beverages mixed with soft drinks ...'

He pauses. 'To be a trademark lawyer', (he adds), 'you've gotta be ingenious ...'

For instance. One of the longest recent cases arose when Coke hauled a soft drink called Cup-O'-Cola to court. There ensued a ding-dong in which the Coca-Cola Company lost the first few battles but resoundingly won the war.

The miserable Cup-O'-Cola made some play of the fact that their beverage was supposed to be drunk *hot*. Much of their packaging depicted a steaming cupful of the stuff, as their lawyer pointed out. It availed him little.

Indeed, this exhibit dramatises the similarity of the marks [as the *Federal Reporter* summarises] *for appearing on the side of the cup is the word 'Cola' not in the block letters of appellee's registration but rather in a script so similar to the familiar 'Coca-Cola' script that a close, side by side comparison is required to perceive the few minor differences which may be present.*

Cup-O'-Cola finally ran neither hot nor cold, but dry.

'His thinking is so much above ours that—*I can't comprehend it*,' says a Coca-Cola man with total and terrible sincerity. He is a junior, and brimful of zeal. 'It is above the day-to-day working,' he says: '*A synergistic view!*'

The exec respectfully lowers another glassful. *Plus royaliste que le roi.* The king, in this context, being **Paul**

Austin, chairman, and effective boss-of-bosses at Coca-Cola.

Austin is a tall man, with a sort of handsome and statesmanly *gravitas*. He is in his middling 50s, was at Harvard, an Olympic oar, and commanded a PT boat in the Hitler war. The Camelot resonances have not gone unnoticed, and one British publication has wondered why a man of this calibre isn't in politics rather than selling soda pop.

This observation caused much chortling among company men. The business of the nation is business. No wonder the UK is up the creek, with this sort of thought around. Anyway, the Coca-Cola Company *is* in politics. Unhappily, but unavoidably.

'We are based squarely now on the multi-national concept,' says Austin, orotundly. 'We will become less and less parochial to America, more and more oriented to international trade.' Coca-Cola, adds Austin, should not be 'an American company exporting products into another country. We should be *identified with the country in depth.*'

Statistics are reeled off in support of this. The low proportion of US citizens amongst overseas Coke men. The fact that foreign franchisees have invested 'their own pesos, marks, francs, and what have you, into our business'.

Despite which, the view that Coca-Cola is just a fizzier part of US foreign affairs, a sort of carbonated CIA, is annoyingly deep-rooted. The tendency of the foreigner to confuse Coke with its mother country is a source of justifiable pride to the company, but also, occasionally, of embarrassment. As recently as July 1971 a row erupted in the Indian Parliament during which irascible politicos claimed that the company had been raking annual profits out of the country fifty times higher than their investment *in toto*. Other MPs leapt to the defence of the beleagured beverage, among them that sometime anti-US Radical, Krishna Menon.

At once Menon's foes demonstrated the superior virtue of *their* radicalism by diagnosing this new and horrid deviation: *Coca-Cola Socialism.*

'It's a matter that is solely politically motivated,' Austin says, sagely, 'and a relatively small left-wing party has gotten some very valuable publicity out of it.'

78

What of a suggestion by yet further sources that the whole imbroglio had been stimulated by a rival soft drink firm?

'Those things happen,' Paul Austin says, taking the synergistic view. 'I'm too far away to comment on them really.'

However identified-in-depth Coke gets to be, it remains a multi-national firm with multi-national problems. One instance. There was a comical commercial showing two Arabs in the desert, which was on the point of release when, zap, the Arab-Israel War.

A McCann-Erickson adman tells me the doleful tale. 'The Coca-Cola Company were as unhappy about that, and the War, as we were. *The Coca-Cola Company takes no political position on anything.*'

'They're in the position of making soft drinks. They don't have a position on who's right and who's wrong in any encounter.'

So unlike the home-life of, say, IT&T, I feel. 'And anyway they were just *Hollywood* Arabs,' the exec elucidates, adding with a high-pitched buzz-saw of a laugh, 'It certainly wasn't that the Coca-Cola Company was in favour of the *Arabs. Or anyone—*'

The film was never screened.

The real nature of Coca-Cola's interest in the Third World is much more positive than one might glean from this genre of diplomatic finessing, or the occasional scrap that surfaces in the Press. There has (for instance) been the attempt to grapple with the global feeding problem.

'Let me start back aways. About five years ago,' Austin says. 'We have these periodic office seminars. I suppose we number about forty or fifty, and we get away from our offices, and go to another place, a resort area. But not for the sports, just to get *isolated*. And then we put on programmes that feature some of the top intellectuals in the world.'

Like—Well, Paul Austin is reticent, not wanting to make publicity capital, but he cites a handful of economists, a State Department specialist on Latin America, and a number of experts on multi-national populations.

'It's a whole long list now,' says Austin. 'I guess I'm talking about forty or fifty luminaries, and the purpose of the meeting is to do anything but talk about selling Coca-Cola. It's a *mind-stretching* affair.'

Obviously, the talk frequently gets around to company matters, Austin says, but these are not sales talks. No way. 'This is a chance to let men get away from exactly that, and have a chance to think as individuals, under the guidance of someone. *These are directed discussions.*

'Now at the end of one of these a particular professor said —what we should do now is list your capabilities. And people would hold up their hands, and say this, that, and the other thing—advertising, marketing, sales promotion, all of which is true, and the professor said I'm still waiting for the genius I haven't gotten—

'And some chap said *distribution*. He said—Correct! You have the most unique distribution system in the world. Now what do you do with that? You make a lot of money out of selling soft drinks, but is there something else you want to do?'

An unnecessary question really. Coca-Cola is (I repeat) a concerned company. 'We had had discussions at this same meeting about obligations that the company has to ... let us say, pay its social rent, and discharge its responsibilities. Move from the area of accountability to the balance sheet to accountability in increasing degrees to the public at large.

'If you make money for fifty thousand shareholders, you've done a very good job, and that's what we're supposed to do, but should you do something more? Well, we decided that it would be foolish for us to do something that was totally foreign to our basic capabilities as we would just create expectations in the public. And we came out this way, that perhaps the three very wide areas of activity that were very much in need of assistance were, one—*Education*, in its broadest sense; and another was *pollution* of the earth's surface, and atmosphere and water, and what have you, and the third one was *malnutrition*.'

Well, malnutrition was obviously Coca-Cola's bag. Austin explains: 'From then on it was only a matter of structuring the company to do something about it.' Otherwise they might just have had 'a fine brain-washing four days, and gone back, and not done anything'.

What they did was to find 'the man most knowledgeable on protein in the world'. This was an Indian doctor who, understandably, 'was very excited about the idea of coming to us and using funds to pursue his work in protein technology'.

In the course of time, the excitable technologist produced a drink which, Coke hoped, might be 'engineered to appeal to the people who wanted and needed it', but pretty quickly they decided that there was no point in pushing this as highly nutritive etc. etc.

'Unfortunately,' Austin says, philosophically, 'people will not do what is good for them just because it's good for them, so it was our aim to create a soft drink which they would buy because of its *taste*. It would, however, contain a meaningful amount of nutrition, which ours did, and does. It's half the daily protein and vitamin requirement of an adult.'

Otherwise, it did leave a little something to be desired, as Paul Austin conceded. The drink was test-marketed in Brazil where, alas, 'it got off to a very bumpy start'.

Because the Coca-Cola company was not the only US giant doing what it could for this gigantic starvation sector of the global market. The magazine *Advertising Age* examines the state of play in the Third World at the beginning of 1971.

COKE MARKETS SAMSON IN SURINAM; PUMA GREAT IN GUYANA, IAA TOLD runs the headline, IAA being some esoteric advertising agency, or something.

Coca-Cola Co., which has been experimenting in Brazil with various formulations of a nutritional drink called Saci, has now brought out Samson, an enriched soft drink with a high nutritive value, in Surinam.

The launch of Samson was revealed here by Graham Williams, director of investment development, Overseas Private Investment Corp., at a meeting of the New York chapter of the International Advertising Assn. Overseas Private Investment is a new Washington corporation comprising many governmental agency functions formerly handled by the Agency for International Development.

81

Later a Coca-Cola official contacted by Advertising Age said that Samson is a clear, reddish-colour non-carbonated drink with a tutti frutti flavour. He said that despite its nutritive value, it is being promoted simply as a soft drink, rather than 'something that is good for you', because of frequent resistance to such appeals.

Mr Williams noted that another nutritive drink made from a soy concentrate, Monsanto Co.'s Puma, which is being marketed in Surinam's neighbour, Guyana, is now outselling Pepsi and Coke there. Priced at about 10c, Puma sells approximately 10,000,000 bottles per year in Guyana, he said.

Another soy-based nutritional drink, Vitasoy, is outselling Pepsi in Hong Kong, Mr Williams added.

He went on to say that General Foods, which has been test marketing corn noodles in Brazil, is now putting up a pilot plant in that country to produce the product locally. 'It is cheaper than the wheat such products are usually made from, and has a higher nutritional value,' he said.

A General Foods man suggested to AA that Mr Graham must have been referring to its golden elbow macaroni, (sic) with which it has been experimenting in Brazil for more than four years in co-operation with government authorities. He said that the pasta form was selected for its high protein content and because of its popularity. Actually made of corn, soy beans and wheat, it is distributed free to Brazilians. The product also is being tested in low-income groups and institutions in the US the GF man said.

Mr Williams said that CPC International 'didn't do too well' with its Cerealine high-protein cereal, introduced in Brazil in 1968, and is now going into full production with Duryea, a similar product, in Colombia.

Archer Daniels Midland Co. encountered a 'tremendous problem' in trying to market an imitative hamburger product (made of soy beans) in Thailand and decided against moving into that market but may go into another country, Mr Williams said.

Coca-Cola's exemplary behaviour has been a relevant part of Operation Arden—especially relevant considering such recent PR setbacks as the Hi-C affair.

82

The trouble with Hi-C was, essentially, a disagreement as to the permissible amount of free enterprise in advertising copy. Hi-C is a line of fruit drinks, and Hi-C is adman-speak for High In Calorie C. It was this, and certain other suggested claims, that attracted the interest of the Federal Trade Commission in 1971.

First the FTC asked the company to drop the use of the name 'Hi-C' entirely. Later, this uncharitable proviso was dropped but the commission still requested that Coca-Cola *avoid advertising which says or implies that its fruit drink products are uniquely suitable for children; that any such product is the equivalent of, or superior to fresh fruit or fruit juice and may be consumed in unlimited amounts in place of nutritious foods. FTC also wants the company's advertising to avoid representing that the product is made from fresh fruit when the fruit has been processed. The percentages of natural fruit juices in the final product should be disclosed when it is claimed that the product is made from natural fruit juices.*

The Coca-Cola Company did not find themselves in agreement.

'Nothing in the proposed complaint issued today by the Federal Trade Commission questions the wholesome quality of Hi-C,' they state. 'The Federal Trade Commission has not ordered Hi-C off the market. Reports to the contrary are entirely false.

'The Coca-Cola Company Foods Division will continue to market aggressively the product Hi-C and will make an immediate and vigorous objection to the unwarranted allegation of the Federal Trade Commission ...

'The Company is proud of the product Hi-C and the fact that we have pioneered the concept of vitamin fortified fruit flavoured drinks for the American consumer.'

Take that, the Feds! Nor did they fare much better over the earlier case, which was when a Senate Sub-Committee on Migratory Labour accused the company of 'callous disregard' on the citrus fields of Florida. The way Coke tells it, the legislature and the company realised that the workers were having a rough deal at more or less the same time. Paul Austin had asked Luke Smith—then manager of the Foods Division—to go and have a look around the groves.

'I had a funny feeling that something was happening there,' Austin recalls, 'and this is absolutely true ... I had been through those groves half a dozen times, and seen permanent housing that was very nice. It was just a *hunch*.

'Luke Smith is a wonderful, conscientious guy and must have sensed my nervousness, so sure enough he went down there and demanded to see every roof that anybody we paid lived under.

'When he left there, instead of going back to Houston, which was his headquarters, he took an aeroplane up here— Called me from the airport, and said *I've seen*! He sat at that desk, in one of those chairs,'—he indicates a chair—'and he said, Paul! What's going on is totally—to use his expression —*totally alien* to the Coca-Cola Company. And we can't have it!'

There is no reason to dispute the Austin version. What with the Cesar Chavez grape-workers' campaign there were enough straws, so to speak, in the wind. And the Florida conditions really were a shocker, Coca-Cola discovered. They own some 30,000 acres of citrus grove and employ three hundred regular workers but, during the eight-month season, perhaps another thousand would be hired every day. The housing consisted of this huge and dirty dormitory or a huddle of bug-infested tarpaper shacks, and the hours were interminable. Coca-Cola swung into action. Scientific Resources Inc., a consulting firm from New Jersey, was hired to probe the migrant point of view.

This emerged as 'Don't trust anybody. Especially if he's white.'

A multi-pronged attack was got under way. The permanent workforce was increased, and such comforting paraphernalia instituted as vacations and pension schemes. Likewise, child-care centres, and mobile clinics staffed by registered nurses. Regular worker-management meetings were organised, and Community Boards set up such worthwhile programmes as Voter Registration, Reading, Legal Services, and Cultural Enrichment. A housing scheme began to erect a great many

84

economic model homes, several of which are due to be occupied—with Coke handling the financing—in the community of Frostproof, Florida.

But giving credit where credit's due has never been the medias' forte. This plan had been under close scrutiny for nine months when somebody alerted NBC to the whole migrant deal.

'We got out our plan. It was as thick as a telephone book,' Paul Austin recalls. 'We gave it to Mr Huntley'—of Huntley & Brinkley that was—'and said, You will be interested to see what one company is going to do ...

'And that's the last anybody ever heard of our plan. In fact, we had to ask about four months after the documentary, please to send it back. And anybody who saw the documentary, every living soul, figured that the company was the most callous abuser of labour!'

Directly because of this video muckraking a Senate Sub-Committee of Migratory Labour was set up under Senator Walter Mondale. Austin was called and admitted that, yes, things were pretty rugged down there, but—he repeated—Coca-Cola had been sorting the situation out for a year.

The Congressional Record reads as follows: *'I think I can speak for most of my colleagues on the sub-committee,'* Mondals says, *'when I say that we were impressed and encouraged with the ambitious efforts and intentions of Coca-Cola.'* Interestingly, not even the good senators, I observe, seem to make the distinction between company and product the way that Coca-Cola would like. *'We are all deeply concerned that Coca-Cola will institute the plan as soon as possible, and that it be carried forward to fruition without undue delay.'*

Senator Mondale wraps it up with, perhaps, the merest breath of menace. *The sub-committee will continue its interest in the plan, and we intend to maintain a close watch on its progress.*

The prospect doesn't displease Paul Austin. 'I could say to you', he says to me, 'that this is the only welfare programme in America today that is actually *working.*'

Other, and still unresolved, problems lie elsewhere. Namely in the populist/consumerist upheavals concerned with such code-words as the Environment.

This is an area wherein the interests of Concerned Coca-Cola and Commercially Profitable Coca-Cola do not inevitably coincide. The dialogue might, perhaps, be described as a head-on clash. Coca-Cola as a commercial organisation is not disinclined to a certain breezy pragmatism. One broadsheet that the PR department hands me is called *The Disaster Lobby* and is circulated by the Illinois Manufacturers' Association. It represents a frontal assault on Naderism and the headings—*Threat to Free Enterprise, Threat to Freedom, Mixed-Up Extremists, Nader's Interests*, and so on—are good beefy backlash stuff. Coke's uncharacteristic interest in this literature is that they are cited as follows.

Just recently the Coca-Cola Co. felt it necessary to reply to environmentalists who demand immediate replacement of glass and metal soft drink containers with something that will self-destruct. 'A degradable soft drink container sounds like a fine idea,' said Coca-Cola, 'but it doesn't exist. And the chances are that one can't be made.'

The problem is the massive growth-rate of non-returnables. 'We would be delighted to go back to the returnable bottle,' Austin says, 'if that's what the Consumer wants ...'

And since he manifestly doesn't?

'Here's an example where you cannot do what the pure ecologist would have you do, and withdraw all non-returnable containers. That would be *catastrophe,* and the company would be so weak that it wouldn't be able to do anything good for anybody. So there is a commercial side ...'

He is, however, a bit less pessimistic than the Illinois Manufacturers. Persistent experimentation is going on in this very building. A room is chock-a-block with new containers, new sizes, new conceptual shapes. Already in the Fall of '71 the new 32-ouncer had been launched. It was made from glass especially suitable for recycling, and jacketed in foam plastic. Nor need the word 'plastic' give one the shudders.

'What we have developed is a particular plastic which discharges no noxious effluent. It is', Austin expands, or rather abbreviates, 'totally nox-free, and disposable through the municipal effluent system.'

86

It is—that is to say—destructible?

'Yes. As a matter of fact, it *feeds* the flames, and the heat is what destroys the matter. The bottle just returns to its natural composition of some glass, and some natural resins. It's been on test for some eighteen months.'

These issues are naturally much aired in *The Coca-Cola Bottler,* since this is one area where the company's interests are not necessarily identical to those of the bottlers. Bottlers have to make their profits too, and swollen with millionaires though their ranks may be, there are not a few operating in more benighted terrains who might well go to the wall if Coke was to outlaw the non-returnable on a conservationist whim.

Under the circumstances, the magazine seems admirably civic-minded. *Omaha and Boston paving streets of 'Glasphalt',* runs one snippet, *as ecology efforts continue through the country. A heavily travelled street in the heart of Omaha was reported as the first municipal project to use discarded jars and bottles in this manner. Many privately sponsored projects, including several parking lots of Coca-Cola bottlers, have used the new experimental material.*

One whole issue is dominated by *the latest developments in consumerism. Now, more than ever, bottlers must stay tuned in to this critical subject.*

Creative thinking has included efforts to educate the great drinking public. One series of ads would show a pretty young thing bending over obligingly, picking up a Coke bottle.

The caption runs BEND A LITTLE.

But—I inquire and, frankly, with some scepticism—does Austin really imagine that this sort of (profit-paring) thing can really be left to the companies concerned? Even at lower echelons of Coca-Cola itself I have found eddies of discontent at all this 'fashionable' Naderist busybodying, and can Business be regarded as entirely equipped to police itself?

'No, I don't think so,' Austin agrees. 'But I don't like to ask for government regulation either. The pollution problem is so vast ... Let's assume that the US cleaned up all effluent tomorrow afternoon, we would still receive a significant amount from the Japanese complex. To state it another way, suppose Europe decided—as London did, not too long ago—

you just can't simply fog up the atmosphere, and you won't be *allowed* to do it.

'So Europe cleans up and America *doesn't*.' Helpless gesture. 'And *we* would be dumping all *our* nitrogen oxides over there ...

'What I'm getting at is that there has to be an international control mechanism that will evaluate the seriousness of the problem.'

Austin alludes to UN Ineffectiveness. He mentions Guidelines, Purpose, and Sober Concentrated Thought. Also the Nuclear Stalemate, and the dodgy condition of the Biosphere generally.

Everything he says is inarguable. And in the meantime the Coca-Cola Company has to wage war on Pepsico, Royal Crown, Seven Up, and those other effervescent armies of the night across a battleground deep and thick with zillions of crunched containers.

What else—in all realism—is a working corporation to do?

But things (Austin feels) may be changing, not just for Coke, but for the entire country. The nature of the change is something else again, and Paul Austin is capable of pondering the End of the American Era etc., but rejects it, decisively.

'I'm not preaching that kind of pessimism which you can commercialise, and get paid for writing, but I do worry. About a nation that has never had a trauma. Never!

'And it has taken for granted that it was the Number One nation. I have a feeling and *I do worry*. I mean politically ... the *political* structure, the *economic* structure, the *psychology* of the people.'

Paul Austin relaxes a bit, brightens. The mantle of Elijah assumes a jauntier set on his shoulders, and transforms into the cape of a commander.

This is not (one senses) the pessimism that lodges in the marrow of the bones at three o'clock in the morning: it is the coach's half-time pep talk when the boss team has been fumbling the passes.

Also, it does explain why the statesmanlike Austin is *not* in politics. It was 'Engine Charlie' Wilson (who, at the time, admittedly *was* in politics) who delivered himself of the pithy

line: 'What is good for the nation is good for General Motors.'
The same, Paul Austin believes, is true of Coca-Cola. And
—as Engine Charlie is usually misquoted—*Vice-Versa.*

Unlike certain other businesses—consider the lost *meisterwerke* of Hollywood—Coca-Cola is properly respectful of its
past. The museum archives occupy a couple of rooms in the
new Atlanta building, where they are cared for and cata-
logued by Wilbur Kurtz Jr.

Kurtz looks rather like Otto Preminger, but more benign,
with a Southland panache of yellow shirt and striking tie. He
was the natural choice for the job. Wilbur Kurtz Sr was a
military historian and artist who was taken by Margaret
Mitchell to the Coast to act as technical adviser on *Gone With
The Wind.*

'She said that she wanted him to see that General Sherman
didn't marry Scarlett O'Hara,' Kurtz recalls, fondly.

There have been archives of one sort and another for a
quarter century, but the current nicely mounted display only
dates back two or three years. How was it preserved? It was
put away in warehouses, Kurtz says. A lot of the old-timers
kept track of it.

Kurtz was actually hired to do this job thirty years ago, but
there was one thing and another. The War. Kurtz shuffled
around the company doing every sort of job: 'But I had this
archives in the back of my mind, and I operated a lot out of
my hip pocket until I could get it organised.'

What is now organised is a documented display of memorabilia, in which the dominant item is the Coca-Cola bottle
itself. Here are those first sturdy bottles, the sort that are still
used for ginger-beer, and the later, slightly slimmer jobs with
diamond labels, and then ... *the bottle.* The Samuelson
Classic. Certainly the best-known bottle, if not the best-known
shape in the world.

*Believers in the efficacy of words may find the attempt to
describe the shape of the bottle a humbling experience,* remarks Craig Gilborn in an article devoted to the Coca-Cola
bottle in *Museum News,* which points out that *the bottle is,
by any practical educational standard, a model vehicle for the*

89

performance of those operations which are basic to the system-
atic analysis of objects.

And a systematic analysis is just what we get. There are
two *'methodolgical objectives'*, it seems. One is to provide a
written and iconic record and the other is to involve the
scholar-scientist in *every detail of the object to be studied.* Mr
Gilborn is able to distinguish eleven sub-types and variants in
the upwards-from-fifty-years manufacture, from the sole surviving Samuelson Original on.

These include bottles with 'Coke' on the throat, and bottles
without. Bottles with the bottler's home-town on the base,
then without, then—from 1963 to 1965—sometimes with and
sometimes not. There are blown bottles, on which 'Coca-Cola'
appears in relief, and there are painted bottles, and there are
transitional bottles which are both blown *and* painted. Also,
there are the two main *types* of bottle, which are the green
ones for America and plain ones for The Rest, with the single
exception (no doubt for well researched reasons) of Japan.

Watch out for signs of wear, notes Mr Gilborn. *In the
bottlers' lexicon a 'bum' is a bottle that can be safely re-filled
but that looks disreputable; a 'scuffie' is a bum that is scuffed;
and a 'crook' is a bum with a chipped bottom.*

Nearly 6.6 billion bottles were manufactured in the States
up till 1960, says Mr Gilborn, with a smack of the lips. Raymond Loewy—also known for the Lucky Strike pack and a
Studebaker—called it 'the most perfectly designed package
today'.

*The bottle, unlike most other objects which might be re-
garded as symbols* par excellence *of American culture, is sin-
gularly free of anxiety-producing associations.*

Well, yes. Unless one is tormented by memories of Fatty
Arbuckle, inefficient douches, eco-hazardy, Molotov cocktails,
or whatever. Gilborn, anyway, is pretty big on the Coke bottle
to the extent finally of proposing it as a course of study.

Other questions (he suggests) *that invite interpretation are:*

*What are the sensuous (touch, sight, etc.) and psychological
    qualities that contribute to the effectiveness of the Coke
    bottle?*

*How might archaeologists of a future millennium use the
bottle in reconstructing the events and forces of the
twentieth century?*
*What kinds of ritualised behaviour accompany the drink-
ing of Coca-Cola from bottles?*
*Compare the changing roles of the Christian cross, the
American flag, and the Coca-Cola sign in the non-Western
nations of the world.*

But there are things that even this indefatigable Coca-Colaphile seems to have missed. Like the bottles in *amber* glass.
'Most unusual,' says Kurtz. 'An experimental bottle made
during the War Years. We thought perhaps the colour would
help the product, but apparently not ...

'Only forty-four were ever produced. There are only three
that I know of in existence, and'—that Mellon-ripe glow—
'I've got two!'

It is (I surmise) of value?

'I could sell it right this afternoon for ... $200.'

The immense growth of interest in Coke archaeology began, Kurtz says, in about 1960, and prices have rocketed.
There is a dazzling variety of bric-à-brac: calendars/match-
books/clocks/thermometers/trays—and most soft drink firms
were pushing this sort of giveaway, but none more than Coca-
Cola. In 1903, when Pepsi were spending $1,888 on advertis-
ing, Coke was already spending a quarter million.

Wilbur Kirtz riffles lovingly through folios of ad material.
First, the archaic ones. 'The earliest advertising agency we
had was right here in Atlanta. Mostly black-and-white stuff.
Newspaper copy ...'

These are High Victorian, and brimful of uplift. Doc Pemberton's own belief that his contribution to the sum of human
happiness was of a medicinal nature was celebrated when
Coke was heralded in 1890—a splurge of red type, Coke's first
use of colour—as THE WONDERFUL BRAIN AND
NERVE TONIC.

But already contrary *tendencies* were present.

On March 29 1886 the beverage had been revealed to be:

DELICIOUS!
REFRESHING!
EXHILARATING!
INVIGORATING!

A subversive element, the Pleasure Principle, had slunk on to the scene. As Larry Dietz, another notable Coca-Colaphile, has remarked: *Could the Mustang Convertible be far behind?*

Obviously this would include girls. The Coca-Cola Girl emerges at just about the same time as the Lautrec dancer or Picasso's absinthe drinkers but it is doubtful if they would regard themselves as sisters, even under that pearlised skin.

The earliest Coke Girl was of wholesome proportions and demurely stay-thitherish, like Lillian Russell, the spitting image of Queen Alexandra (so to speak), with ostrich fan and tiara, and there's that massive mammalian thing, all pink silk and lace, who daintily lifts a teensie tumbler in 1907, imploring us AFTER THE THEATRE DRINK A GLASS OF COCA-COLA.

True, the side was let down by the Chicago bottlers in 1904. The Middle Western riff-raff produced an unauthorised tray in which not only did they commend Coke as a mix for High Balls and Gin Rickeys but also featured a girl whose ripple of Dante Gabriel Rossetti hair did nothing to conceal naked tits much daintier than the Russell frontage.

The tray was rapidly withdrawn.

However, together with the century, the Coke Girl began to loosen up somewhat. An important change was that the D'Arcy agency of St Louis began to handle Coke advertising in 1906. 'That was Archie Lee,' Kurtz says. 'He was the man who invented the phrase THE PAUSE THAT REFRESHES!'

Lee masterminded the great decades of Coca-Cola advertising right through to 1956. It was Lee who hired the greatest of the American Pie painters, magic realists like Norman Rockwell, Haddon Sundblom and N. C. Wyeth. The Coke Girl, for one thing, gets younger. Her hair is tidily tousled, and her mouth widens into that demure laugh, like a crossbreeding between Sandra Dee and the Mona Lisa. Often she

92

is caught in a break from some hyper-active scene, but even if she is just sitting there she *looks* hyper-active. A glint of eye and teeth mean that she is actually going to get that bathing suit *wet*. Or—during the War—she hasn't put that uniform on for show, or—after—that she is going to jive like crazy, just a wholesome foot apart from body contact. And even that 1946 brunette in the white two-piece grinning at this hand that appears (left) holding a full bottle—the caption just reads YES, because (Down, Sigmund! Down) what she wants is a Coca-Cola.

Other veins in Coke genre include the element of robust whimsy typified by Rockwell, and by the underrated Haddon Sundblom. Sundblom brought to life such unforgettable characters as 'Sparky'—the elfin bellhop who coruscated with pixie-dust, and wore a metal Coke cap at a sporty angle—and Santa Claus, who was a seasonable Coke favourite for some thirty years.

The model (Sundblom once said) *was a retired salesman named Lou Prentice, who embodied all the features and spirit of Santa Claus ... Lou passed away several years ago and since that time, I have been using my own face as a model for Santa Claus.*

The energy of these fancies is precisely mirrored in the Coke colours. Over the years, there is great consistency in these. Looking through the archives, or walking through the caviar-crepuscular halls and the peccary dazzle of the Atlanta corridors, one becomes absorbed in the thin surface brightness of the Coke palette, the weightless realism of the Coca-Cola homey utopias. The world is detailed, but utterly insubstantial, and it is a world of pale bright yellows, blues, browns, but dominated by reds, from shrimp-pink-cheeked urchins, flushed maidens, to the darkly ruby fluid itself ... A supabrite world, devoid of darkness, or any but the most shimmery of shadows, when even the night is cobalt and firelight ... a facsimile and edible cosmos of pie-crust and Jell-O. Delicious and Refreshing as a nubby bottleful of sugar-and-water itself.

⊠ Coca-Cola!
The Second Part

In which the writer meets an engineer of the Corporate Image in New York and attends the shooting of a Coca-Cola commercial in the Columbia studio, Burbank, Los Angeles.

I meet Walter Margulies in New York City. Walter Margulies has a polished tan, the unyielding smoothness of a chestnut. The tan is complemented by a dark-blue suit, a perfect dark-blueness, Homeric wine-dark seas translated into clothiery. Highly polished black shoes protrude from the bottom, and the top is a white gleam of cuff and collar, settling around a dark-blue boldly polka-dot tie.

The effect, taken with that suave, but distinctive, Hungarian accent, is so dignified as to be a trifle exotic, like an actor, a ducal valet, or a diplomat. What Walter Margulies is ... well, the role is tailor-made for him, as it should be, since he created it himself. Margulies is a scientist and an artist. A technician of the Corporate Image.

Lippincott & Margulies Inc. (It is some time now since Mr Lippincott joined the Corporate Image-Maker Above) were first prospected by Vance Packard in those high '50s times when it was the sociologists who made our flesh creep, and the firm hasn't looked back since. Their favoured self-description runs as follows:

Lippincott & Margulies, Inc.
and Lippincott & Margulies Ltd.
Consultants in Design—Marketing—Communications
Communications Planning

94

Corporate Identification Systems
Interiors—Architectural Exhibits
Market Planning
Market Research
Name Development
Package Planning and Design
Product Planning and Design

Anything, in fact, that the thinking corporation could possibly need. Especially (Margulies indicates) the corporation caught in one of those vexing Identity Problems that plague them nowadays. Corporate patients who have got that healthy glow in the cheeks thanks to L & M include some very fine firms indeed. It was L & M who created 'Group W' for Westinghouse, and it was L & M who metamorphosed the Ohio Oil Co. (not, frankly, in big league) into the infinitely more impressive Marathon Oil and it was L & M who turned the Hudson's Bay Co.—already a bit shrunken from *The Governor and Company of Adventurers of England Trading* into *Hudson's Bay*—into, tersely, *The Bay*.

L & M took on US Rubber, the third biggest, and vendor of such material as Naugahyde, and (soft-pedalling Uncle Sam) turned them into UniRoyal. Thanks to L & M, Haloid-Xerox became Xerox and prospered prospered prospered prospered prospered.

L & M helped Mead Johnson & Co. in a shrewd onslaught on the children's vitamin market. They co-operated with *joint research and package design aimed at penetrating the over-three market with a totally new product. The vitamins developed were, in fact, a new concept, being produced in animal shapes with five different flavours in five bright colours.* L & M redesigned most everything for Eastern Airlines—the Disney World airline, as it happens—including the Inflight Livery and the 'Flying Falcon' symbol on the Whisperjets.

Walter Margulies was the obvious choice, in fact, when Coca-Cola, sensed that they too were suffering an Identity Crisis. The crisis was an odd one. They weren't saddled with some monstrosity of a name—Haloid-Xerox!—nor the frankly unfortunate image of, say, another L & M client, the Internal Revenue Service. (Here, by the way, the intention is to endow the IRS with the glamour of some other government agencies. Like the FBI. There's some way to go, but Margulies is undaunted.)

No. Coke's problem was different. *They were too well known!* They were successful, established—yes, almost stodgy —and what's worse they were so well-known that they were ... invisible.

This was the genesis of Operation Arden. Uneasiness had spread up to the highest company levels. Even the elderly Mr Woodruff, theoretically retired—but how can one retire when one owns a third of the stock? Margulies was recommended by the president of Heublein Inc. (whom I am to meet later with the indomitable Colonel Sanders). Margulies set to work at once.

'The first thing that we did was what we call a Phase Out. A study to make a diagnostic audit of how Coca-Cola is perceived *now*. What its strengths and weaknesses are. Or'— hastily—'were *at this time*.

'And what a projection for Coca-Cola would be. What believable things they could be to their audiences. What the problems are that Coca-Cola creates for itself. Whether there was a need for the re-positioning of the brand in the eyes of the consumers. Or'—the mystic expertise of craft—'should I say a re-positioning in terms of marketing and communications models?'

So Margulies and his team took 'a thorough reading of Coca-Cola'. They examined the whole spectrum of soft drinks. They scrutinised the present, pondered the future.

'What the next decade is going to be like ... the thrust of our environment. Of our world. Of our opportunities!

'This was probably the most thorough job that we have ever done,' Margulies says, and some of the corporate frailties that he bared were familiar, but others came as a bit of a shock.

There are eighteen million outdoor Coke signs, at a conservative estimate. 'The sign was so well-known and so overall displayed that people could go through a street with, let's say forty or fifty Coca-Cola signs, on windows, doorways, and so forth, and you ask if they had *seen* a Coca-Cola sign. *And they didn't!'*

Dramatic underlining came from a hi-jacking incident, in which a dissident Japanese ripped off a plane, and demanded to be flown to North Vietnam. The pilot feigned assent, but —while a ground crew removed all overt signs of filthy capitalism—flew to *South* Vietnam.

Only, when he was about to land, the unwelcome passenger prodded a fire-arm into his neck and requested that he return skywards.

They had forgotten to cover a Coca-Cola sign.

It was invisible.

Global wallpaper!

Walter Margulies came up with two schemes of which the second—and slightly sedater—was adopted. Just for a start, a new advertising campaign was designed. Of course, in today's saturated market campaigns are effective for shorter and shorter series of time. McCann-Erickson (who had taken over from D'Arcy after the death of Lee) had launched THINGS GO BETTER WITH A COKE as recently as 1965. The slogan had a fun feel about it which seemed appropriate to the Swinging Sixties. The replacement—IT'S THE REAL THING—had other characteristics, just as appropriate to the '70s. It is Relevant, and likewise Reliable.

It is, incidentally, a smack in the eye for such unreal things as Pepsi and Royal Crown.

But it wasn't just a new campaign. The entire image was overhauled. There is the new logo, red split by a white whip-lash, which slightly suggests the shape of the classic bottle, and (even more slightly) what a computer might disgorge if it had a crack at reproducing that Spenserian script.

Finally, that higgledy-piggledy global wallpaper, all shapes, sizes, and indeed colours, will be wiped out, and replaced by that crisp market-researched uniformity. And how long (I inquire) will it take for the new device to attain the mass recognition of the original, or rather medley of originals?

'That is one of the good things about this programme,' Margulies reveals: 'The new one has the same recognition *at its*

97

start as the old one did after years of exposure. This was one of the ... criteria of the project.

'Because there are hundreds of millions of dollars of signage—all over the world. And we could not create a completely new look so that people would not recognise Coca-Cola. The job was to up-date Coca-Cola! To make it look ... fresher, newer, more youth-oriented. This was one important criterion: that we do not lose the Youth Market!'

Oh, yes. The Youth Market. And could it be that Coke has become—too wholesome, nostalgic, All-American, *boring* even? Might segments of the Youth Market rebelliously get stuck into other raunchier soft drinks? Margulies assents, joyously.

'It was getting this safe and stuffy image! And this project contributes to ... *unstuffy this image*!

'*Get it svinging again!*'—and how punchy the old word sounds with a V—'But we have problems. Did they show you research studies in Atlanta? A *very large amount* of research was done on this, and we have the problem that the moment we get ... very swinging, and very up-to-date, and very youth-oriented, we lose the quality image.

'And the one thing that Coca-Cola has—more than any competitive drink—ven anybody entertains, ven anybody really vants *quality,* they go to Coca-Cola!'

We go to lunch in the Sky Club, which is on the 56th floor of the Pan-Am building. It is a club beloved by corporation men, and I am to return here often. I find it a profoundly melancholy place, all that Berkeley Square kitsch—rococo mirrors, chinoiserie, green-liveried servitors, and the sort of family portraits you buy by the square foot—and those amiable executives, from embattled corporations and collapsing conglomerates, the subtle chink of silver on china, high in the central structure of an agonised air-line.

The view is, admittedly, splendid. It is also (as Margulies is not unaware of) a sort of Lippincott & Margulies diorama, a tabletop presentation of past, present, and future clientele. Over there on the Avenue of the Americas is American Metal Climax, transformed by L & M to AMAX, and here on Park his own HQ in the Chemical Bank Building, trimmed—at his

98

suggestion—from the Chemical Bank New York Trust. Across on the Rockefeller Plaza is the Radio Corporation of America.

Now this just has not been RCA's year. Finally, after one knuckle sandwich too many from IBM, they wrote off their computer operations taking the largest corporate loss in history (so far). Margulies mentions having just seen a rather drawn-looking Sarnoff—soon, it turns out, to die—who remarked, *en passant,* 'I have just lost fifty pounds and five hundred million dollars.' *Look* magazine is just one other unhappy memento of corporate life and death, directly visible down there from the Sky Club window. For a spooky nano-second I flashback to the stone dinosaurs in the La Brea Tar Pits, Los Angeles, but these saurian presences are the reverse, rending life embodied in three-D steel & marble & glass, clawing, devouring, succumbing.

Or, like Coca-Cola, surviving.

'It's a ... good ... old ... thing,' Margulies says, with sensuous glee. *'It's—the Real Thing!'*

'Yes,' I remark. 'So they say.'

Margulies pauses, deep in his technological arcana, the Marketing Models, Communications Systems, Scientific Structuring and Identification Programmes. 'You know, the Real Thing is not just an *advertising slogan,'* he explains, with the gentlest disdain: 'It came out of Consumer Research!

'People attribute to this product qualities ...'—he corrects himself—*'Dimensions which are greater than the product!'*

The Real Thing, in fact, is inscribed *there,* on the marvellous heart of the Corporate Image, eternally.

Or, at least, so long as it swings.

One of the Coca-Cola Recycling Plants is on East 34th Street. I stroll down there beneath a muggy, gooseberry sky. The plant is down by the East River, a great warehouse of a place. Kids are running in and out. Oil drums are being loaded with empties. These are being brought in anything from scuffed cardboard crates to smart panniers. Aluminium cans are fetching 10c a pound, and glass only one cent, but it's easier to collect a pound of glass. Returnable bottles are a nickel apiece.

One couple arrive in a dented beige Oldsmobile. It is up

to its windows with empties, the detritus of a commune hanging on somehow or other in the East Village.

'I heard that they turn the glass back into sand,' says the girl.

The idea appeals to her so much that I don't like to say that the Coca-Cola Corporation regard this as a wasteful conception, an absurdly roundabout way of replenishing nature's riches.

Coca-Cola, as even company men admit in their more down to earth moments, is a non-essential commodity. It's a myth, yes, but it is also just a bottle of soda pop, and a soda pop, what's more, that hasn't changed in any but the most trifling ways in eighty-six years. Except, that is, in the size of its operations. If anything is a tribute to the power of promotion it is Coca-Cola.

In that first year of operations 'Doc' Pemberton's profits were fifty dollars. In that same year he spent forty-six dollars on advertising, namely an oil-cloth sign. This proportion has been revised somewhat—one has to keep one's head—but it was an omen.

Today, the Coca-Cola Corporation is ranked sixty-nine in the *Fortune* list of top US companies. It is, on the other hand, the twelth top advertiser with an annual expenditure of something upwards of $75,000,000.

Obviously I had to attend to this. The lucky agency is Mc-Cann-Erickson, and I took to hanging around their Manhattan offices. The first Coke art director that I meet is Al Scully. He has a stripey button-down shirt and nifty cropped hair, such as I remember as being almost mandatory in those days before Rock came, and went, and the nuances of style were formulated on Madison Avenue. Al Scully has an unquenchable enthusiasm for Coca-Cola. Atlanta vibes pulse richly through McCann-Erickson.

We discuss various possibilities. One which interested me was one of those Ol' Man Mentholated River numbers: a boy, a girl, and Coke, drifting down a stream, which was to be shot in Little Rock, Arkansas, a township I had never had the chance to visit.

This wasn't to be particularly sexy or anything: not like another recent opus in which Tony Randall drifts lubriciously amongst a number of yachts, each one kernelled with a nubile girl and Coca-Cola. This was unusually overt for Coke, in fact, and the subject of some muted controversy. The river piece, Al Scully explains, was more the 'Huckleberry Finn kind of thing'. Visual problems were that the Mississippi tends to look like chocolate milk, and McCann's were still looking for a tributary that looked the way the Mississippi *should* look.

'We don't want the *reality* of it,' Scully explains: 'Because the Mississippi's too damn *big*. You need it *intimate*.'

Another potential situation was that a black was working on the product. (Coke gets special commendation from the NAACP for its proportional representation on commercials.) When some Arkansas worthies were advised of this they reputedly said, graciously: 'That's all right. Just so's you tell him to keep close ...'

Anyway, as it turned out, the shooting schedule clashed with another assignment, an International Writers' Convocation, held beneath the aegis of Hugh Hefner in Playboy Towers, Chicago. Not even Huck Finn could keep me from *that*. The next opportunity was a piece of domestic humour to do with house-painting. It was to be shot in New Jersey. Somehow, I missed that too.

Then Al Scully suggested the Christmas Message. This was to be a sequel to that number shot on Hillside-in-Italy, the genesis of which was a radio jingle. Scully recalls how McCann's were struggling to find a TV format for it when Harvey Gabor, another art director on the account, suggested suppose it was like a chorus, all the kids in the world ... they want peace, and harmony, and when they are thirsty, they all want Coke.

'We looked at them as if they might be the UN Chorus,' says Scully. 'On the Ed Sullivan Show in the old days.' The commercial was, of course, a smasheroo. Unforgettable. McCann's pondered what this sort of group might do at Christmas Time.

'We decided they would light up a Christmas tree, and

stand around it, and sing in the snow,' Al Scully says, working his hands with forceful *bonhomie*.

'It's only in storyboard form now. We don't know how it will work out in reality ...'

Shooting is to be on the Columbia Pictures studio lot, Burbank, Los Angeles.

And, yes, the tree is *tremendous*. Twenty-five feet of Silver Spruce in vegetable explosion into the luridly blue sky. The producer and the director went down to the Arrowhead Lake —a reliable source—and picked it out personally. The producer is thin, dark, with a confidential voice. The director has longish hair, and exudes nervous energy. They are down from New York with the art director, for a few days and they have the jaunty triple act of people who have worked successfully together before.

We examine the tree. It is still undressed, and it is unbelievably symmetrical. Literally unbelievably, as a matter of fact.

'It wasn't as complete as it is now,' the director says, poking around it with enthusiasm. 'There were areas that weren't ... perfect. So we've fleshed it out, added branches where it was necessary.'

Only God can make a tree, but it takes man to triangulate it.

Grips are hustling around with the truculent bonhomie that characterises the movie unions, and a few executives are here from Screen Gems. Screen Gems is a spin-off from Columbia Pictures which makes commercials, which means essentially that they handle most of the business around here. As a matter of fact, one real movie *is* being shot somewhere on the lot—1776, if anybody cares—and this will be the last in the torpid trickle of features to be made on this doomed acreage of fantasy, since in the not-too-distant future the sets are to be replaced by a supermarket, or whatever, and Columbia moves in with Warners.

But, 1776 apart, things are *jumping*.

'We are shooting six commercials *just this week*,' says the creative director of Screen Gems as we stroll across the backlot. One for Chevvy. An insurance company. He sneaks me on to the closed *Peter Pan* set where Alan Sues, side-splitting star of *Laugh-In*, and looking even more side-splitting than usual in a twirly-toed elfin outfit, is about to launch himself through a kitchen window and dole out great scrumptious gobs of *Peter Pan* peanut-butter.

Further afield we pass the Skeffington House, which is where Spencer Tracy played a politico in *The Last Hurrah*; the Deeds house from *Mr Deeds Goes to Town*; the Western Street; and the Boston Street which, supposedly, resembles Beacon Hill. A morose man in baggy trousers is clipping the grass around the fountain where Charlton Heston got speared in *The Omega Man*.

We return towards the tree. This is situated at the foot of the New York Street where Frank Capra shot his great comedies in the thirties. It is now scuffed and peeling, and the façades occasionally crop up on TV: the Partridge Family, or The Bobby Sherman Show. Behind the tree is a miniaturised wilderness, scrub and crumpled Giottoesque rocks, which have basked in the sun of a hundred Westerns. They will not be visible, being masked by the wintry woodlands of Coca-Cola. Anyway, shooting will be at night.

What is the intention of the commercial?

'It's as if we *discovered* a group of people who are reverently singing a Christmas Carol around a tree,' the director explains, 'and the tree is the most beautiful tree you've ever seen ...

'The people will be holding hymn-books ... They'll have a general, acceptable look, very merry and bright. It's more a symbolic group representing Goodwill.

'You know, I think it's nice,' he adds, earnestly, 'and what I think is nice is that it's a commercial with no pitch in it. It's simply a Christmas tree. It doesn't have a Coca-Cola bottle in it, and all it says is: *Peace on Earth! Goodwill to Men!*'

Goodwill or no, this is movie biz, and inevitably problems crop up. Right now, the tree is being strung with fairy lights by electricians working from a yellow Cherry Picker truck. Shooting is tomorrow night, but can they run a test tonight? Dick Kerns of Screen Gems is non-committal.

The other problem is more vexing. The McCann-Erickson concept is that the tree should be encircled by thirty extras and—in view of the nature of the festival—several of these should be children.

The California Board of Education has other ideas.

The Board is used to protecting that sunkist Californian youthlife from the rapacities—not to say perversities—of Hollywood, and their regulations, concerning working hours and such, are *stringent*.

'The children thing doesn't work out,' reports Kerns.

'What children thing?' asks the producer.

'The kids. Because of the time they're required on the set.'

McCann's finds this literally incredible.

This is Hollywood, for Christ's Sake! They've had kids in movies before. What about Bobby Driscoll? The Partridge Family? What about ...

'That's just how it works,' Kerns says, stolidly. 'It's difficult. Don't tell me, I *know* it.'

'What if I picked five kids from off the street?' the director asks, brightening.

'Then we'd lose our licence where we'd never be permitted to use children again in a studio.'

The director deflates. 'It's not critical,' he says.

'It is so! Critical!' cries the producer unassuaged: 'Why is it not critical? *What is Christmas for but the young?*'

'Yeah,' says the director.

'Yeah,' agrees the man from Screen Gems sympathetically.

'You have any baby-faced eighteen-year-olds?' asks the director, inventively.

Screen Gem says Yes.

'Real small?'

Screen Gems ponders. 'I'll get the little girl we used as a stand-in for Susan on the Bobby Sherman Show. She's four foot ten. We'll get kids like that—'

'It's the *shape* of children and not *children* that's important. If you have small people.'

'We could even hire *midgets*,' says somebody, with a brainwave.

'If we have ... small-limbed people, four or five of them,

and dress them in children's clothing, and put them with their backs to us. Small bonnets, and knickers, and stuff like that—'

'Even midgets.' (Perseveringly).

'Or midgets.'

'Or midgets,' concedes the director. 'We've got to make do with what we've got to make do with. I'd really like some people that look like young people because, you know, that's what Christmas is all about.'

'Why don't we make that pitch to them?' the director says, with a spurt of enthusiasm, meaning, the California Board of Education. 'Say, look, this is for *Christmas*!' He looks around the table. Gloom. 'They don't care, right?'

'You're dealing with the *government* this time,' says Screen Gems.

'I go for three girls and two boys,' says the producer.

But the director has rethought the midget situation.

'You're asking for trouble,' he says.

'I'm not, I know what I'm doing. I know exactly what I'm doing.'

'You're gonna have midgets singing around the tree?'

'If he looks *right*.'

'If he looks *grotesque*?'

'If he looks grotesque, that's *wrong*. But if he can pass—'

'They'll give a dumpy look maybe,' agrees Screen Gems, rethinking also.

'A midget is *stumpy* looking,' the director insists. 'I think it would be grotesque, midgets around the tree—'

'But who needs a nice Christmas more than midgets?' says somebody else from Screen Gems, genially.

'Right!'

'*Right!*'

'Now among those children, you have two blacks. Don't make me look for *black midgets*!'

The midget solution is abandoned amongst general mirth, and a telephone search is mounted for small-limbed extras. It is, as the producer says, a matter of making do.

Next day, the long dressing of the set starts. The Green Man is examining the trees. There are the smaller conifers which cluster around the big tree and stand on cross-pieces, Toy-town-fashion. The Green Man is, in fact, greying, and has an amiable withdrawn manner, rather vegetable in fact. He hammers a couple more branches into the Big Tree. Per-fection.

The Cherrypicker is wheeling around and fifteen hundred bulbs in primary colours are strung along the branches. Also the Snow Men are at work. They are shovelling snow by the spadeful. It glitters white in the broiling heat, and the Snow Men are slick with sweat. The snow comes in fifty-five card-board crates, with fifty pounds of snow to a crate. It consists of white plastic shavings. They feel light and dry, like desic-cated coconut, and hardly smell at all.

Why (I ask) bother to come to Hollywood? This macabre backlot, the constipated motions of the multiple unions, the regulations dating back to L. B. Mayer?

'We thought at first of doing it in New York,' the director agrees: 'Or if not New York, a place which is accessible to New York. But we decided that the *simple control*—which you begin to see—is important in a thing like this.

'Where we have the snow in the right place, the lights com-ing on, you know, on cue, and everything going at the right time. We have ...' he says, definitely: *'We have to have a completely controlled situation.'*

Certainly the snowscape is beginning to look pretty con-vincing. The plastic is being heaped on to sheets of white material, deep and crisp and even, or not even exactly, more a hummocky effect. This is, after all, supposed to be a North-land forest in the dead of winter.

Has it actually occurred to anybody to try and do this out in the woods somewhere?

The art director is patient with me.

'If you have the illusion that fake snow gives exactly the same illusion as real snow, why would any crew want to go into the woods at twenty degrees below zero? This'—he gestures at the glittering plastic—'will look *more* like snow than real snow.'

How would real snow look?

'*Worse!* Because the lights would have melted some of the snow, or there would be tracks, or somebody would freeze their ass off. Because you have no control!'

It would be too easy to underline the ironies. Art has always had its quotient of artifice, since that first painterly anecdote in which bewildered birdlife pecked at the painted grapes of Apelles. Artifice-as-the-Supreme-Reality. W. B. Yeats is just one who has spent time grappling with the problems that face McCann-Erickson.

Consider one of the art director's earlier *œuvres*.

This was a product of the time when he was still in the stills department, and it was during McCann's Dutch-Still-Life Period. Briefly, this was immediately after McCann's took over the account in 1955. The market research had been done, and they had spent a quarter million on experimental colour photography, and then they launched this lip-smacker of a campaign. Sometimes, the spreads would accessorise the Coke with a hamburger, or a trayful of cold cuts, or some humdinger of a multiple-layer sandwich, positively leaking good things, and sometimes there would just be the essential centrepiece: the Coca-Cola.

Anyway, this particular set-up was to be shot at Big Sur, that loveliest of North Californian beaches, and the concept was a purist one, just a Coke bottle stuck in the sand.

The bottle was seductively chill, wreathed in mist, and condensed droplets of mist, a frosty bloom that suggested it had just been fished up from some Antarctic deep-freeze.

This, pedantically, is of course Not On. There is no way that a bottle can retain that icy appeal when rooted in a sand-dune. 'But that's beside the point,' as the art director says, reasonably enough: '*Technically*, it couldn't. But *emotionally* you want it to look cold.

'You know, it became a whole craze. How to bead a bottle! Guys wouldn't share secrets, guys just wouldn't tell me what they put with the glycerine, you know!

'Then a guy came along, and it was the most bizarre thing, a guy came along that had developed a *plastic* bead—'

'He fired them,' the producer amplifies: 'He would fire the bottles with the plastic beads *on* them.'

Anyway, here was this small troupe from McCann's sticking the Coke bottle into the sands of Big Sur. They were positioning it just so: that equilibrium of sea, sand, sun, and the sensuous chill of the Coca-Cola itself, and some of the Big Sur crowd began to drift over to see what was going on.

'There were all these kids around, and they were ... *completely out of it!*' the art director mimes a kid who is absolutely zonked, bombed, blocked, in fact a characteristic seaside condition of the Mid '6os. 'We had put the bottle in, and we had all those spritz on, with glycerine, and we were just sticking it in, and—one of these kids came up.

'He was ... so *groggy*, man! He was out of his mind. And he stood there, and said: *"Man, now I've seen it all ... I've finally seen it!"*'

They break up, laughing.

'And he backed off,' the art director says, with amiable wonderment: 'Like we were turds or something.'

'Those are the sort of guys I *use* in my commercials,' says the producer, '*Plastics!*'

Later, we go to the Columbia Props Department to get some suitable Christmas gear for the extras. There are rows and rows of overcoats, plaid jackets, mufflers, furry boots. Here is the overcoat that Bogart wore in *The Caine Mutiny* and Ty Power's uniform from *West Point Story*. The authentic astronaut's helmets from *Marooned* are hugger-mugger with Roman helmets from unidentified spectaculars. A row of prison uniforms which must have figured in innumerable cellblock riots include the one that Burt Lancaster wore in *Birdman of Alcatraz*.

In the female area there is a signed picture of Ann-Margret, and the vicuna and fur creation worn by Ingrid Bergman in *Walk in the Spring Rain*.

Somebody idly picks out a pink feather stole. It was worn in a Matt Helm movie by Sharon Tate.

The extras begin to arrive. There are thirty-five of them, a skilful mix of shapes, colours and sizes. They greet each other with delighted cries. The delight may be a touch impersonal, but is none-the-less sincere for that, a group dynamic, like debs huddling at an intimidating dance. A great many people do extra work, but the hard core—the ones that telephone in every morning—are numbered in hundreds only. They seem resigned to the business, and the decline of it.

Except for some of the girls. These are lined up in a Frank Capra doorway while a former Columbia costumier checks out the chunky sweaters and knitted hats with those pompons. There are young ones, small-limbed as per order, and some matronly character types, but mostly they have the hard, bright eyes of the hopeful actress, that sta-prest unflinching smile.

One girl with a starletty cascade of Joan Crawford hair has an anxious query for Screen Gems. Should she wear the hood of her parka up or down?

Why not down? says the Screen Gems man tactfully. He doesn't say she will hardly be more than a blur.

Now an assistant director forms the extras into a circle around the tree (not a full circle. The producer is working the lights from a console right at the back.) They open their black St Basil's Hymnals and bend their heads, reverently. The arcs are lit, and the brutes. All around them the snow glows in the simulated forest. Right behind, the berm—or artificial hill—has been draped with white sheeting which lends it a folded Mantegna look. Agony in The Forest.

California insects batter away at the lamps, while the Snow Men tidy the snow with branches. Somebody tests the effect of a handful of the stuff held in front of a wind-machine, and the girl with the parka and the hair is unlucky enough to get a flake in the eye. She retires.

The fairy-lights on the tree are synchronised, and the camera makes smooth practice runs up and down the ramp, starting way in there, close on the treetop. *'I want To Buy The World A Coke!'* repeats the playback unit, generously. The starlet returns, parka hood still down. The Show Must Go On.

Shortly before shooting, a rocket mounts behind the tree. It has an odd, looping trajectory, an eccentric signature, which coils and spreads and thins with painful sedateness. Later I discover that this whorl—now diffusing into a sleeve of yellow silk—is an aborted satellite, a weather capsule launched from Vandenberg, and code-named ITOS, the Improved Tiros Operational Satellite. Being insufficiently improved, ITOS wrote off $10.5 millions, but here and now the problem, equal in relative magnitude, is: How long will it take for the blaze to die down enough not to diminish the fairy-lights on the Coca-Cola Tree?

Things are ready. There are four towers of tubular steel, all manned. The camera is aloft with the director close into the tree. The arcs are switched on and flood the place with a silvery fox-fur light. Last adjustments are made to the extras.

'There's a girl in a white coat—'

'Yeah?'

'Is she too *hot*?'

'We're working on that.'

'And right there! The girl in the pink coat and pink pants. Change her for something dark.'

To the extras: 'Hold up the hymn-books at both ends. And look forwards, kids.'

They start shooting. They do it the director's way in which the great silver star at the top of the tree turns on at the beginning; and the producer's way, in which the star comes on at the end, in time for the Goodwill Message.

The director doesn't think that's quite right.

'I don't think that thing is right,' he confides to the art director: 'It has no spiritual uplift *at all*. With the star going on at the end it isn't beautiful. It's cute, that's all ...'

They shoot it again, and again, and again. Filming is always laborious work, and usually tedious, and filming commercials is no exception. 'If that guy on the end shakes his goddam head one more time, I'm gonna kill him,' grouses an assistant director.

There is a break. Snacks, hot drinks. It is maybe ten o'clock now, and really cold. A couple of the smaller girls demonstrate their dancing talents by jiving to the jingle on the Playback machine.

'All right, take your places, kids! No talking now,' says a Screen Gems man on the loud-hailer.

They re-group around the tree. 'It's an American group,'

somebody tells me: 'It's—*John Everyman.*'

Another take. The star glitters, and the lights twinkle on, red, bright orange, and sky-blue, and there is a far-off hint of sleigh-bells on the wintry air, and John Everyman stands in a warm, close circle, the old and the young, man, woman, and, uh, small-limbed person, and they are holding the coal-black St Basil's Hymnals open and gaze up at this somewhat re-constituted spruce, Yggdrasil, the Tree of Life, imported for seasonal celebration by Prince Albert the Good, and now starrily incandescent with colour and light. *And they sing* ...

The Coca-Cola jingle wells out pure and sweet from the Playback machine and fills the Los Angeles night ...

'Cut! Print it!' the director says. Further work lies ahead, but he has an instinct.

'That was the take,' he says, contentedly. 'It was *beautiful.*'

✖ *Trust Texaco*

In which the writer observes an oil company shrewdly counter-attacking the eco-consumerist lobby with an All-American Spectacular involving a great many cheerleaders, flag twirlers and drum majorettes, filmed in the Rose Bowl, Pasadena.

It was during the shooting of the Coca-Cola goodwill commercial, during one of those *longueurs* when nothing much seemed to be going on, that I found myself in a Screen Gems props shed. I knew at once how Howard Carter felt when he set eye to aperture and first perceived the fabulous fitments in the tomb of Tutankhamun.

For one thing, it is pleasant to see that certain of the embattled Hollywood values are safe in televisionland, not just the Stars and Tycoons which can be as rapidly made as unmade, but those irreplaceable arts and crafts, those elaborate truer-than-true simulations, or the super-rococo grotesqueries, nowadays so snootily ignored by contemporary moviemakers on their reality trips (In New York recently a screenwriter acquaintance met an aged man who was treated with great respect, handled in fact like a Sung tea-cup. He was, apparently, the last Feathers Man in the world).

Here, for instance, in the Screen Gems shed are the Apple Trees from McDonaldland. These are the trees amidst which waltzes the jester of fast-foods, Ronald McDonald, and they are to be found amongst the french-fry bushes, the hamburger shrubs, and the bubbling fountains of cola. The trees are anthropomorphic, all popping eyes and stretcho wrinkles, just the sort of thing that Edvard Munch might have turned out had he been working for a creative advertising agency, and I thought they were superb until I saw the Can.

The Can was a colossus, a spectral bluish-grey, and as yet unenhanced with typographic detail, so that it had that enigmatic latent air of the slab in *2001; A Space Odyssey*. Inquiries elicited that this was to be the centrepiece in a Texaco commercial to be shot in the Rose Bowl, Pasadena. With fireworks, and one hundred and fifty extras. Girls mainly. The most grandiose commercial ever.

It seems an interesting project, and I discuss it at lunch with a representative from Texaco, a bright and amiable man from the Back East. We lunch in a Los Angeles club much in favour with executives. It has a stately air, not to say subdued. The furniture is dark glossy, and the approved wear is of Wall Street sobriety, free of the studied casualness of Beverly Hills or the rest of L.A. In fact, despite the disadvantage of the California weather, this could be a superior businessmen's club just about anywhere.

Inevitably, the talk gets around to ecology. This is again hogging the news since, judging by the papers, most of the California coast-line is knee-deep in sludge.

My host distrusts these sensationalist attacks. He agrees that there is a problem, but, he assures me, the oil companies are very concerned about it indeed. As to the ecological hysteria it must, he believes, be just another passing fad.

During luncheon we get hellos and beaming smiles from three or four other guests who all, also, turn out to be with oil companies. Competitive companies, but—my host says with pleasure—oil is a tight, friendly world.

Rehearsals start the following Monday. Shooting is at night, but already in the early afternoon the Rose Bowl pullulates with activity. Globules and segments of the Long Beach band are walking around trying to master the Texaco jingle, and two willowy blondes in bellbottoms are marching up and down, apparently counting steps.

The chief cameraman is marshalling lights, and the director who is tall, with a pink face and a ginger moustache, is organising the crane which is to contain one cameraman. This is bright yellow, and is (I am told) a forty-five-ton rig with a 150-foot grab. Beneath the rig and grab a great number of girls are on their backs, rhythmically working their limbs in the air.

'Americana!' says Milt Trazenfeld. Trazenfeld is from the ad agency, and this is his Concept. He describes how it was revealed to him, how he fought for it through scepticism and opposition, and how the Concept won through. Galileo had it easy. His assistant is a slight girl, a New Yorker, with the New York face, dark, and fine-boned to the point of neurasthenia. She wanders among that alien and splendiferous California youthlife, shiny faces and shiny hair, even the brunettes seeming another colour of blonde, bouncing around their clean and monstrous yardage of thigh, buttock and bosom, and she says, 'This is the *real* America. Not New York.'

I look at her a moment. I have heard this from New Yorkers before, but generally what they mean is Thank God, New York *isn't* like the rest of America.

No. She is enthralling.

'They are so—wholesome,' she says.

Well, yes. This is 1972, and the Sixties are way behind us. There were lean years in the sour old Sixties, the cheerleaders say, but now recruitment is again on the up-and-up. Americana is, in fact, all the thing.

Trazenfeld agrees. This is what the Concept was about. We discuss a few of the previous Great Commercials, like the quarter-of-a-million dollar airline ad, and the Stan Freberg soup spectacular done in the mode of Busby Berkeley, and the Alka-Seltzer *œuvre* starring George Raft.

But this is—the biggest. Appropriately, the lights are switched on. It is night, and chilly. Out on the pitch, an assistant director, Jerry Bernstein, is now rehearsing the Can, which is partnered by an equally colossal Pump. Both are based on stripped-down Volkswagen dune buggies, whose wheels are concealed by vivid skirtings of red and white roses. I purloin one of each. They are made of reflective plastic and *Made In Japan*.

There is no way the drivers can see. Bernstein tries to direct them with a Motorola walkie-talkie. The Can lurches forward, almost running over the hindmost cheerleader and devouring a mouthful of pink-and-white pompon. The Can's motion is indescribably evil, evocative of a slew of Sci-Fi movies, that Coming-of-the-Things glide, which is at once clumsy and unstoppable.

'When we finish shooting,' Tranzfeld says. 'We're gonna take over Los Angeles.'

'Not Los Angeles,' someone corrects, 'THE WORLD.'

Tuesday means last arrangements. The Screen Gems conference is in a screening-room, with Saarinen tulipstem chairs and an oval table around which sit the creative personnel in trim ties or open Malibu shirts. Madison-Avenue-meets-Famous-Monsters-of-Filmland.

The balloon, it is decided, is unnecessary. Right now, the problem is the troupe of girls from Santa Monica High and *dirt*. When they go down on their backs for those energetic callisthenics will their white sweaters get grubby? The merits of sacking, grass mats, aluminium foil and green plywood are weighed.

These are, as somebody points out, moistly, the Cream of American Youth. It would never do if they got *soiled*.

Wednesday is the first day of shooting, and the Rose Bowl is snap/crackle/popping like a bowlful of Krispies, what with one hundred and fifty Cream-of-American youths done up in their finery at last. The band wears that Napoleonic kitsch which is *de rigueur*, all button, braid and striped pantaloon, and the two willowy blondes are now wearing Deathshead Hussar helmets in shiny vinyl, and white microskirts. They are carrying the Texaco flag which is topped with a brazen eagle and looks heavy, but fits snugly into a leather pouch situated midway between navel and crotch.

There are twenty bit actors playing Texaco retailers, and they are hamming it a bit for the girls.

'Once more into the breach, dear friends,' declaims one, while another says, 'Once more, maestro!' to the music playback machine. A third does a witty Chaplinesque shuffle.

'He can dance,' says somebody from the agency. 'Pity he can't march.'

Mostly, they are likeable fellows, finding the going heavy

in their moribund industry.

'It's difficult for the no-name actors,' says one. 'When even name actors will do commercials for the money.'

'I'm going to get to *the Top*,' says another fiercely, capitalising the phrase, Harold-Robbinsesque. 'I wouldn't stay in This Town if I didn't *know* I was going to get to The Top. My friends', he confides, 'tell me I need more lines in my face.'

Another, a good-looking black, and himself a sometime baton-twirler, reminisces about the time that in the day he shot a Dristan commercial and in the evening he went to the Oscar Ceremonies in a party that included Carol Channing.

'That,' he says, 'was the happiest day of my life.'

Yet another actually prefers acting in commercials.

'It's more money. And it doesn't take as long.'

It is drizzling now. Goosepimples blemish those Sunkist thighs, but now is time for the first Big Shot, the Parade, and everything slots into place. The kaleidoscope resolves—

It is Cindy the Twirler in front there. White boots and white armlets, skintight in sequins, and the sort of glittery tiara that (some) debs' mums used to wear. Cindy's first baton lit up but was a bit of a disappointment in motion, the ghost of a firefly, so this is the standard chrome model, and up, up and away it goes, spoking through the sky.

Next come the two blondes, flags erect, and Marvin the Bandmaster, and the band, and the girls with the smaller flags, in primary colours, and now the Giant Pump. Behind the pump is another twirler, Debby, who is a major in maths, and who has a great hi-stepping style, her bottom apparently immune from gravitational pull, and whose twirling is altogether different ... close-order, up, down, around the body, with a weird spin off the back of the neck.

Then the Texaco salesmen, their marching finally together, and now the Giant Can. Around the can the cheerleaders from the University College of Los Angeles are doing their thing. A much milder thing once had me thrown out of a nightclub in Accra. There they go, exploding, a supernova of limbs, and the whoosh-whoosh-whoosh of pompon, in time to the nearest nano-second. Each cheerleader has a big red letter on her bosom. Together the letters read TEXACO.

116

Behind the Can is a girl of the girth I associate with Heroines-of-the-Soviet-Union. She is flag-twirling, slicing the air with this great flag like a demented signalman. Behind her is the Hex. This is a swath of material of roughly the size laid down for helicopter landings in the jungle, and it is carried by fifty-one girls in crushed velvet hotpants: California girls, but there is no cheap chauvinism here. Each one wears a banner inscribed Maine, or Arkansas, or wherever, and the hex itself is inscribed, yes, TEXACO.

The parade moves right down the Rose Bowl into the beady eyes of the three cameras, and the girls maintain that great gleaming grin, not that simian stretch you get from overtired models nor the dentifrice joy from beauty queens, but that supersmile which doesn't mean Fun but Clean/Clean/Clean.

Anyway they march on through, and the Can narrowly avoids running into the Pump, and it's a great take.

'You were beautiful, beautiful,' shouts an assistant.

The two blondes are striding back, Kate and Sally, Texaco flags still *in situ*, and they slant their necks sidewise and redouble that perfect smile, saying—

> 'Thank *You*!'
> 'Thank *You*!'

Friday. Not a day of rain, but forcing wind. The Old Gods of Movieland are, I daresay, angry. Skirts fly, and orange feathers, and girls huddle uncomplaining into blankets.

'I *live* in Hollywood but I've never been this close to show-biz before,' says one. Cindy the Twirler is buried in a fake-fur coat, her liqueur-chocolate hair still crowned by the tiara. She is nineteen, so these are the twilight days of twirling.

'At twenty-one they expect you to be married or something,' she explains. She is studying Sociology and, between takes, dips into a tome entitled *Contemporary Social Problems*.

After graduation? Cindy desires a job as air hostess. Any preference?

'Oh, I hope United.'

Fly the Friendly Skies with United goes the amiable slogan.

Slowly smaller set-ups are being completed. In one corner the Tumbler is tumbling. She is called Michelle, and she is compact with polished black hair, and she has brought her mini-trampoline which is the size of a washbasin.

A cameraman lowers himself into the strategic position, which is the upwards slant with which starlets are snapped descending from aeroplanes, and Michelle launches herself towards him a flip, backflip, and double flip-flop, ending up with knickers millimetres off the lens.

'The same again,' counsels an assistant director. 'And this time a nice, big smile!'

Elsewhere, the last and grandest tableau is being constructed. The Giant Can and the Giant Pump have been positioned side by side, silvery-green in the indirect Rose Bowl light. In front of them, the human jigsaw is being got together, the Band, shivering mutely, and the Cheerleaders, still dancing all-systems-go.

Tommy Roberts is forming up the letters.

'Come here T!' he bawls.

The T girls scamper over and form up.

'R! S! Where are you, S?'

'I've never seen so much S,' mutters a technician, lewdly.

The girls are handed their Easy-Lite Gold Sparklers, which are a foot long, and of the width of a cocktail sausage.

Everything is ready at last, and there is a hush, Reverential, almost. This is, after all, to be the *tour de force* of commercials, adland's answer to Bondarchuck's *Waterloo* or King Kong falling off the Empire State. *Except more so.* This is a One Shot Only, and it's now or never ... 'Ready when you are, CB' jokes make their appearance, uneasily.

This is Tommy Roberts' moment. The spectacle is his affair.

'*Be proud!*' he says on the loud-hailer.

The cameras roll.

First, the sparklers are lit. The girls hold them erect, in the Statue-of-Liberty pose, which is also not unlike the Columbia Pictures logo. And the centrepiece flames into life.

Now there has been a certain amount of trepidation about this centrepiece. My own feelings for instance are based on those Guy Fawkes celebrations in which the cheap squibs could be relied on to perform whereas the more expensive affairs could equally be relied on to topple sidewise into the mud or generally fizzle out. How much technological defeatism is implanted by this conditioning I wouldn't like to guess.

But Tommy Walker is no mere science-master or other sub-variant of NASA man, but the former Director of Entertainments at Disneyland where Fun is organised to within an inch of its life.

First there are the rockets, and rockets and rockets, orgasmic trajectories, and wheels and whorls, and superb smudges of variegated smokes, all very Late Turner except orchestrated around this simple message at the contraption's explosive heart, letters of fire reading TEXACO.

So that from the arse-freezing seat at the grab-end of the rig, this, and the massed rank of female Americana spelling out their one word, and the whole together reads—

TRUST
TEXACO

⊠ *The World That Hilton Built*

*In which the writer meets Conrad Hilton, a founding
father of the New World. He attends the inauguration
of two pleasure domes and visits many, many more.*

In Xandu did Kubla Khan
A Stately Pleasure Dome decree
S. T. Coleridge

World Peace Through International Trade and Travel
Slogan of Hilton International

It was hardly to be expected that Hilton would ignore Outer
Space. There has never been much wrong with their nose for
a trend and, anyway, they are as reverentially overwhelmed
by man's assault on the cosmos as anybody. (Amongst the
obeisances that the Business Culture pays to the rituals of
technology the Space Programme ranks high, having almost
acquired the status of a Royal Family.) And, even if the
honed Hilton sense of values hadn't provided lift-off, a host of
cartoonists, sci-fi writers, columnists, and Stanley Kubrick—
who in *2001* credited them with at least five floating edifices—
have already spread them among the stars.

Down in NASA–land itself, of course, this sort of cosmic
joshing is a way of life. In the lobby of the Cape Kennedy
Hilton during one of the periodic (if waning) irruptions of
launch-fever, there was a table sporting brochures which
solicited advance bookings for moon vacations 'sometime
after 1973'. Travellers would be put up in the Lunar Hilton
which was to grace the Sea of Showers.

So Barron Hilton, son of Conrad, and president of the

Hilton Hotels Corporation, created fun, but not much surprise, when he gave a talk about 'Hotels in Space' to the American Astronautical Society at a meeting in Dallas, Texas, and handed around eight-by-ten glossies of the projected designs.

These were not mind-boggling. There was an Orbiter Hilton, which resembled a floating Hoover. Barron Hilton quoted a Douglas Aircraft executive to the effect that *'Outer Space should be regarded basically as a medium for travel'*. and companionably suggested that he and his good friend, Don Douglas Jr, should get together.

The Orbiter Hilton (mused Barron) would be for short stop-overs, rather on the lines of a Hilton Inn. A hyper-space motel, in fact. But the Lunar Hilton would definitely be a more lavish affair. The sketches show a subterranean structure, cruciform, with an entrance like a gun emplacement. Facilities include a Beauty Shop, a Drug Store, a Gift Shop, and—sensibly—a hefty hospital. They derive from a feasibility study of the vaguest sort and are not of compelling interest. So far, one might have been forgiven for assuming that the main sort of space that interested Barron Hilton was newspaper space.

But, then, the note of authentic passion sounded.

Barron had been speaking, perhaps just a touch simplistically, of some of the bugs, like the need to economise on power, which would mean no elevators.

The multi-storied underground hotel will come later, Barron Hilton reassured the star-men, *But—and this is very important—in almost every respect, the Lunar Hilton will be physically like an earth Hilton.*

But, one feels, of course.

We know that most guests are uneasy unless their accomodations are a reflection of their style of living. We will have none of those science-fiction 'cells'. The rooms will be large, with carpets and drapes and plants; the artificial lighting will reflect the sunlight. There will be wall-to-wall television for programmes from earth and for views of outer space.

Guests in the Lunar Hilton, or in an Orbiter Hilton for that matter, will not dine on vitamin or nutrient capsules.

Perhaps they'll have to wait until they return to earth for some extra fancy items. But for the most part, they will eat at home.

This home-cooking will be thanks to Hilton's know-how with the new food technologies. *Great strides are being made in dehydrates, freeze-dry foods. Today, for example, a four-ounce hamburger can be reduced to 1/5 ounce; a steak to the size of a silver dollar. When reconstituted, these foods will be as tasty and nourishing as any served on earth.*

Cookery will be done by nuclear-reactor, and wash-up with a small Laser unit. In the bar, a mixture of ethyl alcohol and distilled water will be flavourised by a tablet of, say, Scotch. The whole lot will be chargeable to Carte Blanche, the Hilton credit card.

Nor is the picturesque aspect of Outer Space forgotten. *If you think we're not going to have a cocktail lounge, you don't know Hilton—or travellers,* quips Barron, *Enter the Galaxy Lounge. Enjoy a martini and see the stars.*

The concept is a dazzling one, and more surreal in its way than anything to be found in the fantasias of sci-fi. It rings totally, *but totally,* true. Space Hiltons. Martinis in the lounge, and Naugahyde furniture, jumbo-burgers in the Grill Room or a London broil, astral postcards in the Gift Shop, then a re-run of *Bonanza* on the TV or—just for laughs—*Star Trek* ... Galactic Hiltons reduplicating through the Infinite the Jupiter and Pluto Hiltons, and each one *'physically like an earth Hilton'* ... and yet further Hiltons, domesticating the pure sub-zero banality of Outer Space, innumerable Milky Way Hiltons and further out Hilton on Rigel, Betelgeux, Aldebaran ... a homogenised and cosy cosmos. The Hilton Universe.

There were, actually, just a few eyebrows raised in the organisation at the *pensées* of Barron Hilton. The thing is that the Hilton Imperium, like the Later Roman Empire, is no so much bifurcated as literally bisected. There is the Hilton Hotels Corporation, which operates within the confines of the continental United States with Barron Hilton as chief executive, and there is Hilton International, of which the president is Curt Strand, and which was acquired as a separate entity in 1967 by TWA. Conrad Hilton remains as a titular chairman of both companies, and they are on the jolliest terms, but one can see that to the suspicious flyboys of Trans-World, already bruised by decades of dealing with Howard Hughes, it might look as if Barron Hilton was staking a claim to starry business which—by all logic—should appertain to Hilton International.

Not that either group has much real cause to fret. The Hilton Hotel Corporation owns, manages or franchises some ninety US Hiltons and Hilton Inns—These being a cheaper sort of affair, usually close to an airport—and as for Hilton International ... Well, they number fifty-seven currently, namely the establishments in Acapulco, Addis Ababa, Al Ain (The Emirate of Abu Dhabi), Amsterdam (two), Aswan, Athens, Barbados, Berlin, Bogota, Brussels, Cairo, Caracas, Curaçao, Dusseldorf, Guadalajara, Guam, Hong Kong, Honolulu, Istanbul, Jamaica (Ocho Rios), Kuwait, London, Luxor, Madagascar, Madeira, Madrid, Mainz, Malta, Manila, Marbella, Martinique, Mayaguez (Puerto Rico), Mexico City, Milan, Montreal (two, one at the airport), Munich, Nairobi, Nicosia, Paris (Orly), Paris (Paris), Rabat, Rome, Rotterdam, San Juan, Sao Paulo, Singapore, St Thomas (The Virgin Isles Hilton), Tehran, Tel Aviv, Tokyo, Toronto, Trinidad, Tunis, Vancouver and Zurich.

The nature of the Hilton International involvement varies widely. A few hotels are owned outright by Hilton—or TWA, which comes to the same thing—including the Brussels, Orly and Kahala Hilton, and the upcoming edifice in Holland Park, London. In others, Hilton may control a piece of the action, like the Zurich hotel, where the company owns a slice of the ground-base; or the Nairobi, where TWA co-operated with El Al; or the second Amsterdam Hilton, out at Schiphol airport, where TWA co-financed the hotel with such prestigious partners as KLM, Philips, Heineken, BEA and the American Express.

But, for overwhelmingly the most part, Hilton International are a *hotel operating* company. The money will float in from elsewhere. Investment funds. Individual financiers.

Diversifying businesses. The London Hilton, to name but one, was initially financed by Charles Clore and, later, flogged to other property interests. Hilton International owns none of it.

Hilton are brought in to ... create a Hilton. Sometimes they use one of their own architects. Sometimes the architect is part of the deal, and the Hilton Architectural Office, which is in New York, gently exercises what they like to call *persuasion*. After all, if people bring in Hilton International, as an executive says, presumably a Hilton is what they *want*. Hilton are selling ... expertise, know-how, and (of course) the Look.

I have stayed in perhaps a dozen Hiltons, and one Hilton Inn, though this was being managed by Walt Disney Inc. at the time, so perhaps it doesn't count. And somehow these memories have unified. Congealed, even.

There are the big blocks themselves, gridded and marmoreal, like fossil kitchen graters and transistor radios. Inside, gone is padding over wall-to-wall carpeting, the colour of vegetable soups, and there are doorknobs which Pavlov warns me may well unleash a bolt of static. There is stuff on the walls, sort of a silky grass, and boutiques filled with pastel cashmeres and *Objets d'Airport Art*. There is the trembling blue jelly of the Pool, and the Lobby which—in the less developed countries—fills with locals goggling at the Glory of Western Culture and—in the *more* developed countries—management is always battling to keep free of hookers.

There is the Bar, where somebody travelling in Business Machines is eyeing the Pan-Am hostess, but fruitlessly, because she usually says that at birdsong sharp she is off to Hiltons elsewhere. And there is the scenic club with a blobby plateglass panorama of ... Abu Dhabi, Zurich, the Surface of the Moon.

The Beverly Hilton, Los Angeles. Picture a slab of layer-cake, or a marbley simulacrum of layer-cake, eyeball white against the sky. You leave the hotel, and move into Wilshire Boulevard. Automobiles pass in that non-stop ominous ripple, a machine-gun belt aimed at the Ocean, but you turn right, towards Hollywood, and walk chin-deep in roiling wheatfields of exhaust.

Soon you reach a building, which is low, and emphatically discreet. The exterior wall is a mosaic, apparently put together from sugar-lumps, but inset here and there are gold segments which flare in the sun like matches, and there are glass slabby doors.

Stupidly, I wait a moment, half expecting them to swing open, but this is what students of California would unhesitatingly identify as the Bel Air style, which means a fine feeling for values, so the doors don't open till you push them. Inside you are faced by a picture of Uncle Sam. He is on his knees, in prayer. Uncle Sam's prayer begins so.

AMERICA ON ITS KNEES
not beaten there by hammer & sickle, but FREELY,
INTELLIGENTLY, RESPONSIBLY, CONFIDENTLY,
POWERFULLY, America now knows it can destroy Communism & win the battle for peace.

These are Conrad Hilton's private offices, and this is the prayer that Conrad Hilton wrote, after discussions with Norman Vincent Peale and Fulton Oursler, author of *The Greatest Story Ever Told*. It is much asked for, and several thousand copies are sent out annually.

And it seems a message from another time, Uncle Sam—drawn with the deft magic-realism of the Rockwell School as a polychrome cross between Abe Lincoln and a Kentucky Colonel—and, not the prayer itself, but that uncomplicated appeal, the forthrightness. Like Conrad Hilton himself, a survivor.

Actually Conrad Hilton attributes the current stature and status of the Hilton name directly to that otherwise gloomy period in the national story, the Great Depression.

'During this period, eighty-one per cent of hotels in the United States went broke,' he says, earnestly. 'And I think we acquired some great hotels after the Depression which it would have been very different for me to acquire if it hadn't been ...'

These include, especially, the Waldorf Astoria.

125

The Waldorf is on Park Avenue, Manhattan, and it is now
the Stateside HQ for Hilton International. It seems a bit con-
congruous at first, the lava-flow of *modernismus* being controlled from the plummy and diamanté interior of the dowager
hotel but, as Conrad Hilton repeats *Every Man Needs A
Dream!* (The first chapter of his breezy autobiography, *Be
My Guest*, readily available at most Hiltons, is entitled
'You've Got To Dream') And the Waldorf Astoria was Conrad
Hilton's Dream.

'I still think that's the greatest hotel in the world. I just
came back from there,' he says: 'And I looked around the ball-
room, and you could see—the beauty and the grandeur. I
don't think there's another ball-room in the world can equal
it.'

He had anatomised it previously. 'This was my biggest
dream. And I made it come true. It took me years . . .

'But finally there was this group. And they wanted to sell,
and I wanted to buy. They were entitled to their profit, I was
entitled to my bargain. And between them was the fine mar-
gin, the honourable price, for this great deal.

'That's the American Way,' added Hilton simply: 'Any
man who does business in God's name is helping to build
Peace on Earth. This may be Idealism, but it is Practical.
And it is our right to make money, make a profit . . .

'I sincerely believe that we are doing our bit, to spread
World Peace, and to fight Socialism.'

It is quite moving. The unspoken is spoken. The Creeping
Red Menace has its heavies, cerebral and interminable, Marx
& Engels & Lenin & Trotsky and now dense dust-clouds of
ism from contrary ideologues, but Capitalism has its creeds
also, and it's nice to know that those fires of moralist Darwin-
ism are—though banked low—still burning, deep in the pink
styrofoam belly of the Great American Dream.

Conrad Hilton is a large man, six foot two, a bit stooped
nowadays, but with dark alert eyes and a skin of rosy leather-
ette. His bristle of moustache is worn in the mode that we
used to call an Anthony Eden, and he has a winning smile.
Naïf, almost. He is eighty-four, and bashful about his age. A
not unusual vanity. He has been known to attend functions

in a snappy reddish toupée.

He is wearing this unobtrusively expensive medium-grey suit, with the inky-black quatrefoil of the Order of Malta peeping from a lapel. Like the moustache, the ensemble is somehow Corps Diplomatique, apart, possibly, from a glint of gold cuff-link engraved CNH—Conrad Nicholson Hilton— and the same embroidered in blue on the shirt-cuffs.

This happens to be the first time I have come across mono-grammed shirt-cuffs. It seems not inappropriate. Conrad Hilton, after all, has written his name on a more far-flung assortment of variegated global real estate than anybody since Queen Victoria. 'Now they tell me'—he says, with that child-like zest—'that no new country dares to think that it has got going until it has a seat at the UN, a national air-line, and a Hilton hotel.'

Athens Hilton lore. A friend swears that he was chatting up two American birds down by the pool, and they asked to be taken to see the Pyramids. They thought they were at the Nile Hilton.

I myself heard a guide point out the best view of the Hilton from the hill of the Acropolis.

A Brief Biography. It all began on the Old Frontier. Hil-ton's father, Augustus, had emigrated with his family from Norway. Aged ten, Augustus arrived in Iowa. Later, he met Mary Laufersweiler. She was a local Queen of the May, and the daughter of a German emigrant, a store-keeper who advertised such real necessities as Metallic Burial Cases. Love bloomed.

Augustus left Fort Dodge for a rumoured mining boom in Leadville, Colorado. The rumours were right enough, but he looked around and Leadville was no place for a lady. South, then, to New Mexico. Albuquerque. Socorro.

'That was Frontier Country, and real wild,' Conrad Hilton recalls: 'Some real wild Indians around. My father was one of only two survivors in a party of seven massacred by Apaches.'

Again, no place for the future Mrs Hilton. Hilton *père* moved to San Antonio, where he set up as a trader, dealing in groceries, hardware, meat and furs. Just about anything. Mary Laufersweiler came West, and they were married on Lincoln's Birthday. No less archetypically, the former May Queen gave birth to Conrad two years later on Christmas Day. Fate moves in mysterious, if occasionally banal, ways. It is like watching the lineaments of a *Reader's Digest* profile being hewn out of the Wilderness.

Augustus Hilton was a six-footer with a handlebar moustache. He was called Gus by Mrs Hilton and 'El Coronel' by the natives of what was still The Territory. Mrs Hilton believed in Prayer, says Conrad, but Gus believed in Work. 'He gave me a pretty good example about working. He was up in the morning at five-thirty. And I remember him telling my mother one time I was sleeping till seven-thirty that he didn't think I would ever amount to anything. I was sleeping my life away!'

None-the-less, Gus was doing well, with the store, and a part share of a coal-mine, and there were plans to send Conrad to West Point. Then it all went. That particular débâcle was the 1907 currency collapse caused by the Knickerbocker Trust. The giddy switchback of Mid-American Capitalism peaks and slumps through the Hilton chronicles—rags/riches/rags riches —heady, and essentially harmless, because in those days you *knew* that the Good Guys win in the end.

Anyway, the family—two sisters and a couple more brothers by this time—struggled, and one prophetic note was struck. Gus jammed them tightly up in their great adobe house and turned it into a hotel. 'With me as bell-boy,' Conrad Hilton says.

So the Big Money began to roll back, and the young Connie Hilton got involved with the Democratic Process. 'I was elected to the legislature when I was twenty-three, and I decided that I was gonna put a *bank* in this little town.' The junior Representative's attempt to push through a law banning crime-movies was a failure, but the bank went well. Even so, Conrad sold it, after volunteering for the Great War. He celebrated Armistice Day in Paris, and then there was a cable to the effect that El Coronel had been killed in an auto wreck. Typically, just about the first in the Territory.

'So what to do? The business was gone. The bank was gone. There was nothing in Mexico for me. So I went up to Albuquerque to see a friend of mine ... who was very ill ... *and on his deathbed he told me this—*'

Conrad Hilton pauses.

'And he raised himself up, and he said—I'm not long for this world. The Good Lord is going to take me soon ... *But, if you go to Texas, Connie, you will make your fortune!*'

Hilton only had $5,000, but he was on the next train. 'I knew this was to be my New Frontier.'

This was when the great oil boom, the boom that was to cave in the Rockefeller monopoly, was under way. But Hilton had already made up his mind that he wanted not an oil lease but a bank. 'I found a fellow from a bank. He lived in Missouri, and he had staked two sons-in-law in the bank, and they weren't doing too well. He said he'd sell the bank for seventy-five thousand.

'It took quite a lot of nerve to go and buy a bank in Texas for five thousand dollars,' confesses Conrad Hilton; but as always people trusted his judgment. In particular a rancher with whom he had been involved over that first bank in El Paso. 'He said—Go ahead and buy that bank, you damn fool! he says, and draw on me for all the money you haven't got ... So, I sent this fellow a telegram and said we'd take the bank.'

The fellow answered thus.

Price up to $80,000 and skip the haggling.

A man who went back on his word. It was to change Conrad Hilton's life. Bringing about ... this office, with the signed celebrity photographs, and the funky memorabilia, like the silver dog mounted with startling effect on the telephone. The national and civic freebies, Ceremonial Keys, and the framed Légion d'Honneur some class or other, and the Freedom of the City of Istanbul—'There's only three of these been given in *five hundred years,*' says Hilton, overwhelmed at the graciousness of the Turkish municipal fathers—and the plaque which reads *Conrad Hilton—This Is Your Life.* And the rocketing graph which depicts the fortunes of Hilton International. And the great Hilton-studded globe itself.

'That evening,' continues Hilton, 'I went back to the hotel, and I saw the crowds around there, jammed up, and sitting around, people trying to get a room. I met the owner and I said you seem to be doing big business. He said, Well, I am, but if I had any sense I'd be out in the oil-fields where I could *really* make some money!'

Oh, that oil madness. The hotel, Hilton discovered, was turning over $2,000 a month. He liked the idea, and he also liked—*the idea of hotels*, he says. Meeting people. The owner was persuaded to take forty thousand dollars, cash on the barrel-head.

'And I was only in it for twenty-four hours when I said— This is it! My life's work. And not just one hotel. I want a chain!'

That first hotel was the Mobley in Cisco. It was (Hilton says) a crock. 'A two-storey building and it had, oh, I would say fifty rooms.' And one-bath-per-room? Air conditioning? Hilton splits into a grin. The days of tooth-mugs mummy-wrapped in those weird diapers, and bales of Turkish towelling, and lavatory seats *Sanitised For Your Protection* lay deep in the unimaginable future.

But the Mobley was cleaned up into a good earner, and one Texas flea-pit after another was acquired and metamorphosed. Partners were also acquired, like Jay Powers, an army buddy, whose misfortune it was to be gunned down by another (former) partner in a Hilton hotel situated in, of all places, Dallas, Texas.

Undeterred, it was in Dallas that Conrad Hilton decided to build for the first time in 1925. The first real Hilton and the first million-dollar deal. The Truly Big Deal. Conrad Hilton tends to talk of it in images, Sailing-round-Cape-Horn and Climbing-Mount-Everest, how it was put together; his own tenth part; the enlistment of backers, and how—with the hotel halfway up—the money ran out.

Conrad tossed a coin for guidance, and fought back, paring costs to the bone-marrow. Fortune twirled, and up the hotel went.

Is Mr Hilton specifically dedicated to hotels? ponders Curt Strand. I would say he is creatively dedicated to making deals.

But HOTEL deals.

In celebration, Conrad married for the first time, and announced the start of the El Paso Hilton. An even Bigger Deal at $1¾ million.

Nineteen days later the Stock Market collapsed.

'But we kept on building, fighting ... And we got it built,' Hilton recalls, with a gritty melancholy, because the hotel was built, but Hilton lost control. The bricks had been dropped in Wall Street, but the ripples built into almost irresistible waves. Except, nothing is irresistible.

'I travelled from hotel to hotel. I did everything I could to cut down expenses. We closed up rooms, took the telephones out ...' Hilton saved five of his eight hotels when the national average stood at one in five.

Meanwhile another great hotel had been going up across the country with the doomed insouciance of the band playing on the *Titanic*. It was, of course, the Waldorf Astoria. Hilton cut its picture out of a magazine, and wrote across it—*The Greatest Of Them All*.

And the Depression waned, and Hilton waxed. Those marvellous hotels started tumbling into his lap. Like the Town House, a Chicago aristocrat, at a knock-down price of twenty millions and, in the same city, the Stevens which had cost twenty-five millions to put up, but which Conrad got—*an absolute steal*—for seven. It was, and remains, the largest anywhere so was, inevitably, re-named the Conrad Hilton.

A second marriage to that seminal celebrity, Miss Zsa-Zsa Gabor, was well, brief. Hilton still speaks of her with wry affection, and notes that the divorce cost as much as the Sir Francis Drake in San Francisco. (Less sentimentally, in 1968, the London Hilton sued the talented Hungarian for an unpaid, but properly splendid, bill.)

More fruitful liaisons included further and yet grander backers. Henry Crown was one. 'Another man with a Dream!' namely to acquire the Empire State Building, all for himself, which indeed he did ... The giddy switchback! When last heard of, Colonel Crown was fighting for control of General Dynamics.

1949 was a very good year. Conrad Hilton finally became

the Man Who Bought The Waldorf. And as he breathes this phrase, he *marvels*. As if the news had just broken, the printing-ink still moist ... As a matter of fact, there had been quite a ruckus at the time, around the Waldorf's Peacock Alley, a degree of ruffling and crackling amongst the ladies of fashion rather as there was when Mr Hugh Fraser stormed Harrod's, but actually the visible effects of both these rapes have been similar—*negligible*. And the titanium-plated battle-cruisers of the Social Registers continue to grace the Waldorf with their teas and cotillons—'Conrad Whatshisname or no Conrad Whatshisname,' as one was quoted as saying, testily.

It was not cheap. Three million dollars. 'My board tried to dissuade me. A White Elephant, they called it,' says Hilton, who led, but by no means controlled, his board. They went along with the Waldorf deal, but more trouble was under way this same eventful year.

'I got a letter one day from the governor of Puerto Rico, saying that they wanted to build a hotel down there, and was I interested?'

Conrad Hilton was New-Mexican-born. His reply was deftly couched in that flowery business Spanish, and went down splendidly with the Puerto Ricans. His board were less impressed. 'One man got up, and he said—This is a dangerous thing! He was with Paramount Pictures, and he said we're having trouble all over the world ...'

The others concurred. 'They talked of wars, and anti-Americanism, and inflation. They said I was an Idealist, and I said "Yes, but it's *practical* idealism".'

Oddly enough, this dragging of corporate heels also used to plague Walt Disney. It sometimes seems as though the Napoleons of the American Dream have functioned almost in spite of those sage old heads clumped around the boardroom table. 'I said I'll tell you what we'll do,' Hilton remembers, crinkling as he focuses, on the rear-view mirror, this historic tableau; 'Give me five hundred thousand dollars, and I'll form a separate company. I won't ask you for any more money. I'll paddle my own canoe!'

The measly sum was voted, and with this modest start— plus a spanking new slogan '*World Peace Through Inter-*

national Trade and Travel'—Conrad Hilton marched out of Fortress America. Firstly, preparations were set afoot in Puerto Rico. Then, on a jaunt through Europe for the first time since the Armistice, Conrad pressed flesh with a variety of presidents and other local powers and scouted around for likely locations.

So the Caribe Hilton had its opening in 1949, duly star-studded and speechified, which was, surprisingly, not attended by the eldest of Conrad's three sons, Nicky. Why? Because Nicky was in the process of courting and then marrying Miss Elizabeth Taylor, a union fated to be rent by Miss Taylor's familiar demon, Publicity, even then in strapping form.

The first European beach-head, the Castellana Hilton opened in Madrid in '53, to be followed the next year by the Istanbul Hilton.

The momentum, what's more, is picking up. Of the fifty-seven hostelries in operation, no fewer than twelve have been launched in the last two or three years, while a further fifteen are in varying stages of being moved towards the pad. An additional Hilton is planned for Abu Dhabi and two in Amsterdam. There is the uplifting prospect of a Jerusalem Hilton. Also one for Khatmandu which will, no doubt, cater for the more material needs of that influx of Westerners searching for spiritual (or vegetable) Oneness. There will be Hiltons for Kenya, Kuala Lumpur, Kensington (London), Melbourne, Okinawa, Quebec, Stratford-on-Avon, and Sydney.

Further possibilities for the (later) '70s include Bali, Bahrein, Djakarta, Dubai, Kano (Nigeria). Lahore, Lisbon, and the venerable capital Vienna.

It is a formidable spectacle, and my mind is wrenched back to science fiction, particularly that much-worked-over scenario in which the World is menaced by a Thing that seems to have the capacity of spontaneous, multiple repro-duction. The scientist-hero is wrestling against time to find out How It Does It—Airblown spores? Telekinesis? A kink in the space/time warp? Still the blobs keep appearing, and they grow until ... There it is! *Another Thing—and just like the first!* And they multiply, quantally, until—

With the Hiltons too, first there is an amorphous blur, where the brainforce of the corporation meets the brainforce of the president of whatever or wherever, a gelatinous glimmer of Platonic Hilton, and it ... fructifies, and up there pops Another One, those 3-D pearlised bilda-blox, beckoning in Trade & Travel. Because where the Hiltons differ from the weirdos of sci-fi is in a matter of intention. These are, unquestionably, benign.

'As I see it,' Conrad Hilton says, succinctly, 'we are sharing the benefits of the American System abroad.'

Another time, he said much the same, but with just a touch of gleeful patriotism.

'Each of our hotels is a little America.'

This is not (I think) the way that Hilton International would state their position nowadays. The global HQ is on the nineteenth floor of the Waldorf. I wait for a bit in the corporation lobby, and examine the almost mandatory cosmic reliques, a set of six medals presented in 1969 to Astronaut Buzz Aldrin. These are silver, and mounted on perspex, and they show 'Milestones In Manned Flight' including the (conceptual) ascent of Leonardo da Vinci and that of Montgolfier, the celebrated balloonist.

Curt Strand, the president, is shortish, stockily built, in a dark suit of airweight sobriety. His office is muted, soothing, and his manner both lucid and crisp.

'We are a multi-national corporation,' Strand says. 'In fact, we were before the word was coined. Because, you see, we are domiciled here, but we are not *operationally* an American company at all.

'The number of American nationals in the company is actually very small, and our operations are all abroad ...'

Certainly it would be difficult to query the Internationalism of Hilton. This can be seen in a refined state at the opening of new hotels, which can be quite a production when they— and the economy—are in the mood. I have attended a couple of these: the inauguration of the hostelries in Rabat (1967) and in Tunis (1965) and the over-all style is the comforting bazzazz of the Grand, Gala Première, as brought to perfection in the Old Hollywood.

Firstly, the guests. These are picked with finesse. One list which I happened to come across was graded, for convenience's sake, Celebrity, VIP, CIP and Press. The middle initials distinguished the Very Important Persons from the just Commercially Important ones, and what distinguished the VIPs from the Celebrities was a matter of that subtle instinct that distinguishes good publicists from bad ones; and the treatment was a blend of the privileged and the perfunctory. It's a bit like being the bottle of Bollinger used to launch a ship.

If my memory of the two fests seems to have merged. Well, I can plead cause. Rabat and Tunis occupy adjoining stretches of North African soil beneath the identical blue swelter of sky. In both events we were introduced to the dignitaries and the locale. This involved a fair amount of well-programmed mosque trotting, plus watching craftsmen at their ancestral chores in the more picturesque *souks*.

Rabat—itself by no means the pearl of Africk cities—is within striking distance of Marrakesh and Fez. Tunis has Hammamet, the ruins of Carthage, and languorous beaches. Specific celebrations included feasting on cous-cous and other Arab delicacies in authentic tents, not to mention the Fantasia, in which the splendidly mounted horsemen of the desert launch a charge at the Guest Celebrities, pulling up in the nick of time, and perfect camera range.

It is difficult to imagine, say, César Ritz going to this sort of detailed trouble. Examples of that first wave of International Grand Hotels tended to be just plonked down any old how in glorious indifference to the surrounding terrain. Strand, on our first meeting, expressed it pithily.

'The prototype of the Old, International Grand Hotel? Always the same. Four or five employees to every guest. High ceiling, Louis Quatorze or Quinze or something. One dining-room, very soigné, with the classic French menu. And, if you had any idea of *fun*, a noisy cheerful bar or something, just get out of the hotel.

'Basically they were designed for a smart set, say the 1925/

1928 crowd and, well, there are some of them left, but hardly *enough ...'*

He settles back into the greenish sub-aqueous light of his office.

'Those old hotels were always fairly aloof from the life of a country. Not us. We feel the pulse of a country ... The Hilton Manager is a big man in a community. Not perhaps'—reflectively—'so much in London ...

'And we try to attune ourselves to a country. For instance, we don't just offer that classic French cuisine, but both quick American meals *and* local delicacies, *which you can eat in perfect safety*! And our tourists are a bit—cautious about that.'

Strand relaxed back, into the aquarial calm, and added magnanimously: 'Not in London, of course.'

Local delicacies which you can eat in perfect safety. This is almost the leitmotif of Hilton styling. The blend is incredibly skilful. Examine the buildings themselves which are basic Functional-Baroque, like a Los Angeles insurance office but into which the Hilton architects and interior decorators have gone to appalling pains to incorporate local *motifs.*

The stylistic diplomacy of the Hiltons is illuminated by the brochures, *'In the center of Tananarive, rising 18 stories along the side of a hill'*, reads one, *'is the Madagascar Hilton. By far the largest and most luxurious hotel on the island, the Madagascar Hilton subtly blends the best in modern décor with traditional Malagasy motifs in each of its 200 completely air-conditioned guest rooms.'*

In the Athens Hilton the innumerable bars and coffee-shops serve the staple hamburgers and steaks, and are backed up not only by Ta Nissia, a Greek speciality restaurant with an *'Atmosphere of the Aegean islands'* but also by a Pizzeria, and—of course—the rooftop Galaxy Bar where a perfect view of the Acropolis was at one time a bit obstructed by a perfect *model* of the Acropolis.

Another superlative example of having your cake and eating it is the Brussels Hilton which is *'the tallest building in Brussels—a 27-storey pinnacle that visitors have learned to use as their "homing" point above the marvellous confusion of streets'*. (As rather often one is put in mind of Oscar Wilde's observation that the Eiffel Tower was the best place to be in Paris, because it was the only place you couldn't see the Eiffel Tower *from*.)

The new Madeira Hilton again, is *'a delightful blend of contemporary and traditional Portuguese décor'* and has the added enticement of *'international cuisine with a British accent'*.

Other British accents, no doubt, are to be heard in the Nairobi Hilton. This is rather a striking building, white and cylindrical. *'Even the architecture is adventurous,'* the hotel leaflet puts it, justly: *'A uniquely circular, 17-storey guest room tower, inspired by tribal legends that life is a perpetual circle.*

'You will be captivated by the Nairobi Hilton décor. Dramatic murals of majestic Masai warriors'—none of the Kikuyu I am interested to notice, although they showed the war-like bent much more recently—*'imaginative Afro-modern sculpture, ancient tribal symbols on wood, splashes of safari colors and zebra skins. Everywhere brilliant masses of exotic flowers accentuate the beauty.'*

Also, of course, the Pool, the Sun-Deck and the Sauna. And the usual variety of chop, which is to be found on the second level. *'Here in the Ivory Lounge, sit and swap stories of your safari experiences or, if you like, discover delightful dining in the Tsavo Restaurant and the Amboseli Grill, stunningly designed to represent the interior of a huge native hut.'*

Not for nothing do gastronomes, folk-lorists, and other travellers to antique lands look forward—with mingled emotions—to a day when cultural cross-communications will have become so free and easy that in the entire terrestrial blandscape only the Hiltons will stand a proud and determined guardian of native manners and *mores*. It will be the Hilton interior-decorators who will be a repository of the artistic motifs of times gone by, and it will be Hilton Tours who will furnish an audience for colourful local ways. Traditional craftsmen will ply their archaic trades by courtesy of Hilton Gift Shops, swords will be beaten into ashtrays, and dying customs will live for ever on Polaroid. In the Hilton coffee-shops, skilled food technologists will find ways of preparing local delicacies which you can eat in perfect safety, and they will be brought to the table by waiters sporting, perhaps, a touch of authentic costumery ... in the last genuine Greek Tabernas, Suki-Yaki houses, Nordic Smorgasbords, and Old London Pubs in the whole wide world.

Not, of course, that some of the problems that Conrad Hilton's board anticipated in '49 haven't come to pass. Some of these have been simple enough matters of finance. It is, perhaps, in-sufficiently understood that Hilton International is in the business of *managing* hotels. It does not necessarily own them.

'We own the Orly Hilton ... the Brussels Hilton ... the Kahala Hilton,' says Robert Henderson, 'and, often we have some sort of an interest ... We have sixty per cent in Zurich.' Henderson is a Canadian, formerly a native of Winnipeg, and now Area Comptroller for North Europe, France and Iberia. No two deals, Henderson explains, are likely to be quite the same.

Naturally Hilton feel free to withdraw if a deal begins to look a touch dodgy. For one reason or another, the Hilton name is no longer associated with the Chevron in Sydney, the Bangkok Rama, or the San Geronimo in Puerto Rico. In March 1971 Hilton withdrew from a Hamburg deal with the building already up. (The abandoned waif is now part of another American chain, Hyatt Hotels.)

It is, of course, not possible to separate cash from politics. Hiltons once scheduled for Tripoli and Benghazi have been quietly shelved following the Libyan coup. The Beirut Hilton has bitten the Lebanese dust and the Dublin Hilton has been another sad write-off, apparently because of Erse in-transigence *vis-à-vis* North American flights, or something. Anyway, the corporation has finally sold the wedge of the Ould Sod that it hung on to for seven years in the neighbour-hood of the Balls Road.

In some ways, though, Hilton have been pretty lucky. In Dacca and Amman, the rival and larger Pan-Am-owned chain of Intercontinental Hotels have been involved in two shooting wars. In both cases, the hotels proved great vantage points for the world's Press, so the bar takings broke even, but tourism over-all declined. Not that Hilton have remained entirely un-affected by the ebb and flow of world affairs. The Malta Hilton has been fading a bit recently and the Berlin Hilton, once quite the treasure-trove, has never recovered from the build-ing of Herr Ulbricht's Wall. During the Six Days' War there were some tense moments in the Tel Aviv Hilton but—as a staff member confided to a British journalist—the main anxiety wasn't that an Egyptian pilot would *bomb* them but that an Egyptian pilot might *hit* them.

In other respects, the Arab/Israeli situation shows Hilton diplomacy at its unobtrusive best. Since they have been able to show that they don't own hotels, but just manage them, they have been spared a Middle East boycott. Other firms have been less lucky.

It is not these larger accidents of war and peace that disturb the corporation so much as more personally directed events. This is, of course, a tribute to their success. Hilton might perhaps no longer claim to be spawning far-flung Little Americas, but the hotels are inescapably seen as concrete em-bodiments of the American Way.

Their status is literally proverbial. Up beyond the Arctic Circle I have swilled hot wine in a hutment crudely lettered *Lapland Hilton*. A scrofulous Vietnam bivouac is christened the *Khe-Sanh Hilton*, and at the Isle of Wight Rock Festival a structure put together from several cardboard crates was enticingly labelled the *Nirvana Hilton*. Things happen in Hiltons that could happen anywhere—caches of arms found in London, armed whores in New York, Gene McCarthyite heads busted in Chicago. It was in the London Hilton that the Beatles first hearkened to the Maharishi, and it was in Hiltons in Amsterdam and Montreal that John and Yoko, several karmic cycles later, had their Bed-Ins. As I say, they could happen anywhere, but happening at Hiltons they acquire a symbolic status. Hiltons are perceived as neural centres in that ... amoeboid poly-vinyl slurb ... Identikit figures in a blandscape of shopping plazas, Chemical Banks, metro stations, open-plan offices, multi-media gobbledy gookodromes, New Town bus stations, corporate fiefdoms, palaeobauhaus office blocks with areas in front, supposedly to create a humane horizon, though littered with appalling lumps of sculpture like brontosaurus turds ... and—most especially—Hilton Hotels and Airport Terminal Lounges ... *the metamorphosis into a global Terminal Condition.*

Feelings of this nature are distressing to Curt Strand.

'That sort of thing is usually said by people that haven't stayed in a Hilton,' he says, just a bit snappishly: 'Because if they had, they wouldn't have that impression. These samenesses that people notice—In other words the elevators function, the hot water comes out of the tap. And, personally, I can't see anything wrong with *that.*

'There is', he adds, with resignation, 'a sort of inverted *snobbism.'*

The impact of Hiltons on planetary culture should (he feels) be seen in a very different light.

'Building a Hilton hotel has an enormous effect. Because it says to the local people and to the world at large that— *We are now part of a World-Wide Picture ... Worthy of Modern Times.'*

Strand speaks with a pale gleam, and the words are resonantly capitalised, but I'm sure the evocation of Charlie Chaplin is unintentional. There are, of course, occasional twinges of self-doubt. In one sense, Hilton hotels, Strand says, are Status Symbols; but Status Symbols come expensive.

'I was out in a new country in Africa the other day,' he had told me on our first meeting. 'They had asked me to advise, and I said, "Go ahead. Spend a million dollars on a new hotel." And a man from the Ford Foundation took me aside and said, "How can you? They need hospitals, schools, sewers. Why tell them to spend a million dollars on a *hotel?"* That shook me up a little. But, well, for a start, they had begun anyway. And, secondly, what would they have said. Except we won't live that long—we are newly independent, and we want some of the fruits of that now. It will take a hundred years before we have enough sewers. And the hotel will bring people in, and earn some foreign exchange, won't it?'

The question of prestige, Strand says, is not to be under-valued.

'If the president of Country X gets invited to Country Y, if he hasn't got a place to put up his counterpart for a return visit, he is *embarrassed*. That may sound like a small thing, but a country's embarrassment lowers its standing in the international community ...'

There was, to name but one, the inauguration of the Tehran Hilton which coincided with a lavish monarchical gangbang thrown by the incumbent of the Peacock Throne. This was attended by fifty heads of state, eight kings, three queens, and thirty-two assorted princes and princesses. 'We can now boast that almost every one of our guest rooms has been occupied by a member of the Royalty,' the Hilton carolled happily, thoughtfully supplying room numbers.

But all this, Strand concedes, is icing on the cake. The real benefits of joining the Hilton imperium lie elsewhere. In the inevitable proliferation of trade and industry, development and tourism. It is, naturally, a bit tricky to prove the benefits in hard cash, but Curt Strand asks me to consider the case of *Spain*. 'When we opened on the big, broad Castellana Avenue eighteen years ago, all you could see out of the window were ... 1928 taxis, and donkey-carts, and the occasional street-car.

'Today Spain has approximately eighteen million visitors a year. You can't attribute all that to the building of the Castellana Hilton,' Strand says, duly moderate: 'The fact however remains that it was the first international hotel that was built in Spain at a time when Spain was by no means the place to go. So it's difficult to say. But it has to start somewhere ...'

Well, does it? Opinions, of course, vary. Reactions to rampant Hiltonism have run the gamut from the aloof to the vindictive. London has, predictably, tended to the aloof mode.

'It took me ten years in London,' Conrad Hilton recalled, on my first visit. 'I could have bought the Savoy at one time but, no, I wanted to build a new hotel. The question was where? And how to get a permit. It won't take long, they told me. Good, I said. How long? Oh, just a few years ... *A few years.*'

Nor was there much rejoicing when the Park Lane site was acquired, and the Hilton finally built. It's a slightly weird building with a curve to it like a '30s cinema. *Moderne* rather than Modern, and the snooty neighbouring hotels, like the Dorchester and Grosvenor House, reacted like a dowager who finds herself forcibly attending a Tupperware party. Hilton has his consolations, though.

'But now it makes more money than any other, and we have a very fine patronage, and we are *packed*.' He riffles through his memories: 'Just like the old Mobley ...'

Anyway British passions seem to have been exhausted in that one sharp snap. Not even the Stratford-on-Avon Hilton has drawn much by way of attack. Cartoonists have seen it as a half-timbered skyscraper, and novelist Anthony Burgess said that Stratford should be made over to the Poor, who like Shakespeare more than the Rich do. 'I asked on what ... *sociological research* he based such a conclusion,' says Strand, with an amiable snort.

Other reactions to an impending Hilton have been less genteel.

'They write an awful lot,' Conrad Hilton said, with a merry twinkle. 'They would say—What the hell! Here was this fellow Hilton coming in, and, you know, *interfering* with them.

'*Coming in with the very opposite theory!*' He elaborates on the political leanings of the anti-Hilton crowd. 'They like to control, and we're free. A free country, see! That's why they gave me hell when the Berlin Hilton was built. The Communists thought it was an *awful thing*.'

Others who thought Hiltons an awful thing included President Charles de Gaulle, in a rare instance of accord with the Federal German Republic. He was as obstructive as he could possibly be, and Strand says frankly that had any patriotic French group put up plunge money for a badly needed new hotel, Hiltons would never have got a sniff of

French air. But none was forthcoming, and with patent reluctance de Gaulle succumbed.

Not so, President Nyerere. Such a storm broke when the building of a Tanzania Hilton was announced that the project was swiftly dropped. Tanzania was going through rather a rabidly Maoist phase at the time, apparently. Such phases do not last for ever. Hilton can wait.

Nor is waiting a bad idea on occasion. Because once every obstruction is removed, and the Hilton has actually been built, well, the electricity doesn't necessarily subside. Hilton are justly proud of their identification with the American Way, but it does tend to make them a surrogate target for emblematic or real half bricks. Fidel Castro remains the only head of state actually to have *liberated* a Hilton, but Hiltons all over are subject to a fizzle of everything from snide comments to sit-ins and bomb-threats.

This is even true in that placid capital, London. In the course of some chilling speculations about the 1968 'October Revolution' it was revealed by *The Daily Telegraph* that *Police have not discounted entirely reports that groups of anarchists plan to occupy certain buildings ... Obvious targets for the anarchists are the American Express offices, the Hilton Hotel, the BBC, and the offices of certain Fleet Street newspapers.*

Diabolical. But that particular revolution was aborted, as so many have been. Conrad Hilton and his executives of Hilton International tend to optimism.

'Mr Kruschev wanted me to build. Over in Moscow,' Hilton says, wistfully: 'And we made a deal. Just before they kicked him out of office.'

Kruschev, I find later, was also on calling terms with Colonel Sanders, hot gospeller of Finger Lickin' Chicken. It is interesting to speculate how things might look in the USSR by this time if Nikita had remained in the driver's seat. Would Conrad really have collaborated on this revisionist project?

'Why, yes. I would have' (firmly): 'Because it would have been on my terms.'

World Peace through International Trade and Travel! It's a seductive picture. The Moscow Hilton, with Kremlin ashtrays and minuscule waxen Lenins in the Gift Shop. Hiltons in Leningrad, Kiev and Samarkand, with Armenian specialities in the Pushkin Coffee Shop. Peking and Shanghai Hiltons, and Hiltons in Leipzig, Bucharest, Tirana. Reliable ice-water in the reclaimed Havana Hilton and the Hanoi Hilton, an artful blend of Western knowhow with traditional Viet motifs.

But even the most optimistic of Hilton executives would agree that the Hiltonisation of the Eastern Bloc is not immediately on the *tapis*. Other changes, of equally profound importance, are more directly on the way, Curt Strand says. Some of these relate to that whole mess of computerisation/automation.

Computers, for instance (explains Strand) will be able to store large quantities of instantaneously available information about Hilton guests. Just helpful trivia for the most part, of course. Likes, dislikes, birthdays, whatever.

The changes wrought by automation will be rather more visible. The Kensington Hilton, now under way in Holland Park, London, has been made a vehicle for much experimentation. Now the thing is that Hilton expertise has always been based on a mastery of hotel mechanics. The ultimate mileage is squeezed out of space and materials, inch by inch. Often, of course, a local architect will be used, but Hilton have their architecture and design group right here in the Waldorf Astoria.

The picture is clarified by Ali Kolsal, a nattily dressed Turk, who is sitting here surrounded by swatches of material, and blueprints, photos and drawings of Hiltons the world over. The architect employed on the job enjoys, of course, much autonomy. But (it is delicately inferred) seldom is Hilton professionalism ignored.

'After all,' says another executive, 'if you don't want another Hilton, why bring us in?'

The Kensington Hilton will, for one thing, be cheaper than the Park Lane establishment by about a third.

'We set out consciously to do just that,' Strand says, 'and before we even started, we made probably the most exhaustive piece of building study that we've ever made.'

The bar has had to go for a start.

'Bars are always very lucrative, you know. But we have cut it out because we know from experience in London that we can make more money per square foot in a restaurant. So in the space we originally allocated for the Pub, we'll have instead an authentic Japanese restaurant.'

Room Service is another area apparently ripe for economies.

'Frankly,' Kurt Strand says, frankly, 'take the breakfast you serve people in their rooms. It would be cheaper to hand everybody a dollar, and say—*Here's a dollar! Don't call Room Service* ... It would be cheaper for us.'

Later, in London, I examine the replacement. It is a machine over six foot in height, with see-through windows and veneered in plastic wood. It has the look of an exceedingly inexpensive computer. The machine is called a *Bell Captain*, and when the guest inserts his key, he can help himself to croissants, or Danish pastries, or miniatures of Seagrams or whatever takes his fancy. One of those reliable computers will instantly adjust his bill.

Bell Captain also has a built-in infra-red cooker, for those that want their croissants warmed up. A sign reads *Please Do Not Operate Without Bun In Place*, with other instructions. Some of the more squeamish members of the London Hilton staff have suggested that all this stuff about buns-in-ovens might be reworded but, so far, this tiny example of Anglo-American misunderstanding hasn't been cleared up.

No question but that the future is a rosy one. Approvingly, Curt Strand quotes Buckminster Fuller's observation that whereas the average American moved just 1,640 miles per annum in the teens of the century, right now his quota is more like ten thousand.

And this is just the motorcar set. Flying is something else again.

'When you looked at an airport crowd ten years ago, it was an *occasion*. You were dressed up, you were excited ... Today, you go in blue jeans. It's a matter of adjusting to the reality of the times.'

Is the reality of the times, then, that travel is somehow getting *boring*?

Curt Strand finds himself in agreement. 'Exactly!' he says: 'This is one of my real concerns ... that people who are travelling now do not enjoy it as much.'

Like fucking, in fact, people are doing it more and enjoying it less. Another bit of Modern Times *angst*. But not, Strand feels, irremediable. More efficiency is the answer. Cheaper fares. Cheaper hotels. More Hiltons. Many, many, more.

'Travel enriches the quality of life—tremendously,' enthuses Curt Strand. 'If you stop somebody in the street, and ask—*If somebody handed you a thousand dollars, what would you do with it?* I'll bet the majority would say—I'll take a trip!

'And it is simply common sense! People who have seen other lands ... know that other people have other ideas, other achievements ... and have created some beautiful things. This means some kind of increase in international tolerance.

As to the Travel Experience, so called, well, 'You know there are about three billion people in the world,' Strand says, reasonably. 'And how many of them have actually seen the Taj Mahal? Even if all of the projections of the airlines should materialise, which they probably won't, *by 1985 only six per cent of the population of the world will have gone up in an aeroplane* ... You want to see the Travellers of the Future?' Strand shuffles jubilantly through some papers, and produces a centre-spread airline ad from that day's *New York Times*. 'You can see them *now*—'

The advertisement is headlined so.

BOSSES OF AMERICA: LET YOUR PEOPLE GO.

The People number four. There is a guy in garage-hand overalls, with a middle-period Steve Cochran look, off for five days in London; a more ascetic-looking man, balding, with a slide-rule protruding from a laboratory-type smock, off to Spain; a fellow with a stripey tie and an arsenal of pencils sticking out of his shirt-pocket flying to Paris; and a girl, with horn-rims, a shy grin, and hands clasped over her, er, lap, understandably off to Rome.

No longer, in fact, will travel be a matter for the vacation-

146

ing bourgeoisie, or execs with morocco brief-cases and crease-less suits, nor even those juves in swinging blue jeans ... The Strand credo is, of course, unabashedly motivated by corporate profits, but still it has a nice populist ring, and as I examine the Travellers-of-the-Future I get the eeriest flash—*Déjà Vu*. There is something antique about the scope and scale of these huge, expected peregrinations, mass movements such as have hardly been seen since the obscurer Dark Ages when tribes would shuffle grimly over the landscape, just a nose ahead of War, Plague, Famine and Death, obliterating cultures as they moved.

But this is to take the negative view. There is more uplift about the Travellers-of-the-Future. They are pilgrims almost, and there is something positively Chaucerian about the Hilton Vision, the wayfarers bound for their available dreams, riding this aerial cafeteria, a *caravanserai* on the move ... the Miller, the Reeve, the Squire, and (clutching a week's worth of contraceptives) the Wife of Bath ... *Longen folk to goon on pilgrimages,* as Geoffrey Chaucer so justly put it, and if they longed to go on pilgrimages which might assist with bliss in the hereafter, what of the allure of the Hilton world, bliss in the here-and-now?

Down in Los Angeles, Conrad Hilton too has a vision of the Shape of Things to Come. 'Well, I'll tell you how I see the future,' he says, joyously. 'You see, we don't put the word "hotel" any more. We just put "Hilton". We opened the new one in Spain'— this is the Marbella Hilton, which is currently enriching local life, cheek-by-cheek with the projected Marbella Bunny Club—'and all I saw was ... *"Hilton"!*

'And that's all I saw in Amsterdam ... and at Rotterdam, they didn't put "Hotel", all they put was "Hilton".

'Hilton stands for hotel as far as Europe is concerned. And other parts of the world. *Hilton means hotel!'*

He leans back. Outside the swollen sun hammers a hole in the hurtful cobalt Raoul Dufy sky, broiling the juices out of the fruit, broiling the earth to chicken-colour, Deep-Southern-Fried.

It is orange-juice-breakfast-by-the-pool time in the Beverly

Hilton. I have consumed a breakfast which—a Hilton news-sheet shows me—is identical to that eaten by the King of Lesotho at the Tehran Hilton jamboree. It is lunch in New York, and bankers are soaking up Martinis in the Bull and Bear at the Waldorf. In London there is still just time for tea, and in Paris there are the pre-dinner cocktails. In the Tokyo Hilton the last (free) Welcome-Drinks are being mixed at the bar. And at the Hiltons in Hawaii and Honolulu it is still very early morning. The world is segmented into time-zones, like an orange, and it is pipped with Hiltons. A ripe, warm orange, filled with promise. The sun will never set on the World that Hilton Built.

⧉ *Pleasant Days*
in
Pleasantville

In which the writer spends time in the estate where the Reader's Digest is produced for the delectation of its many millions of readers.

It's a special drive, the drive to Pleasantville. Pleasantville is the community where the *Reader's Digest* is got together. One of the company limousines would pick me up at the Pan-Am building—where the *Digest* have located such activities as *literally have to* be done in New York City—and we would cruise along the feculent river, past the rotten-peach mud, Alcoa, the Palisades Amusement Park, and out of the whole glassy and fuming city, which feels like drifting out of the neck of a Molotov cocktail.

It's a forty-mile ride, and it has phases. One stretch is prickly with pylons and higgledy-piggledy with industrial plants. Antonioni's *Red Desert*. There are lurches into the pop-up vernacular of the freeways, and then one is traversing a tumbled terrain, rocks shelving down like glaciers, split here and there into fossil floes and ice-cubes, and hectic with dogwood, maple, oak, birch.

On the approach to Pleasantville itself the landscape becomes oddly familiar. White houses, tiled, with black shutters. Motor-mowers gleam on lawns, and mail-boxes on gates. Birds carry on their bird-life ignorant of impending ecocide, and cumulus floats overhead in clumps of aerial cauliflower. It's the World-according-to-Norman-Rockwell.

It usually seems brighter around Pleasantville. The brightness catches a rotunda suspended above the trees. This is

149

slim, a distant but not disreputable descendant of Rome's Temple of Vesta, with custard-yellow Ionic columns supporting a sea-coloured cone. It signals Journey's End, and appropriately enough, because at times the trip seems to belong to one of those gothic tales in which The Traveller from some humdrum place or other finds himself in another region/time/dimension, anyway the Perfect World where everybody is happy, and everything is organised and good.

Nor is the feeling entirely eccentric. The *Digest* occupied these green acres long before IBM went to Armonk, Bell to New Jersey, and General Electric, Western Electric, American Can, Pepsico, Shell Oil, Borden, UniRoyal, Olin, Nabisco (maybe), General Dynamics, General Telephone and Electronics went wherever it was *they* all went, and certainly long before Mayor Lindsay was motivated to announce at a Press, conference that Harper & Row was *not* planning on leaving, the *Reader's Digest* had established itself at Pleasantville, one of the first of the regulated oases, the feudal fiefdoms of the Late Capitalist State.

Swinging into the drive one sees that the rotunda surmounts the main *Digest* building. This is a handsome building, made of bricks the colour of smoked salmon. It was erected for the Digesters—as the upper echelons fondly refer to personnel—in the later 'thirties by an architect much impressed by the colonial chic of Williamsburg, in particular the Governor's Palace; and a college designed by Sir Christopher Wren.

Sir Christopher himself might, or might not, have put the rotunda on the roof. Here it does belfry duty being programmed with an electronic carillon. At its foot are four winged horses, marine green, Pegasus, the symbol of the magazine.

As the fountainhead of literary inspiration (remarks a brochure) *Pegasus still watches over writers as their words cast new light where needed, often arousing a thunderous response upon the awakening of those who have slept too long. So is it that Pegasus most appropriately symbolises the* Reader's Digest *today.*

Pegasus might well be feeling his oats. It is now fifty years since the *Digest* began its stint as a fountainhead. For fifty years life and learning, fact and opinion, have been artfully reduced into the compact confines of what Digesters like to call, with a cosy twinkle, 'The Little Magazine', and if anything the responses they are arousing are more thunderous than ever. The *Digest* sells 28 million copies in 13 languages in 170 countries to upwards of one hundred million readers. One hundred million readers! Pegasus has every reason to soar.

And if this memorable fifty-year anniversary hasn't provoked much comment, well, comment in outside media has never much interested the *Digest*. DeWitt and Lila Wallace, the couple who started the mag, have never been ones to make a show of themselves. The reverse in fact, though this is no variation on the Garbo/Hughes style. It's just—Digesters explain—that the Wallaces are plain folks. They just can't abide ... fuss.

A certain amount of discreet euphoria has emanated from the magazine. The relevant issue, February 1972, has an all-gold cover, and contains a 16-page 'Birthday Album'. This includes (properly condensed) 'Greetings From World Statesmen', the statesmen being Nixon, Heath—'During the past half century *Reader's Digest* has spread much knowledge and given its millions of readers a lot of Pleasure'—and Sato of Japan. Also Willy Brandt, Chaban-Delmas, McMahon, Golda Meir, Marcos (The Philippines), and King Hussein. There are also colour pics of Pleasantville—*'a greensward abloom with tulips'*—for instance, and, also, of some 'Homes away from home', namely the lavish edifices in Milan, Paris, hard by the Imperial Palace in Tokyo, and in Berkeley Square, London.

Finally, there is a potted history, and a summary of *Digest Philanthropies Over the Ten Years 1962 Through 1971*. These total $19,677,000, and are followed by the message: 'A corporate responsibility: helping to strengthen USA.'

As to the Wallaces themselves, they celebrated quietly enough, except for a white-tie shindig thrown by President Nixon—the Wallaces are friends of Nixon, as they were of Eisenhower before him—in the State Dining Room of the White House. Guests included the following: Attorney General and Mrs John Mitchell; Charles and Anne Morrow Lindbergh; J. Paul Austin (president of Coca-Cola); Colonel Frank Borman; Billy Graham; The editor of *The Detroit News*; Dr Sidney Hook; Mr and Mrs Bob Hope; Mr and Mrs Irving Kristol; Mr and Mrs Fred McMurray; James Michener and Mrs Michener; the Rev. Norman Vincent Peale; the Laurance S. Rockefellers; the president of J. Walter Thompson; and Clement W. Stone, billionaire proponent of the Power of Positive Thinking.

Quite a dazzler, except for that notorious Nixon luck. It sometimes seems as if no attempt to restore Camelot is complete without some naughty thing showing too much bosom. On this occasion music was being provided by one of the Ray Coniff singers, hardly a protest group, except that a Miss Carol Feraci suddenly reached down her dress and produced a sign reading STOP THE KILLING.

She then expressed support for Jesus Christ, the Berrigan brothers and Daniel Elsberg. Cries of *Throw her out!* were heard amongst the assembled illuminati, and Mrs Mitchell judiciously decided: 'I think she ought to be torn limb from limb!'

Miss Feraci left. The Wallaces had, apparently, remained silent through the incident, favouring the young lady with only the briefest of icy glances. A subversive demo right there in the State Dining Room, among the crystal, silver, white ties and Norman Norell gowns, is just about par for the course nowadays in this unruly, verbose, disorganised and dangerous world. *The Terrorists* (as a recent *Digest* reminds) *among us!* As they are acutely aware, the *Reader's Digest* is almost alone amongst media in standing four-square for law and order, truth and beauty: the positive decencies, in fact, and Feraci-type antics may occasionally rate a scary feature, but one thing's for sure. They'll never make 'Life's Like That'.

My first Pleasantville day begins in the Guest House. 'Just a li'l ol' farm house,' Bob Devine says as we approach it across the astroturf perfection of lawn. The little old farm house exhales a comfortable charm, a hundred years aged-in-the-wood, white horizontal planking, and a Colonial portico.

Today, by happenstance, there is a briefing of this year's visiting Fellows from the World Press Institute. This is a group of a dozen youngish journalists. They come from anywhere from the Argentine to Switzerland, and they are on a nine-month course aimed to give them 'an open and unfettered view of American society at every level so that they may return home with a new-found ability to report and interpret US affairs more accurately and with deeper understanding'.

The course, by the way, is sponsored by the Avon Foundation (the cosmetic foundation, so to speak); EI du Pont de Nemours & Co; The First National City Bank Foundation; the Ford Motor Company Fund; the General Mills Foundation; IBM; Minnesota Mining and Manufacturing Foundation Inc.; the National Cash Register Foundation; the Olin Corporation Charitable Trust; RCA; the *Reader's Digest* Foundation; the Signode Foundation Inc.; the Standard Oil Company of New Jersey; the Union Carbide Corporation.

The Institute is headquartered at Macalester College, Minnesota, which gives it an extra-special link with the *Digest*. This was the college of which the president was Dr James Wallace, DeWitt's father. It was not, frankly, very consequential. Now—as a major beneficiary of *Digest* largesse—it is a very rich place of learning indeed.

Anyway, the journalists assemble in one of the rooms, and we sit down, and are introduced to a number of senior Digesters. The first speaker is Bob Devine. Devine is the Public Affairs director of the *Reader's Digest Association,* and a long-time confidant of the Wallaces. He is by way of being Virgil to my Dante as I move through the *Digest* infrastructure, and he is a Good Guy, with suits of Tory-elegance, that crisp and creamy wave of hair, and eyes of the hard blue candour one associates with rear-admirals and Peter Arno's clubmen. Devine loves the *Digest,* and will unblinkingly repeat its history as often as necessary.

'People who try to track down the genesis of the *Digest* usually wind up in an Expeditionary Force hospital,' he says.

This was the hospital in Aix-les-Bains where the young

DeWitt, a convalescent volunteer, checked out his early convictions that just about every published thing was—too long, and where he industriously began those first condensations.

One by one, Devine conducts us along the votive stations on the *Digest* journey. How DeWitt and his young wife. Lila, laboured in a Greenwich Village apartment, reading up the periodicals they couldn't afford in the New York Public Library.

How the Wallaces raised eighteen hundred dollars, and how the first magazines were put into envelopes in this windowless basement underneath a speakeasy at 1, Minetta Lane. How they were mailed. 'And only the other day,' Devine recalls, with a twinkle, 'Mrs Wallace was telling me how she remembers so well sitting on top of those mail-bags!'

And how—after one year in the Metropolis—the Wallaces came to Pleasantville. Not the present green acres, but a flat above a garage. And how the magazine grew, and grew, but how, essentially, that first idea never changed—*An Article A Day Of Lasting Interest!*

Fulton Oursler Jr—'Tony to us here at Pleasantville'—is next on his feet. Oursler is the senior editor of the Condensed Book section, and he has the rumpled, no-nonsense manner of a don who also shines on the admin side.

Oursler sucks at a pipe, amiably, and begins peppering us with hard facts. The fifteen Reading & Cutting Editors (for instance) regularly work their way through 'five hundred and fifty-nine periodicals, newspapers, journals, quarterlies, and magazines'.

He explains the role of the Department Editors: 'They are responsible for putting the regular and irregular features in the magazine.' The department editor in charge of the 'First Person Stories', for instance, receives on average thirty thousand submissions a year.

The alien penmen subside wowing gently at the thought of all this freeflow input, but Tony Oursler—no beginner with a dramatic effect—is just getting into his stride.

'On "Life in these United States"'—known over here as 'Life's Like That'—'submissions average 185,000 per year ...

'The Excerpts Department'—which handles those great

Digest one-liners and much of the anecdotage—'receives six hundred thousand separate pieces of mail a year. And that is not truly representative, because you open one, and inside there are twenty or thirty.

'I remember counting, one fellow sent in two hundred and twenty submissions with one piece of mail! So we are really talking about millions of bits of items here—*every one of which is read!*'

There are a few more dense and wheeling clouds of statistics, and then Oursler pauses, adding modestly: 'This process which I describe is really just a technical nuts-and-bolts process,' before leaving this basic engineering stuff behind.

'I hope I've given some idea of the size ... the scope ... the *energy*, that goes into the creation of the magazine. There isn't time to talk about the—informing spirit of the *Digest,* or the wisdom of DeWitt Wallace, and they—not what I've been talking about—are really the secrets of our success!

'I haven't been able to talk about the impact of what we publish, or the lives that we've been able to save by our pieces. By pieces'—he amplifies—'on mouth-to-mouth rescuscitation, and warnings on the hazards of smoking cigarettes that have really changed the smoking habits of this country!'

Oursler puts away his pipe, and lights a cigarette with a rueful chuckle, and luckily finds himself able to *make* a bit of time. He talks about this lady he met at a cocktail party in South Carolina, and how emotional she became when she discovered that he worked for the *Digest.* Apparently some years back she had been going blind, and she went to seven separate doctors, and not one of them could help. Then a copy of the *Digest* came her way and—as luck would have it—the issue contained an article on glaucoma.

The piece, being a properly researched *Digest* job, mentioned a couple of unusual symptoms, and they were the symptoms that she had. So she had a couple of operations. By now she was weeping, but she said—*I'm crying through eyes that can see!*

'Virtually every editor of the *Digest* has a story, or stories, like that,' Oursler says, all too truly, and adds: 'In 1949, Albert Schweitzer, the medical missionary and musical genius who has given so much inspiration to this century, wrote a piece for the *Digest* which he called *Your Second Job*. And in it he said everybody should have a first job—that is, your professional career—but he should also have a second job. And that is to help other people!

'And Schweitzer's Second Job is our *first* job. The *Digest* is an American magazine that has become an International Citizen of the Free World. And it circulates in one hundred and ten countries, and it speaks in thirteen languages—*and everywhere it says the same thing!*

'The same good news!' Oursler pauses again. Not for nothing was his father, Fulton Oursler Sr, the author of *The Greatest Story Ever Told*, which was—along with *The Robe* and the De Mille *œuvre*—a crucial text of the post-war Jesus Freak movement.

'We publish pieces basically to help people. To help them relax. To help them bear suffering. To help them dream ... laugh ...

'Hopefully to give more meaning and purpose to their lives. Whether it's in English or the other languages that we have, that is the universal message of an issue of the *Digest*.'

The main building is reached by strolling back across the manicured lawn. Creepers frame the Greco-Roman door, and inside there is a circular lobby swimming with that oyster-coloured light which derives from marble or vinyl. Plants weep, and a bronze clown stares at me hollow-eyed from a plinth, as a receptionist—briskly friendly as a hospital matron —directs me to the waiting room.

This is to the immediate left of the front door. I am to get to know it well. It is a smallish room, and soothing. Two piebald ceramic greyhounds adorn a mantel above which hangs an oval mirror. A huge orange chrysanthemum stands in a viridian Sung bowl. A book-case is filled with those musty brown books which nobody ever opens, but which somehow transfer culture through osmosis.

Other reading materials are on a side-table. Copies of the *Connoisseur. Réalits.* A neat wodge of *Reader's Digests* and larger vols, the size of headstones, which turn out to be further

Digests rendered, respectively, into Enlarged Type and Braille.

Best-selling magazines do get published in Braille. I have heard of a Braille edition of *Playboy*, for one, and certainly the *Digest* can't pose anything like the same problem with the visuals (can Hef employ the same sort of contour-coding for the centrefolds that geographers use for maps?). As to the content, well, I can only speculate how fearsome 'The Terrorists Among Us' must seem to the unsighted.

The whole effect is that of a country house, but not quite. There is something almost too faultless about Pleasantville. If some conceptual future archaeologists wanted to recreate mid-20th century culture and had nothing to go on but a few copies of *Country Life*, they might come up with something like this. It is like an expensive sanatorium where everything is curable. A Health Farm.

Except, that is, for the paintings.

In the waiting room, a Modigliani is facing the door, and —poised over the Braille mag—there is a duskily floral Matisse. But the room is dominated by *Les Chaumes*, a late Van Gogh, a rural scene, a farm amongst writhing trees. The unprepared might assume that this was just more Good Taste courtesy of Medici prints or somebody. That German process which simulates the paint surface, say. A closer look shows that this is the authentic hand-made article, and these are just three from the Wallaces' collection, the best private corporate collection of impressionists in the world, which is lavishly hung throughout the Pleasantville offices.

The morose clown in the lobby (for example) is the work of Pablo Picasso. Other belongings include: Three Bonnards, two Braques, one Cézanne, one Chagall, two Corots, two Degas, one Derain, two Gauguins, one Manet, one Matisse, two Modiglianis, three Monets, one Pissarro, one Redon (of, what else, Pegasus), one Renoir, one Rouault, one Seurat, one Sisley, one Soutine, two Utrillos, one Van Dongen, two Van Goghs, two Vlamincks, one Vuillard.

A formidable array, in fact. The artists, some of them, were difficult enough in their youth. They were womanisers, like Van Dongen, drop-outs like Paul Gauguin, drunks like Modigliani and Utrillo, but time has sanctified them, and they have become exemplars of painting, as massive as Schweitzer, Einstein, Eisenhower and Bob Hope are in their other worlds, with all those quirks, eccentricities, rough edges, somehow ... edited, condensed into wry anecdotes. 'Personal Glimpses.' 'Life's Like That.'

Jeremy Dole is an Issue Editor. There are four Issue Editors, shortly to be swollen to five, if not six. (The *Digest* masthead is the only feature of the magazine intractably difficult to condense.) Dole is young, obliging. Before arriving in Pleasantville, he was a junior editor on *Playboy*—'No. It's not the norm.'—and on the *Ladies' Home Journal*.

Tony Oursler has already described the routines of an Issue Editor. 'If I can use a fanciful image,' he had said, zestily, 'I like to think of the Issue Editor as a kind of a—*chef*, who is surrounded by the world's greatest delicacies and foods. Everywhere he turns there is temptation!'

Each Issue Editor, Dole explains, does three or four issues a year. 'You strive for variety. I don't think you can pin it down to any hard-and-fast formula, with one thing in every particular category ...

'Sometimes you have two strong articles in the field of, say, "Art of Living".'

This, it emerges, is just such a month. The decision was whether to run two articles, both of which were pretty strong. One was a piece by Norman Vincent Peale on 'Procrastination': 'The idea being that you should not procrastinate,' explicates Dole; and the second an article by-lined Bob Hope, and entitled 'The Importance of Having Fun'.

Both were included. As was (for instance) a think-piece entitled 'Wait a Minute—Let's Not Go Overboard On Ecology'; two health and efficiency items, one on a new diet, and another called 'Striding: The Most Natural Exercise Of All'.

There were profiles on Arthur Burns, the economist; Carol Burnett, the TV celebrity; Vincent Van Gogh, the deceased painter; Bill Marriott, the hotel millionaire; Joe Frazier, the champ.

Political issues were touched on, with a piece about police

corruption; a personal piece by Jerry della Femina on how his daughter was injured in a New York park by a radical's pipe-bomb. The *Digest* was gloomy about Northern Ireland, and yet gloomier on 'Why We Must Meet Russia's Naval Challenge', and 'Teeth for the Red Chinese Tiger'. More cheerily, the condensed book related the exploits of a major who escaped from the Viet Cong.

And if an individual issue must be put together as an immensely skilful balance of wholesome frivolity, the occasional warning note, and an over-all sterling optimism—not for nothing has the ideal, still unwritten, *Digest* article been called: 'New Hope For The Dead'—well, the actual assembling of the written product is something else again, a process of laborious finesse unknown elsewhere in journalism. Materials with the mandatory *Digest* finish are only arrived at through a multiple-phase process which takes the writing biz a goodish distance from the Romantic Agony, and puts one in mind of a combination of a Du Pont lab and a Detroit assembly line.

In the case of those pieces which still are actually digested —e.g. condensed from elsewhere—there is, firstly, that industrious editing and cutting staff. The possible ingredient will be read, and check-read, and check-read again, and—if it seems necessary—again check-read.

If it passes, it will go to the first cutter who will, yes, cut it and send it on to the second cutter: 'Usually two people work on it, and then it goes to the man we call the Check Cutter for that particular issue. And he would work on it, and get the final typing on these yellow sheets ...

'At that point, he gives it to the Issue Editor, who goes over it. And usually it's in very good shape. He'd just maybe strike something out here and there or add a laconic phrase.'

Laconic phrases are, evidently, the prerogative of senior staff. I examine one of these yellow MSS. It has been duly initialled by cutter one, cutter two, the check cutter, and somebody else who is, I find, the typist.

'Now I put my initials on it. After I've worked on it, it goes to the executive editor in charge of the issue. At present there are two people who alternate doing that, Walter

Mahony, who is the Managing Editor, and Harry Harper.
And then it would go to the printer ...'

And DeWitt Wallace?

'He reads them in proof. They're sent for printing, and
they'll come back in proof. And then he'll look at them.'

A magnificent job of processing, in fact, and one which
shows up certain other magazines for the slipshod, personalised things they are. And what is perhaps even more curious
is the way that the artificial process is now being duplicated
minus the first step. Real reproductons of synthetic pearls.

It is no longer a secret that—in the strictest sense—the
Digest is not exactly a digest any more. The furore when
John Bainbridge 'exposed' in the *New Yorker* the manner
in which the magazine would commission writers to do long
pieces, plant them elsewhere, and then 'digest' the material
themselves, has long since subsided. Nowadays the mag admits
to originating 70% of its own material, and walks tall.

The germ of an idea may be suggested by the editorial staff,
one of the trusty writers, or by all of them, just creatively
messing around. As an example, Cornelius Ryan was enscon-
ced with a bunch of editors one day, it seems, and running
through a few ideas. None of them seemed quite right. Then
the editors made some suggestions, but none of them really
turned Cornelius Ryan on.

Isn't there something, asked one of the editors—DeWitt
Wallace, as a matter of fact—Isn't there *something you really
want to do?*

There was, as it turned out.

Whoever tells you this story, and it is a favourite when
Digesters are discussing the way that creative juices flow here;
and whoever tells you this will usually smile disarmingly at
this point, because what had been at the back of Ryan's mind
was finally to be called *The Longest Day*, and was not only
one of the best of Best Sellers, but also a top-grossing movie,
produced by Darryl F. Zanuck, and containing innumerable
Stars.

It is at these preliminary stages that another important
cadre is involved: the Research Department. Like most
media research departments this is a corps of perky but

serious-minded girls, and one of them will be assigned to the writer for as long as may be necessary.

The writer will then produce the First Draft.

This will proceed through the mills and be sent back, with suggestions for a re-write. At least one re-write.

'If the writer really—boshes it up', Dole says, 'it might go back three or four times. But there's a Point of No Return there. You milk all you can out of your author, but there comes a point where you've got to decide whether it's worth it.'

And, if it isn't, well, the piece may be re-assigned elsewhere, or it may be ... no, not *killed*, that has an un-Pleasantville ring to it, but filed away. And if the piece *does* work, then on to the production belt it goes.

But isn't there the merest danger that the pure perfection of this process, the meticulous multiple-phase precision, might somehow render things down, too far down, reduce them to an identical bland consistency?

Jeremy Dole considers. 'I don't think so,' he says. 'It seems to me that whenever the writing is superior, whenever there's a *real stylist* at work, you'll find that we hardly ever change his *wording*.

'In that case, we will block-cut. We'll just take out paragraphs that don't seem relevant to ... well, the quickness and effectiveness of the piece.' He grins, reassuringly. 'We won't monkey with his adjectives or anything like that. We won't fiddle with *his style*.'

Six thousand readers visited Pleasantville last year. 'Readers and editors are really members of the same sprawling family,' as the *Digest* puts it. I see a few readers there every day, comfortable folks with warm, respectful smiles. A girl, will escort them around the premises, not including the roomful of banked computers humming away underground, but including the idyllic offices of Lila and DeWitt Wallace.

The girl is informed, polite. Somehow reminiscent of an Intourist guide. DeWitt's office is blue-green, an orchard in the shade. The girl points out that the painting is by Marc Chagall. There is a chandelier, Waterford, as I recall, and a glazed horse. 'This particular Pegasus,' she says, 'comes from the T'ang Dynasty.

'The mirror, I believe, is French,' she remarks in Lila's office. Because they claim that most of the furnishings in her office are French, with the exception of the desk, which is a Sheraton.

'And this is a photograph of Mrs Wallace with the Little Angels of South Korea. They had just been on the Ed Sullivan Show ...'

Later, Bob Devine takes me off the tourist route, down to the subterranean reaches of the building. It is all much larger than it seems, an expanse of rooms, corridors, and rest-rooms, functional, but done up with true Pleasantville chic. Like the Cheyenne nuclear mountain groomed by David Hicks. In the banked computer-room there are some impressionists on the walls, repros of course, but tasteful. Infinitely tasteful.

Back in New York I visit the site of one of the *Digest* philan-thropies, a small green park which is to be in the middle of Harlem. Literally, the middle, between 139th and 140th on Lexington. It's a drab-looking place right now but this, it seems, is where the Landmark of Harlem once stood and opposite, on the site now occupied by a Woolworth's, used to be the Savoy Dance Hall, 'Home of Happy Feet', and birth-place of the Savoy Stomp.

'What we're doing,' Devine explains, 'is spending 240,000 dollars so far, to make a completely new, and interesting, and usable green park right in the middle of Harlem.

'There'll be a little area for basket ball ... and old men to play checkers and chess ... and greenery, and fountains, and when it's finished it will be a perfectly delightful, beautiful little park.

'It'll give them a community centre for music, and Sunday afternoon concerts. It's *small*, but it's gonna be a little oasis of simple beauty in the middle of Harlem.

'Isn't that something? That DeWitt Wallace wants to do? They want to help with urban problems in some way. And the whole thing—the design, the contracting, *everything*—is being approved by a neighbourhood black commission. So

we're not coming in arbitrarily, and building to our specifications in their neighbourhood. The contractors are black
contractors, the suppliers are neighbourhood suppliers ...'

A small plaque records that this is being funded by DeWitt
Wallace and the *Reader's Digest*; and the local blacks, Devine
says, want to call the area the 'DeWitt Wallace Memorial
Park', but Wally is dead set against the idea. The chances are
that it will be named after a black leader. Probably Whitney
Young.

It's a nice idea, and as vandal-proof as it can possibly be.
Already though, a bench, designed to withstand anything
but nuclear strike, has suffered and, of course, nothing can
protect walls from the pornographic or political aerosol, nor
the branches of trees from the bored, the bombed, the mad or
the bad.

It's a nice idea, a quarter-of-a-million-dollar upper. When
I mention the vandalism, another Digester looks at me with
an odd, but not untypical expression. The forthright do-
gooding gleam is mixed not so much with resignation as with
a sort of high peevishness.

What more (it seems to ask) can we do?

I have been studying that very first issue of the *Reader's
Digest* which is now, by the way, quite a valuable bit of goods.
The formula really doesn't seem to have changed much.
There is 'Advice from the President's Physician', and a scien-
tific piece on 'The Future of Poison Gas' by one Brigadier
General Amos. A. Fries, Chief of Chemical Warfare Service,
USA.

Human interest comes in with 'Useful Points in Judging
People', which is abstracted from the *Art and Science of
Selling*. One scarier think-piece is called 'Can We Have A
Beautiful Human Race?' The author, a eugenics theorist,
feels gloomy and—in true *Digest* fashion—he has done his
research in depth.

'*I have studied thousands of women unloaded at Ellis
Island,*' he reveals, Ellis Island being the immigrants' Check-
point Charlie. '*They are broad-hipped, short, stout-legged
with big feet; broad-backed, flat-chested with necks like a*

prize-fighter and with faces as expressionless and devoid of beauty as a pumpkin.'

Trenchant stuff. A bit too trenchant for the *Digest* nowadays possibly, but the willingness to take up arms in causes unpopular with the 'Liberals' has survived. Increased, perhaps. Reading through past and present copies of the *Digest* one senses an increasing politicisation.

Not that the magazine has ever held back from expressing its views. These are, broadly, Conservative (in the American sense, that is. US Conservatives regretfully consider the British party much rotted with Socialism). This is to say that they combine a proper respect for law and order, the successful and the powerful, with a strong helping of Middle-Western populism. Also implied is a watchful, and sometimes jaundiced, eye on the limousine liberals of the East Coast and the excessive growth of government power in Washington. The *Digest* is of the folks, folksy.

Even so I sense a change of tone. In past decades, the *Digest* knew that it spoke for the consensus. Vigilance was constantly necessary, but the tone was confident, contemptuous, even placid. Right now, the threats have multiplied. The huge *Digest* audience is still waiting out there, but—for the first time—a bit fearfully. The consensus is fissured every which way, and who is to blame the magazine if it sometimes sounds hectoring, even querulous?

I discuss some of these matters with a senior editor, John Allen. Allen is a pleasant, no-nonsense type. He admits that the *Digest* has changed with the times, and comes up with a non-political instance.

'A case in point,' he suggests, 'would be our *nature* stories. They are a lot more hard-nosed—or perhaps *hard-beaked*—than they were in the 'thirties, when birds sang love songs to other birds etcetera ...

'We preceded Ardrey in the whole Territorial Imperative bit, you know, and so a dear, sweet writer, who shall remain nameless, but used to hit us quite frequently, still keeps trying and wonders why his love-songy birds don't get in any more. That's just one example of changing because the information changes.

'Occasionally we can run a piece that we ran back in the 'thirties because they were so universal and timeless, but I think we're getting much more sophisticated—I think if you *look* at us we are more—because the *readers* are more sophisticated. Because they're getting supplied with so much information thrown at them ...

'At least that's the feel. And yet I went back and looked at 1936 for some reason and there were a lot of current pieces then—"Why I'm Going To Vote For FDR", and things like that, which are hardly timeless.'

Why (I inquire) is the *Reader's Digest* such a frequent object of hostility? A recent issue of the *National Lampoon*, for instance, shows Nixon as Moses descending from Sinai clutching the *Digest* in place of the Tables of the Law.

'You see, a number of people ... One way to look at it is that college professors—teaching the freshman year at college —have got to knock *something*. And it's easy to knock something that's popular, and the *Digest* is an easy knock, and a lot of people get their last look at the *Digest* when their college professor snots on it—because, you know, that's his bag! *He's looking down on things.*'

Allen shuffles fretfully through some papers on his desk, and digs out a letter. Not all of those millions of bits of mail, it seems, are amiable. The *Digest* also gets its quota from 'Disgusted' of Budleigh Salterton, though the disgust is usually differently motivated.

'I was just answering a letter, which was probably a waste of time to do, but some young—I take it—reader out in Lamont, Illinois, wrote in. And he's a college student, you see, and he's knocking the magazine.'

Allen sighs, as he reads out a few derogatory sentences. 'Most students are well aware of the shortcomings of the *Reader's Digest*,' opens Lamont, Illinois: 'e.g. the extreme prejudice in outlook, low intelligence appeal, general defender of most establishment mistakes ...'

And so on. Some articles were found particularly distasteful.

'He picks five articles to knock that he hates and, you know, thinks we're being *fascist* ...

'Like "Must Our Churches Finance Revolution?" You see, one reason, we are knocking the World Council of Churches is that they are financing some black revolutionaries who are *themselves fascists*! I mean, they are paying for their guns through the World Council of Churches!'

It is, indeed, a surreal world. Another couple of criticised pieces were 'Quiet Heroes of South Vietnam' and 'Let's Get Off Our Soldiers' Backs'. Neither of these, Allen points out, is gung-ho and war loving. The first is about the 'poor, limbless people that got shot down in Vietnam and how much courage they have', and the second is actually anti-war, but just says don't blame the lads for it. It is furthermore by George Ball who is, as Allen points out, a known dove.

There is also a piece called 'Why I Don't Smoke Pot'. 'This was written,' Allen says, 'by an *incredibly* liberal guy, who happens to be religious. And who is probably through his group "Young Life" doing more to help in the ghettoes than anybody I've known ...'

Finally there is the alarming 'The Terrorists Among Us' which deals with the Weatherman Conspiracy.

'It's a pretty good piece. We have checked it out, and I feel strongly I'd like to sit down with this guy and *discuss* it. Because he's *on* campus, and he knows whether there are groups on campus as we claim, and as we can *prove*.'

John Allen hopes that the Illinois student will reply to his letter, but he is none too hopeful. There is a lot of negative energy around right now.

What (I ask) is his definition of the positive society that the *Reader's Digest* stands for?

'I'm not good at putting flash titles on,' he says, bluntly, 'but the people that you've talked to, and seen around here, are loyal *Digest* people. They all believe that man is improvable, and that their lot is improvable ...

'It can be an in-depth level or it can be, to an extent, a superficial level. Like the importance of having better posture! Now that's not a world-beating article and yet, what's incredible is that you go out and find people who have read a particular article which even you may have felt was a bit idiot, and they've gotten something out of it, and it may

166

have changed their lives for the better ...'

John Allen casts around, and comes up with the mouth-to-mouth resuscitation article, and the various dietetic pieces. On a more serious level, he says, there are the works of Clement Stone, the millionaire adherent of PMA: 'He just drives you up the wall because he's so idiot at times but, Goddam it, it works, and he can prove it because he's got half a billion dollars!'

I leave for lunch with Devine and Paul Thompson. Thompson is the retiring Vice-Chairman and former General Manager of the *Reader's Digest* Association beneath which come the advertising, the books and record albums, the computer operations and educational projects, everything in fact bar the running of the magazine.

Thompson is a former Brigadier General in the Marines. 'He's something of a folk hero,' Bob Devine has briefed me. 'He's running the YAF.' The YAF is, of course, the Young Americans for Freedom and was initially seen as some sort of counterweight to the SDS. That particular threat seems to have, well, subsided, but the YAF are *vigilant*. 'We are helping them out a bit,' Bob Devine says.

We drive to a near-by restaurant with some sort of spaghetti-Western cuisine. Thompson's first taste of journalism was when he had some sort of supervisory role over the rambunctious US military paper *Stars and Stripes*.

'They were a hell of a bunch of fellows, but they were against the Establishment,' Thompson says of the journalists: 'It was a headache from morning to night.'

He recalls terrible bawlings-out by Patton and Bradley. Enough, it would seem, to implant a distaste for anti-Establishmentarian journalism forever.

Our spaghetti arrives. Thompson is duly optimistic about the army today which is, he believes, on the mend. He is also somewhat cross about a recent *Digest* feature which was a good slambang attack on the land appetite of the Army Corps of Engineers.

This was one of those features in which the *Digest* appears in its populist guise, and Thompson and Bob Devine argue the finer points politely for a bit, before discussing certain

167

Digest operations overseas. Like the post-war acquisition of land in Tokyo—'which must have been one of the bargains of the century,' Devine says, and is now worth thirty-five million dollars. A recent mutual fund that the mag launched in Germany was less successful, a victim, Digesters feel, of IOS backlash.

Most foreign magazine operations are totally *Digest*-owned, with a few diplomatic exceptions. The *Digests* published in Korea and Cairo, for instance, are published under franchise, as is the Finnish edition.

The Finns, in particular, have to tread cautiously, what with their delicate relationship with the Soviets. 'We have to be very careful how we set up our table of contents,' Devine says, 'and if our partner out there recommends against something, we never press the point ...'

It is not probable that they will be reading 'Why we must meet Russia's naval challenge' out there in Helsinki, for example. Even 'Teeth for the Red Chinese Tiger' must be considered a doubtful quantity.

Washington (I suggest) might be just about as happy to see the back of particularly some of these Chinese pieces as Helsinki. Don't they represent some sort of attack on the new China policy?

'Well,' Devine says: 'These pieces on the China policy really amount to a *warning*, you know.'

'I don't think we hesitate—do you, Bob?—to be critical of the government on *any* policy,' General Thompson says.

'I sent a copy of it to Henry Kissinger,' Devine says and adds, with a quarter smile, that he never got a reply.

What political impact can the *Reader's Digest* hope for? Can they sense a stirring impact in those loyal millions out there when they let out a blast of the trumpet? What, after all, about that quoted 'thunderous response'?

Well, no. It's the dieting articles that really collect the thunderous response, Bob Devine thinks. 'I just can't think that people read the *Digest* to get their political opinions ...'

'It's more political than it ever used to be,' says Thompson.

'I think', opines Devine, 'if you examined the results of the polls we make among our readers about which articles they liked and which articles they didn't, I don't think you would find the political articles ranking up high *at all.*'

'Every so often,' says Thompson.

'But in effect,' Bob Devine says, 'we are supporting the present administration when most of the public journals are attacking it. Whether or not we support the new China policy, we support the system.'

'We stand,' agrees General Thompson, simply, 'for the Free Enterprise system.'

In New York, the *Digest* is housed in three floors of the Pan-Am Building. There are long battleship-coloured corridors podding off into numberless compact offices. It's all a bit like those information-theory charts.

Gertrude Arundel's office is right on the bend. Today chiffon scarves of fog are whipping past, and the wind is whistling. The *Digest* floors are only in the 30s but even down here the Pan-Am Building can make quite a Gothic racket of a windy day.

Gertrude Arundel is the Research Editor. She has an elfin, but tough face, and a green dress, like a pixie housewife. Her manner is friendly but, well, cautious, which is—I am beginning to find—the generic Digester manner for dealing with outside media.

There is a research staff of twenty, she explains, and another six clipping newspapers. The researchers are all girls, which is one of those time-honoured practices, like editors nearly always being men.

'We have had boys working for us,' Mrs Arundel says: 'I have no objection to hiring boys. But they really don't want to stick to something as detailed as this for too long a time ...'

The work of the researchers is two-fold. There is the pre-interior-decorators who will be a repository of the artistic Lesley Laird, with whom I later share a coffee in the Zum-Zum (Digesters like the Zum-Zum. *Vogue*, which is almost chic-by-chic, being just across the way in the Graybar Building, appears to prefer the Trattoria) and who spent four months interviewing students and the police on behalf of James Michener down in Kent State.

169

The second part of the job happens after the first draft of the article has been delivered to the editors, who shoot it down to research. Gertrude Arundel's favourite writer, she says, 'takes every statement, and keys it to a bibliography, with *numbers*. And then he brings a great big envelope full of stuff, and everything is numbered according to where it appears in the article.'

But such obsessional tidiness is all too rare among scribes, she admits, even the *Digest* trusties. There is usually work to be done though the amount varies widely.

'You could pick up a quick little humour piece, or an *Art of Living* thing that had maybe a couple of quotes in it, and that would be that. Or you could have an article that could take you two or three weeks to get through.'

She shows me some sheets. There are page-long lists of annotated sources to be checked. People. Books. Documents. Some typescript MSS are whipped away pretty sharpish. 'The Soviet Plot To Destroy Mexico', for instance.

This is part of a longer study of the KGB that the *Digest* has devoted much space to (or much space, as space is doled out by the *Digest*). The Mexican opus had to be checked with 29 sources, and it was—as Gertrude Arundel remarks—an extraordinary source-list because almost everyone preferred to remain anonymous.

'Another problem is if a writer gets a quotation in good faith from a person. And then the researcher goes back to that person and says, Did you say this?

'Meanwhile,' Gertrude Arundel says, with a weary grin, 'he's changed his mind, and decides he really *thinks* that, but maybe he shouldn't have *said* it! So this is a very shadowy area, and you have to really evaluate the authors, the source . . .

'Whether it will do real harm to the person if you quote it. In which case, we *would* get in touch with him, and give him a chance, if he denies it, he's denying it for his own protection.'

But is it not (I inquire, diffidently) sometimes the function of journalism to do a bit of harm here and there?

There is, of course, that. Gertrude Arundel allows that the content of the piece occasionally interferes with the etiquette. 'If we were writing a piece about the Mafia or something like this, that'd be different, I guess.'

Nor is there much trouble with getting *Digest* articles checked right up to the top, it seems.

'We have very little trouble getting information,' Gertrude Arundel says, with the sort of starry thankfulness for the plain good nature of folks that is one of the more memorable characterisitics of the whole *Digest* staff. 'Business people ... the medical profession ... people in public life ... They give us *tremendous* co-operation.'

What if (on a hazard) it proved necessary to check out something about Richard Milhous Nixon?

'We would probably check it with his Press Office,' she thinks.

Here also in the Pan-Am nest is John Reddy. The masthead defines John Reddy as a Roving Editor. There are twenty-eight of these, roving away, and essentially they seem to be staff writers. Reddy has pink cheeks, a soft stubble of white hair, and a tremuldous bonhomie that somehow puts me in mind of a plumper Godfrey Winn. Show Biz is John Reddy's turf.

Recent work that he has polished off includes profiles on Flip Wilson, Dick Cavett and William Buckley ('Blithe Spirit of the Right'). Also a study on the imminent decline of porn movies.

Besides this, Reddy has done a couple of Unforgettables. 'Unforgettables' is what Digesters call 'The Most Unforgettable Character I Ever Met', a series of evergreen popularity, so much so that demand on occasion outruns supply. Can it be that too few writers find anybody else particularly unforgettable?

As so often, the *Digest* is motivated towards a spot of literary midwifery here. They ponder a few Characters whom they feel should definitely not go Unforgotten. One such was Louis Armstrong.

'It's what I've done once in a while when somebody is obviously very colourful,' Reddy explains. 'But it has to be done by somebody who knew the person intimately over a long period of ycars.

'So we just explored around, and the most likely person seemed to be the musical director in his band, who had been with him for ten years, but had *known* him since Harlem in the 'thirties. So what I did then was interview him, and get all his recollections, plus any key points I found elsewhere. For instance, there was an anecdote about Louis Armstrong meeting the Pope ...'

One formal problem here was that the musical director had not, in fact, been present at the time, so Reddy just had Satchmo *tell* the chap about it. Catching some of those funky speech-patterns in a couple of concise pages was another poser, but equally deftly solved.

Most of the problems of a *Digest* writer come down to this: the requirement of somehow being at once ample and compact. I am reminded of the crafty Oriental habit of carving cherry-stones except that these stones are carved into the likenesses of Bill Buckley, Louis Armstrong, or—on another occasion—Bob Hope.

This was a piece that Reddy worked on, which was by-lined Bob Hope, and entitled 'The Importance of Having Fun'. Here, too, there were problems.

The thing is that Bob Hope is a great perfectionist, especially about material that goes out under his name. The first problem was catching up with him. 'I saw him two or three times. Sort of on the fly,' Reddy says. 'Once was riding to the hospital, and to the airport. That seems to be the new form of interviewing,' he adds, with a birdlike trill of laughter.

Between them, they agreed the lineaments of the article. It was to be an unexpected piece from the world's richest comedian, stuffed with rib-ticklers, natch, but also a bit reflective, a think-piece almost.

Actually, the first draft seemed altogether *too thinky* for Bob Hope. Too much the sage, not enough the comic. It went back to Reddy for a re-write.

Johnny Reddy is a craftsman. The piece, as it appeared, is a perfect mix. It starts with a snappy one-liner about how things have improved on campus—'The kids are even giving back some of the deans they captured last year'—warms up, and then strikes the serioso note about how much America needs people both with courage and a sense of fun nowadays. Truman is alluded too, and likewise Ike. Hope (and Reddy) stress the importance of fun to GIs and in mental institutions. It concludes with a heartwarmer about 'My former neighbour, Walt Disney'.

A textbook example of collaboration, in fact, with both parties profiting. But what of certain other areas of showbiz where this healthy mutual esteem may not exist in quite the same way?

Reddy doesn't think this a problem.

'Because of its big circulation, the *Digest* has to go for big figures. Like Bob Hope and John Wayne. The *Digest* wouldn't do a ... Jane Fonda. But, I must say,'—helpfully— 'We did a Bob Dylan.'

With the same degree of assistance?

'No, I must say, without his co-operation.'

On the other hand, as Reddy points out, Dylan won't co-operate with *anybody*. He casts around for other untypical projects, and recalls a feature on Blood, Sweat and Tears 'behind the Iron Curtain'. The Rock group hated it there, but the piece never appeared.

'Another person we did who might seem off-beat to you was Woody Guthrie,' John Reddy says, and describes how he interviewed the folk/protest-singer's family with the exception, as it happened, of Arlo Guthrie, Woody's folk/protest-singer son.

'I spoke to Mrs Guthrie. I spoke to a sister ... She seemed to be steering me away from Arlo. I don't know why ...'

But perhaps the main creative department trapped up here in the smog is the Art Department. And this uncanny feel I get in the *Digest*, this sensation of somehow daintily plodding through the methodical innards of a Swiss chronometer, is just as prevalent in the Art Department corridor.

The first person I meet on the Art side is Donald Duffy. He is an Associate Editor, one of four, and his special domain is typography. Donald Duffy is stocky, with a pleasant prognathous visage, and ginger hair in an exaggerated crinkle, like a couple of circumflexes. Pens bulge from the pocket of one of those stripey Ivy-League shirts that were standard in creative circles immediately pre-Pop Art.

Right now Duffy is working on the cover for a Condensed Book. This is one of the Condensed Books that are published inside the *Digest* monthly, and one of Duffy's jobs is to produce a whole-page internal frontispiece for it which will make it entirely plain that the reader is getting two books for the price of one.

Duffy's wall is stuck up with conceptual spreads which may, or may not, work their passage into the mag. There is a natty visual on 'Masterpieces of American Glass' and the artworks for 'Has Your Bank Been Robbed Yet?' and 'Nefertiti, Lovely Enigma of the Nile'.

Duffy speaks with some enthusiasm of *Digest* art. The ideal is harmony. The *Digest* began as a text magazine. The first line illustration didn't appear until November 1939, a time of momentous events. Colour was first used in 1948, but it wasn't until advertising was first admitted in April, 1955, that the floodgates were opened ... photography, full-page pics, white space, typography which, no, doesn't scream —nothing screams in the *Digest*—but certainly clears its throat audibly ... the whole Design & Art Direction gallimaufry.

But—and so unlike the eyeball-popping antics of, er, some other periodicals—Artistic Harmony remains the ideal, Duffy says, that and Research-Soundness.

Both of these desirables are achieved and maintained by frequent art editorial meetings. I attend one of these in a miniature conference room. Ken Stuart, the over-all art editor, is not present, being on a trip to Europe, but Duffy is here, as is Robert Blattner, another associate art editor, Judith, who does the picture research, and John Wells who is i/c the photographs.

The agenda is discussed. Certain lay-outs will depend on the advertising.

'Any word on that, Uncle John?'

Wells considers. He is dourly pragmatic, the cracker-barrel manner.

'Gee! I don't know,' he concedes. 'I just spoke with Hope's PR folks.'

Artworks are circulated.

One humoresque piece in the inimitable *Digest* manner shows a man with his foot stuck in a pot of blue paint. He is surrounded by laughing nymphettes.

The artist is a *Digest* regular, a Puerto Rican, and he is —I am informed—colourblind. There is mirth as a previous mishap is described. An illustration had been needed for a tale in which somebody passes away while watching the TV, and nobody else notices.

'His face was supposed to be green,' says Duffy: 'Instead the artist gave everybody green faces, except this one guy who had a nice pink face! *Everybody else* was dead!'

Now they discuss work to be commissioned.

'Teeth for the Red Chinese Tiger' is type ... No art will be necessary.' Judith makes notes for other areas to be researched. The work is duly meticulous, and there is the usual wastage as the folks at Pleasantville give the thumbs down.

'We'll have a top illustrator! It breaks our heart sometimes,' mourns Blattner, a polite man with a B embroidered on his tie in gold thread, and a perfect creamy wave of hair, a silver Elvis. And then—even when the work is passed—down, down, down it comes, reduced and compacted like the Murillo on a postage stamp.

'When people talk about those little things up there, those are—*big and fully researched paintings!*'

Finally, one of the crucial tasks, a piece of creative artwork to be commissioned.

'We have this *wonderful story* coming in about Bob Hope,' confides Blattner on a warm, high note, 'and I'll need some pictures so we can commission a full-colour portrait.'

'We've got *lots* of pictures.'

'Yes. But always when he's talking to GIs ...'

By the way, the full-colour portrait ultimately used shows Hope looking out at us, the vast reading audience, and it occupies almost a third of the page. Hope is ample and relaxed in a tux, and this is, one senses, not the whiplash professional, but the 'beloved comedian', as the caption puts it, the warm being. Hope's lips are parted in that famous, that irrepressible grin. The glow positively radiates off the page.

The meticulous and hierarchic *Digest* mastheads also represent patterns of power. Power is not a commodity to be sneezed at, even in Pleasantville, and the folksy banter, the first naming, do precious little to conceal that these are some shrewd cookies. I am led to contemplate Walt Disney Inc., where the steel fists are positively emphasised by the home-spun gloves.

Heir-Apparent to the *Digest* is, most folks feel, the current editor, Hobart—'Hobe'—Lewis. As a matter of fact, I run across a few veiled doubts regarding this. 'In neither of the two legs of the organisational chart is there a clear choice,' remarks one executive, not himself on the editorial side, and I am reminded that nowadays the magazine, though undeniably the hub of operations, only accounts for 20% of total turnover.

The inference is that one course of action is at least worthy of contemplation. In the wake of the Wallaces, the *Digest* should go public, and the moneymen should take charge with, no doubt, the same remarkable flair that they brought to Hollywood.

Digest opinion is overwhelmingly against this, as is that of the Wallaces. DeWitt seems set that the *Digest* should continue to be master-minded by the Editorial. Hobe Lewis, being at the same time President and Editor-in-Chief of the *Reader's Digest* and President, Chief Executive Officer of the *Reader's Digest* Association, would seem to have been fairly emphatically dubbed Crown Prince.

'It's policy, and terribly important policy, to let the editors have a completely free hand,' Hobe Lewis emphasises: 'They're not answerable to anybody.'

Hobe Lewis is middling sized with a fleeting resemblance to Tony Randall. He combines an almost aggressive air of competence with a distinct shyness, and shifts from side to side as we talk. Lewis began at the *Digest* writing copy for promotion and for direct mail—'sending people their subscription list when it was time to renew'.

His office is not grandiosely larger than those of the lower editorial strata. As with the British Civil Service, grading at Pleasantville seems to be more a matter of accoutrements, and Hobe's artworks include a Vlaminck, and a superlative Sisley, not to mention—the more personal touch—a bullfighting poster in which the name of Paco Camino or whoever has been replaced by HOBE LEWIS.

We discuss the global spread of the *Digest* which is, Hobe Lewis feels, because the *Digest* is not just an American magazine, in the narrower sense.

'A story in the *Digest* could be, and is, read with as much interest by a *Laplander* as a man in New York,' Lewis observes, and points out that a sense of values is hardly an exclusively American characteristic.

'The Puritan Ethic ... the self help, and individual effort, and sort of reliance on the old-fashioned virtues of thrift and hard work, are fundamental to the *Digest* ... and we think they are fundamental pretty much to human nature—We *hope* they are— and can be shared around the world.'

What (I wonder) are the effects of being surrounded by so many artworks?

They can only be healthy, Hobe feels.

'I mean to be surrounded with works of art and good taste, it inevitably rubs off on your whole daily life, I'm sure.'

We talk somewhat of the rotten state of the magazine industry which Lewis is grateful that the *Digest* is surviving. Does he see any problems with the new generation?

On the whole, Lewis thinks not.

'I don't think we will have to make any drastic changes in our approach. Some magazines have made very drastic changes. Some of my friends, with whom I play golf, try and capture the new, young, somewhat left, movement, and I think probably some problems arose because of that too sudden change. The reading public doesn't like it ...

'The young college student may not be reading the *Digest* as much, but when he gets out of college and starts looking for a job, getting married and having children and personal problems ...

'Our magazine helps people with their personal life, and

if we don't appeal as much to the brash young generation I think we will as they mature just a little bit ...'

Lewis goes on a bit, to elucidate the essential thinking behind the mag. 'The *Digest*', he emphasises, 'comes from one man's inspiration. He is a Calvinist, a Presbyterian, and he was born and bred in the Puritan Work Ethic believing that your rewards come from hard work and honest work. Also he was brought up in the belief that it was important to leave the world a little better than it was when you found it.

'And we'—meaning the *Digest*—'were to try and improve the shining hour so that the purpose behind the *Digest* really is to help people to be better citizens, to do a better job, and to improve their own lives and the lives of their fellow men.' He pauses, oracularly: 'It's a little moralistic, but that's the essential motive behind the *Digest*.'

My last trip to Pleasantville, and suddenly it's the Fall. The day is cold, but bright, and the trees are a moulting pelt, all the colours of earth and fire. A *Reader's Digest* cover, so to speak, *au naturel*.

I am lunching with a couple of junior editors. 'Turn left at the Cézanne,' says the receptionist, pointing me towards the cafeteria. This is a big room, of cleanly chic, embellished with plastic potted plants and a reproduction Renaissance chandelier in bronze. I get a heaped trayful of good things for $1.15. Again, I am reminded of one of the grander health hydros.

We chat about this and that at lunch. Politics, in which Digesters are inclined to express the sentiments of the hawk with the modulations of the dove. An anecdote demonstrating the sheer goddam awfulness of New York City, and a more pious one about Wally.

There is a bit of joshing about the new intake of girls, but with a slight wink, just to show that nothing *gross* is intended. No need. Pleasantville is a bit low on sexpots, frankly. Nymphs and satyrs aren't really part of the scheme of things in this particular Arcadia.

Afterwards, I am walking through that pearly circular

lobby. The vines weep still, and the Picasso Harlequin contemplates me with increased melancholy. John Allen approaches me casually.

'Well,' he says, 'I hear you've covered us pretty thoroughly.'

I demur. There are, I say, a few holes left. Loose ends.

'From the feedback I've been getting,' John Allen says, 'I think you've probably got enough.'

He says it in a friendly, but determined, way.

Even at the *Reader's Digest* research is finite. Even at the *Reader's Digest,* in fact especially at the *Reader's Digest,* enough is enough.

✜ *Marching on our Stomachs*

In which the writer becomes a student of Food Technology. He has converse with Colonel Sanders and Howard Johnson Jr and examines the aesthetic of the Doggie Diner and the Original House of Pies. In Chicago, he attends Hamburger University, where he is awarded an honorary degree in Hamburgerology, and attends rehearsals for a musical devoted to McDonalds Hamburgers with a fine Broadway cast.

Success ... And Then Some!

We have gathered here together
And we're feelin' might proud ...
For the whole McDonald family,
We can tell you clear and loud:
We're so proud that we are Number One
And we're takin' nothing else!
We're not about to settle down
But move up to more success.
(SHOUT) A.T.S!!

We are here to meet, to work, to plan
We are here to learn what's new ...
For you can't learn all you've got to know
Back at old Hamburger U.

We can learn a lot from each other
If we do then we'll progress ...
And from this launching pad blast off
As we rocket to success ...
(SHOUT) A.T.S!!

Opening chorus (as scripted) in the McDonald's Corporation industrial musical. Hawaii, 1971.

Tell me what you eat and I'll tell you what you are.
Anthelme Brillat-Savarin

We in the United States have to recognise—we who are food connoisseurs if you will—that our children are not brought up on the flaming desserts. They are brought up on Mc-Donald's and Kentucky Fried Chicken, and as they get to be older they will only know one thing to teach *their* children. And there's no question, it will, like death and taxes, be the way of the future.

Al Papin Jr president of International Industries, who control (among others) the International House of Pancakes, the Original House of Pies, and Orange Julius.

Moving across the automated landscape, no components seem to be burgeoning more irrepressibly, more *visibly*, than the empires of fast foods. The United States belly has been dominated long since, of course. Now begin skilful incursions into the alien culinary territories of Europe, Asia, the Third World; the beginnings of a war for the global stomach. Mc-Donald's are a sensation on the Ginza, Tokyo, and doing a healthy trade in Holland. Colonel Sanders' Finger Lickin' Chicken is being scoffed in front of innumerable TV sets in Queensway, London. Holiday Inns are vaulting skywards on Primrose Hill, the Monégasque coast, and—for the delectation of the Eurocrats—hard by the Palais des Nations, Brussels. Orange Julius, that indescribable drink, was launched on the Kings Road, Chelsea, with an assist from a number of girls pertly got up as demonettes, complete down to the whisk of scarlet tail.

My investigations began in California, since it is in California that the eateries have taken over the landscape with the most effortless and florid vitality. It's an emblematic world, the world of fast foods. There is the aerial gala of typography like the Denny's sign (Denny's was founded in Lakewood, California, in 1954 as Danny's Donuts. There are now getting on for 400 units, as they refer to them) which is a revolving, and quite indefinable, geometric shape.

Whole buildings become advertisements for themselves. Like the Taco Bells, which resemble Spanish missions in El Cheapo Westerns, and dispense fast Mexican foods which are not—a mindboggling concept—Mexican food at its best. Or Ships. This was founded at Culver City in 1955, and the emblem is a weird aerial shape. I asked Emmett Shipman (the founder) what it represented.

'Some of the others; they are just boxes and squares and oblongs,' he explained. 'We wanted something with a ... rocket feel to it. It was those days.'

What the Taco Bell (for instance) is all about, though, is the Disneyfication of the landscape. This can go to memorable lengths. Few visitors to the US can have failed to take due note of Bob's Big Boy, for one. Bob's Big Boy is a chain of some 650 'Family Restaurants' spread across the States and Canada. In front of each installation stands a monstrously chubby mannikin with checkered trousers, a lollop of quiff, and the cutest little nose. He is holding aloft the main selling-point which is *The Original Double-Deck Cheeseburger*. This is Bob's Big Boy.

His provenance is as follows. The first diner was launched in Glendale, yes, California in 1936 by Robert C. 'Bob' Wian. A distinctive hamburger was evolved by accident for 'some celebrating members of an orchestra' and caught on like billy-ho.

Bob Wian—explains a leaflet—*quickly realised that he had the beginning of a thriving enterprise. All that was needed was a name, a symbol—an identification that would be ap-*

propriate. Several weeks later in walked a chubby lad of six, his sagging trousers held up by reluctant suspenders. Bob took one look—'BIG BOY'. That was it!

Which it certainly is. But the dumpy fellow seems styled by Fortnum & Mason alongside, say, Chicken Boy or the Doggie Diner. Chicken Boy is in downtown Los Angeles, the only bit that could remind one of New York, and I first spotted him/it through two stone scrapers. It was, frankly, a bit of a jolt, a twenty-foot dummy standing on the roof of an eatery, blue pants, red shirt, and muscular arms holding out his chicken dinner ... and a chicken's head. There is a Max Ernst lithograph that has a similar metamorphosis but this is more of an *œuvre* than Ernst, and Ovid, and Bosch, could have cooked up, sorry, created, between them. We drive past, and it looked at me with idiot chicken eyes, and I would believe anything, even, or especially, that the sky was falling, flake by contaminated flake.

The Doggie Diner, on the other hand, is rather jolly. It is a San Francisco chain, with some twenty-three locations, and its main gimmick is hot dogs. Rising from the top of each Doggie Diner is a sort of a flag-pole on which is impaled a dog's head. The dog's head is of some size, about a man's length from muzzle to ears, and despite its uncomfortable location it looks well enough, with a polka-dot bow-tie, saucer eyes, a long dachshund muzzle, and a chef's hat perched atop droopy ears as long as surf-boards.

Doggie Diner number twenty-one is on Third Street and is patronised *faute de mieux* by the staff of the rock magazine *Rolling Stone*. 'You sort of build up a tolerance,' says Stephanie, the English secretary. I telephoned the firm, intrigued by the iconography.

'It was done twelve to fifteen years ago by an artist called Harold Bachman,' an executive explains: 'He was an artist and silkscreen painter in East Bay. He was doing all the Doggie Diner billboards, and he came up with this idea for point-of-sale items. And we bought it ...

'No, it's no particular kind of dog. It's not any sort of dog that I can recognise anyway.'

*   *   *

But things are not necessarily quite what they seem. Examine the case of Jack-in-the-Box, a larger chain than those so far mentioned, with some 650 outlets of which 250 are in the Golden State itself. Even as Disneyfication goes, the Jack-in-the-Box is fairly horrendous, a psychopathically glaring Jack popping out of a box on a pole high above the roadway. Doggie and Chicken Boy do have a certain eerie quality, and the Big Boy is relatively small. Jack is tall, tall enough to dominate a highway for half a mile (Ironically one of their installations overtops the Disney studios in Burbank, even enjoying a height advantage over the Disney US flag) and what's more, it *revolves*.

But there is a fresh set of problems, I am informed by Emery Derhardt, who is Jack-in-the-Box area co-ordinator for Los Angeles. Inroads are being made regarding the liberty of the citizen.

'There are new local *signing* ordinances,' Derhardt says, not without a touch of gloom. 'Some cities just don't seem to like caricatures. Our advertising agency, Doyle, Dane and Bernbach, came up with a model without the head ...'

Which cities?

'A gloomy number of them up in the Bay Area. Most all of them, in fact. We still use the head in Los Angeles. But'—wearily—'the trend is spreading ...'

Yes, Folk-Baroque is sliding into rapid senescence, unnoticed, for the most part, by the illuminati from Europe and the East Coast who arrive to gawk, like bumpkin mandarins, at L.A. excesses. The commercial fantasias are being decimated. One hot-dog stall actually shaped like a hot dog remains on La Cieniga Boulevard, and should be preserved, but by whom? Even the Brown Derby restaurant has been tampered with. Its hatband has been tarted up—and inexorably the blander banalities of corporate chic are even invading the empire of Fast Foods.

One further change seems somehow inherent: Darwinist. Just as the menus are rationalised, and dwindle within the eateries, so the eateries themselves are dwindling. Not in numbers, naturally, but in numbers of chains. The later '60s saw a franchise mania swelling to hundreds of operations.

Baseball stars had their names franchised, also Joe Namath, Rowan and Martin and Minnie Pearl of the Grand Ol' Opry.

'There are two or three dozen now,' Howard Johnson Jr tells me later, in New York: 'In a few years I expect to see three or four ...' He seems confident that he will be amongst them. There will be more and more of fewer and fewer fast-food chains, it seems, multiplicating replica units, like a Monopoly game in which the board becomes dominated by the same red and green cubes. Or like that William Burroughs scenario in which the world becomes dominated by replicas. Theoretically quite possible, of course. Even clones will have to have something fit to eat.

Sad note on the chain that didn't. Alice's Restaurant is in Westwood, which is like Beverly Hills, but a little more twee. The restaurant is 'hip', with old posters of Rudolf Valentino, Shirley Temple in *Heidi*, John Wayne in *Iwo Jima*. Also—from what seems much further back—those flamboyant miniatures from concerts long-gone featuring (ulp) the Quicksilver Messenger Service, Taj Mahal, the Grateful Dead.

I sit over my Alice's Burger and a whisky, since Alice's Restaurant has a liquor licence, unlike the original, but it's an intriguing development, from protest song, to (sort of) protest movie, to funky restaurant, and—almost—to franchise chain.

'Hilly had this idea that we would make a zillion dollars,' says one of the owners wistfully. Hilly is Hillard Elkins, co-producer of that other funky money-spinner, *Oh! Calcutta!*, and his idea was that the time was ripe for some sort of youth-quake chain. But then, of course, came the Recession.

I settle my bill, noting the message printed thereon. THANK YOU FOR COMING TO ALICE'S. IT'S A HAPPY PLACE.

International Industries clearly believe that they will be among the survivors. International Industries is a 'diversified consumer-oriented company' whose operations include the International House of Pancakes (372 restaurants), the 59 Original House of Pies, the 50 Copper Penny Coffee Shops, the 37 Love's Barbecues, the 12 Wil Wright's Ice Cream Shoppes, and the 250 Orange Julius units.

The International Industries headquarters are on Wilshire Boulevard hard by the Beverly Hills Hilton. On my way there I dropped in at the local Orange Julius for acclimatisation. It is done up rather snazzily in buttercup-yellow and, yes, orange, and there are chairs with devil's fork backs. The satanic motif is maintained through the menu, what with Devil Burgers, fish 'from our Brimstone Broiler' and Demon's Delite, which is French fries. There is also the Orange Julius itself which is orange juice mixed with certain secret substances. It is pasty and sweetish, lacking in piquancy, like the essence of every tea-shop cake one snaffled when young. Perhaps it grows on you.

The chairman of International Industries is Al Lapin Jr. We meet in his office, which is Beverly Hills palatial, with walls of darkly veneered wood hung with rather woozy abstracts and the coat-of-arms of the Lapin family. Lapin is in his mid-forties, articulate, with a winning manner. He is wearing one of those ties that are almost standard in the business culture, which is to say it is made of stiffish silk, with some sort of flecked and stippled finish, and an abstract motif derived, be it ever so remotely, from Kandinsky. He speaks of his theory of the food chain with great verve.

'My gut tells me that people aren't just going to get a meal,' he says: 'They're looking for a Happening ... an Event. So we make a big thing of décor ... the whole experience ... how the package is presented.

'In the case of the House of Pancakes I could have built something Modern, but I feel that the pancake image was Early American ... Colonial ... homespun. So the combination of all those elements led to a cottage-looking kind of place.'

The style, by the way, is not unknown in Great Britain, what with having a sloping tiled roof and a fake-timbered façade: By-pass-Tudor, except that the roof is blue and the frontage a sort of smoked-salmon.

'Colours are very conductive to eating,' Lapin explains: 'If you do any research I'm sure you'll find this. You'll find that your favourite restaurant is dark-maroon or something. In the House of Pancakes we went for that orange ... warm, comfortable colours.

'In the House of Pies we have that hot pink. We went for a frothy, gay feel. Using younger waitresses with the shorter skirts for a Contemporary, *In* feeling rather than the cottage appeal.'

The frou-frou, Lapin emphasises, is all-important. 'In our new place in Beverly Hills we've got orange-and-white frying pans to serve the merchandise in,' he instances: 'Gimmicks to make it not just food.'

Also narrow margins in the volume-feeding biz don't leave much of an advertising budget. 'So I felt that the building had to be—*its own advertising*.' Which is to say a recognisable unit on any roadway, and dishing up a standard product. But what (I inquire) of regional foibles in matters of cuisine?

'We have taken the calculated risk—and thankfully we've won—that we would not bow to the regional taste where we ran into it.

'Like for instance in the South, putting grits on the menu.' He pauses, and the faintest timbre of Napoleon, or at least Patton enters his voice. 'We do not have grits on the menu. We do not allow beer to be served in Milwaukee. We do not allow Oregon boysenberries. No scrapple in Philadelphia. *It is standard.*

'We have taken that position, and fortunately we've won. And, therefore, the menu you see in Florida is exactly the menu that's in Seattle, as exactly San Diego, as exactly Washington ...'

And Europe? Britain? Are we quite ready?

Lapin ponders, and admits that a few tiny adjustments may have to be made *vis-à-vis* the menu. (He is unhappily resigned to ladling out beer and/or wine.) But as to accepting the visual uniformity, Lapin is convinced that the British are just about there already.

'I think they already do, and don't realise it,' Lapin enthuses: 'For instance, in London I believe people would hate going to another pub? They would go to the one they're familiar with.'

I assent, and Al Lapin continues: 'So they have already accepted *subconsciously* the concept of liking to be in familiar surroundings. Now here in the United States the concept of the blue roof, and the standard building and so forth, when somebody is travelling along the road in a place where they've never been before, they are more prone to go to a place they know. They know what they'll find. *They do not want to be surprised!* And I say that subconsciously the English people have already accepted that, but don't realise it!'

Lapin pauses, beaming at the logic of it all. In all honesty, I am a bit puzzled by the reasoning. 'Through the pubs?' I ask, feeling thick.

'Through the pubs!' concurs Al Lapin: 'People go to *their pub*. And once you take that pub ... Joe's Pub' (He suggests) 'and if you did a Joe's Pub—which is *my pub*, quote, unquote—and put it on the by-pass, and I'm driving along ...

'I'll go to a Joe's Pub because—*that's my pub!*'

Joe's Pub is Joe's Pub is Joe's Pub is Joe's Pub is Joe's Pub. It's the prophetic and paradisal vision of Automated Feeding, it-self a concept which began ... when? Was it with the first canners, or was it when Dr Dauglish mechanised bread-making in 1856? Was it with the innumerable attempts to automate the slaughter and/or skinning of hogs and cattle, described by Siegfried Giedion as 'The Mechanisation of Death'? Was it when Frederic Tudor, the Boston Ice King, perfected a method for cutting ice into easily-transportable chunks, there-by establishing the US cuisine, or was it when New Yorkers became squeamish about steak tartare, and grilled it, some-how inventing the hamburger?

Regardless of where and how Automated Feeding began, there seems little doubt where it's going. Those perplexed can hardly do better than consult one of the sacred (monthly) texts of the trade, *Fast Food. The Magazine of Restaurant Business.* This is a well-produced glossy, of roughly the same format as *Punch* or *Harpers*, but considerably thicker. Both in its features—which range from weighty legal ques-tions to new modes of creating Shredded Hash Browns—and in its succulent advertising, *Fast Food* magazine furnishes quite the panorma of things to come.

One bumper number, for instance, had a lilac cover, 300-odd pages, and—as its title *Foodservice 75* suggested—was a peek into the middle of the decade. It contained the *pensées* (encouraging, it turned out) of an economist, and some rather imprecise musing about coming life-styles by a fellow at the Hudson Institute, Wiener by name.

'In 1967 the US became the first economy in the world to employ more people in the service sector than in the manufacturing sector,' he pointed out, a trend which he expected to see grow, or as his colleagues at the Hudson might put it, escalate. Quite gratifying, especially when Wiener went on to deny that *'what will be most characteristic of this post-industrial society will be a domination of the national life by intellectuals.'* A lurking fear in the food trade, evidently.

Also, there are interesting anatomies of the new markets. Like the Ghetto Market by the president of All-Pro Chicken Inc. (*'We call in an exercise in black entrepreneurship using capitalistic guidelines to fit the black community,'* he says.) Another piece goes into the problems that private enterprise faces in fast-feeding the Army, but reports an interesting approach from the prison service. *'As far as I know, this is the first time we have had a nibble from the Federal Bureau of Prisons. It's a large market. It's $3 million a day in food value consumed in the prisons of the federal government. And it is a hopeful sign.'*

Other hopeful signs are reported by Mr David Downie, who is the Director of W. R. Grace and Company's European Consumer Products Group, consisting of twelve companies in eight countries. One of these is the Paris-based Compagnie des Restaurants Jacques Borel. *'This company was started in 1957 by Jacques Borel, who is an exceptionally talented and aggressive businessman,'* Downie remarks, with approbation, adding that he runs thirteen Wimpy Bars (under franchise from Lyons of England), a miscellany of cafeterias, coffee-shops, and steak-houses, an industrial catering business with 100 locations, and the biggest meal-voucher company in the country selling 15 million vouchers a year.

Yes, despite the gourmet's ire, Downie feels quietly confident. *'In my opinion, the trend is very clear that the growth in the foodservice market in Europe will be in the fast food category and as is true in the United States, the emphasis will be more on the merchandising than on the food itself.'*

But it is perhaps in its bright bulk of ad material that *Fast Food* comes most truly into its own, presenting the gastronomic future pre-packed and ready-to-serve in umpteen flavours in the here and now. Just what is *this* green scrumptiousness? A Super-Salad, that's what. *Why make salads from scratch?* demands the ad, *Just open a can of Durkee Ready-to-Serve Salad. Scoop out what you need … Thirsty? You can see the appetising colour of your thirst-quencher clear through* if you use the heavy-gauge basket-weave C-Thru plastic cup from Sweetheart Plastics, Inc.

As to Fish 'n' Chips, Britain's solitary contribution to the Fast Food scene: thanks to Dolphin seafoods you can have them *'served in a novel London "newspaper" cone'*, namely a pre-made cone printed up with (are you attending, Printing House Square?) an antique copy of *The Times*. And, as for that disagreeable cleaning up, well, there is always Hobart's Programmed Dishwashing, an automatic system, which includes a U-Shaped Fastrack, described—a bit obscurely—as a *'Time/Space Capsule'*. There is even the Hobart Glutton. *'Disposers from Hobart gobble up food waste you might otherwise have to store,'* burbles the ad, happily.

The revolution, what's more, is only just getting under way. *Fast Food* is full of small, informative paragraphs that prefigure the shape of things to come. Teasers. *A line of 55 varieties of meatless products, said to resemble meat in taste, appearance and texture, includes a bacon, sausage and ham-like product,* runs one such. *All products are cholesterol-free; they come packaged in frozen, canned and dehydrated forms.*

These cannot, I think be the foodstuffs that BP were recently trying to put together from petroleum products since those (they said) were intended as livestock feed. Might there be a connexion with the 'knitted steaks' that Courtaulds were banging on about in 1971? Alas, poignant in its brevity, *Fast Food* magazine just didn't say.

The offices of *Fast Food* are on Lexington Avenue, New York, a fifth-floor suite gently redolent of cooking-smells like a suit too often worn in a kitchen. The editor is a brisk lady, Joan Black Bakos. Her office has neat shelves of books and magazines: *The Progressive Grocer, The Greening of America, the Economic Effects of Franchising*.

Deftly, she conducts me through the franchise jungle, recommending study of a chain here, an operation there ... A & W of Santa Monica, Burger Chef, which hails from Minneapolis, and Burger King—'*Home of the Whopper*'— which burgeoned from Miami ... Pizza Hut, a native of Wichita, now in Australia, and Sandy's, from Kewanee, Illinois, now doing business in Brussels ... the big three of McDonalds, Howard Johnson, and Colonel Sanders' Kentucky-Fried Chicken ... Dairy Queen from Minneapolis and Tasty Cream of Chicago, which is likewise the home-town of Chicken Unlimited ... Dunkin' Donuts which has taken its fifty-two sorts of doughnut to London and (with more éclat) to Japan, all the way from Quincy, Massachusetts ...

Also, a favourite, Bonanza—'They are based on Dallas, and I think they have correctly seen the Market of the Future,' Joan Black Bakos says: 'We're out of the Teen-Age Market and into the Family Market ...'

This is the demographic trend, Mrs Bakos says, and the effects will be widespread. Essentially it seems to mean an end of the grotty teenage look, that whole Drive-In number of the '50s and '60s. In fact, Mrs Bakos amplifies, *Fast Food* did a whole theme issue on this, which was intended to be called: 'The Death of the Drive-In', and was duly published—Why be negative?—as 'The Birth of the Drive-To'.

A certain amount of this upgrading is, however, a little less than voluntary. There is, Jack-in-the-Box is confirmed, a welter of new restrictions governing road-side restaurants. 'They vary with every community, and some of them are very strict,' Mrs Bakos observes: 'There are some that say you can't have a sign on the roof of your building. There are some that legislate the brightness of the sign, or where it can be seen in relation to the road.'

Some communities are peculiarly unreasonable. 'In the

West they are very, very tough. And Detroit is unbelievable. *Very* bad.' Parts of Northern California equally, to say nothing of Baltimore and certain Boston suburbs, where the misanthropic authorities have even legislated against *eating in cars.*

On what grounds?

'That's just what I mean. It's these silly Boards. You see, they are usually comprised of little old ladies, the so-called leaders of the community, who have their own ideas as to how everything should look, and don't even consider the life-style of the public!'

Mrs Bakos sighs, with irritation, but also optimism. Between the little old ladies and the desires of the public she has little doubt which represents the wave of the future.

So—finally—what is the future of fast food? Globally speaking, that is.

'I think it is becoming the world cuisine,' Joan Black Bakos avers, simply.

I leave. A cooking session is under way in the spick-and-span *Fast Food* kitchens. Cooks potter around among the tasties. A sequence is being done on the volume preparation of veal, fresh from the calf batteries

Plates are being tidied up in the photographic studio, and I glean a little technical info. Olives, it seems, have to be painted up before photographing, just a touch of oil, administered with a small brush—'Otherwise, they'd die in the photograph. They're just not shiny enough'. Similar pains are taken with tomatoes, for instance, and shrimps. Shrimps shot fresh from the pan can look very drab indeed. Bad merchandising. Carrots look better raw, and ice-cream is a real problem. Some people have tried spray-coating it, others prefer to counterfeit it with coloured cotton. I leave, as the cameras begin to crackle greedily around the world cuisine of the future.

Slowly I am beginning to digest the rules of the fast food dominions, the golden rules that are incarnate in each Double Mac, London Broil, chicken dinner, defrosted pizza, and in the recessed womb of each Dunked Donut. They constitute, in all senses, a Code. They are Merchandising and Quality Control.

192

Quality Control relates more directly to the product itself, the eatable what-have-you, and the phrase is used in a rather special sense: namely that each single specimen should be of the same quality as each other specimen.

This is, of course, a Platonic ideal. Not all the lurking government inspectors in the world can keep automated feeding entirely free from the world's impurities. Occasionally, there is an unseemly brouhaha in the Press when rats' hairs are found in a plateful of finger-lickin' chicken or whatever.

Governments—with their own necessary interest in automated foodstuffs—do what they can. The Danish Co-Operative Egg Export, for example, with mass caterers in mind, recently announced that they had perfected a machine which will produce 240 cylindrical eggs, 16 inches long, and two inches in diameter, on an hourly basis. Each sixteen-incher, it seems, requires the co-operation of six hens, and various names have been suggested for the *matériel*, including egg sausage, egg zeppelin, long egg, and continuous egg. Just add a little chemical assistance to make sure that the yolk is that rich farmyard yellow and there you are! Enough Quality Control to suit any Continuous Egg franchise.

Not even governments are *sans peur* and *sans reproche. The Food and Drug Administration announced plans for restricting the use of a widely-relied-on colouring agent known as Red No. 2 because of evidence of adverse effects in test animals,* reported the *Wall Street Journal* in the fall of 1971. *Red No. 2 had been shown by Russian scientists to diminish fertility in rats, decreasing the litter size. FDA experts have confirmed these findings ...*

Some food companies have already made the switch from Red No. 2 to Red No. 40. The suspect colouring agent has a wide use in dessert, beverages and other foods. It is also used in lipsticks and other cosmetics.

When even governments err, no wonder Quality Control presents problems in the more private sectors of the automated food trade.

Merchandising covers pretty much everything else. Including, as Lapin demonstrated, the presentation of the unit:

the motif. Also, of course, the service. Dress Codes are fairly universal, of course. 'It's an area we have to police very closely,' confesses Mr Stan Diemoz, the marketing director, of Sambo's, another Southern California operation, with 187 outlets. (Sambo's did have one other image problem, which they have handled with real delicacy. Their name is derived from the Helen Bannerman tale, *Little Black Sambo*, which is no longer the popular little book it once was. The re-designed menu synopsises the adventures of Sambo and the Tigers, with an updated beginning which runs: '*Once upon a time ... there was a little boy in India named Sambo*.') It is mandatory for the waitresses to wear white shoes in Sambo's, and neither excessive make-up nor bizarre hair-styles are tolerated. Likewise the men. 'It's something of a problem in modern society,' Mr Diemoz confesses. 'It's very difficult ...'

Emersons, another operation, do what they can to eliminate the bizarre by issuing their waitresses with a rule-book including the *Famous Ten Courtesy Pointers*.

Increase your tips by memorising these ten simple procedures, decree Emersons. *They are strictly enforced and no exceptions are to be made. Pride yourself in offering the best service and best food to Emersons customers. You MUST memorise and say the following to ALL customers.*

For instance. *(1) Welcome to Emersons. My name is ... SMILE.* Yes, like Alice's Restaurant, Emersons is a happy place.

Promotion and advertising are merchandising's *aides-de-camp*, and tend to be as inventive as one might expect. Howard Johnson's, for instance, zeroed in on junior ecology. In exchange for a couple of frozen-food labels and, I believe, a dollar, the kids procured a collection of eco-games, plus 18 ecology stickers, 3 official badges, an ecology flag decal, a note-pad 'made of reclaimed paper', and a folder made of, um, vinyl.

Even this pales beside the efforts of the North American Pizza Association. This is a commando unit representing those plucky chaps pushing this foreign foodstuff, Italian no less, on the American market. Pizza dealers who join the association, get, by the way, many benefits, including tours

(The Roman Pizza Tour), newsletters, a Code of Ethics scroll, Accidental Death and Dismemberment Insurance at a massive discount, and the services of a Special Information-hunting Task Force.

Their problems are also handled. There was the Alka-Seltzer TV commercial which somehow linked the concept of pizza with the concept of indigestion. Even worse was the commercial in which General Food's Gaines Dog Meal 'was indirectly compared with pizza'. No matter; the Association talked to the manufacturers, and the ads came off the air.

Promotional offers which the public might find it hard to refuse include the whole box-of-tricks. There are T-shirts boldly lettered PIZZA MAKES ME PASSIONATE, and there are lapel buttons in which Peace and Love are, it is indicated, incomplete without pizza. There is also a small series of comic-books of no mean wit depicting the adventures of Superpizza. These begin when Superpizza is persuaded by a top-hatted Spiro Agnew to come to the United States and is met within sight of the Statue of Liberty by a gesticulating Nixon and a great many secret servicemen and police. Seconds later, Super-pizza foils a bomb-plot conceived by—among others—Humphrey Hot Dog, Fins the Fish, Tezio Taco, Hairy Hamburger, and Colonel Chicken, thereby saving his new country from (I merely quote) malnutrition and dysentery.

'Colonel Chicken' in this extravaganza is, of course, none other than Colonel Harland Sanders of the Kentucky Fried Chicken (WOMEN'S LIBERATION as a large hoarding expresses it). This is an implied and involuntary compliment to the promoter supreme, the real fast food magnifico.

I meet the Colonel in the Manhattan Offices of Heublein Inc. who now control the operation. Heublein is the firm that has simplified life by selling, amongst an ocean of other beverages, pre-bottled Daiquiris, Whiskey Sours, Side Cars and 11 to 1 Gin Martinis. Right now, Heublein executives surround the Colonel protectively. He is in his eighties, and magnificent. His suit is of a superlative whiteness, set off by one of those trailing black bow ties. His white whiskers are forcefully baroque. He has a healthy flush, and is agleam with rings and insignia, the Shriners, and both the Thirty-

Second and Thirty-Third Degrees of the Masonic Order.

As I enter a small row is going on. There has been yet another Press report on something or other that got into a chicken dinner.

'Did you see the foller-up there in a magazine?' demands the Colonel, irately. He says it 'foller-up' in a Southernly soft rumble, like an avalanche of treacle, and is reported to have the bluest language in the Southland. Like Burl Ives doing Tennessee Williams.

The Heublein people have, yes, seen it.

'He was afraid to mail me in a clipping,' says the Colonel, *furioso*, speaking of some absent unfortunate.

'Let me read these while you talk,' suggests a Heublein functionary, nervously.

'I don't like to get those damn things I don't mind telling you,' grumbles the Colonel, then turns the rosy beam of his attention on to me. 'Well, that's dandy now,' he says.

Reminiscently, the Colonel told me how it all began. Which was essentially in 1956, when a highway project threatened to destroy his business. The Colonel (the rank is roughly parallel to that of Elvis's manager, Colonel Tom Parker) was already in his 60s. Gamely, he patented his mix of eleven herbs and spices, packed up his pressure fryer—the process takes the fashionable time of seven minutes—and took to the road to sell franchises.

A few years later the Colonel was making $300,000 a year. Peanuts. Then John Brown Jr came along. John Brown Jr bought him out for two million. He is one of nature's salesmen, a man, the Colonel says: 'With the oratory he's got, he could take a greasy pig and make it think it's on its way to Sunday school.'

Thanks to Brown, Kentucky-Fried Chicken had corporate sales of 163 million in 1969. In terms of gross food volume, it came fourth to the US Army, the US Department of Agriculture School Lunch Programme, and the US Navy. It survived, with a few tremors, the franchise upheavals of the later '60s, which saw a flurry of schemes built around the names of (for instance) Joe Namath, Rowan and Martin, and, of course, Minnie Pearl.

'They had no image,' the Colonel explains, prodding the floor with his ebony cane. 'Well, Minnie Pearl was quite an image. She was known in Country Music, the Grand ol' Opry for twenty-five or thirty years. But everyone knew she didn't know nothing about chicken ...'

Brown kept on Colonel Sanders as a 'travelling ambassador', which is to say a magnificent three-dimensional walking, talking trademark.

'I'm travelling ... oh aroun' two hundred thousand, two hundred and fifty thousand miles a year,' says the Colonel, reeling off a strenuous topography. Just recently, for instance, he had been to Athens, Nicosia, Rome, Cairo, Canada, and Australia.

One triumphal tour even took in Moscow whither the Colonel went to have colloquy with Kruschev. The Colonel's plan for world peace was to take over his chicken formula to the USSR absolutely free, and Kruschev, an aficionado of certain Western pleasures—his tantrums when he was not permitted to visit Disneyland were, reportedly, piteous—seemed most eager. Alack, Nikita's influence was at its nadir, and this is only the most finger-lickin' of pleasures which are still beyond the conception of the Muscovites.

'The Colonel', a man from Heublein explains, 'knew there was no possibility of a commercial venture. He is not just a chicken salesman. He's an expert in the area of food nutrition.

'There is much more to the man than the white suit and the black tie. He's sought after by the top corporations in the country. He's a genius. There's no doubt about that. One of the things that people don't know is that Colonel Harland Sanders is the creator of the Motel.'

Really? I ask, fascinated.

'In Corydon, Kentucky, in 1939, I think, he combined his gas station, his eatery, and a place to sleep in one designed building. No, he didn't call it a motel, but the concept was there. I mean he's accredited with it ...'

Back to the Colonel, I ask does he wear his white suit throughout?

Of course. 'I wear them at work,' the Colonel booms. 'It's my prison garb I wear the year round.'

There are uneasy grins from Heublein's. 'Prison garb!' one of them repeats to me, with a deprecatory chuckle.

'You'd be surprised how many people recognise me even in Europe,' the Colonel adds, and speaks of touring the British franchises, even when these were just started with some seven stores, up in Lytham, say, and Liverpool.

'I'd go down the street, and I'd hear the people say—There's Colonel Sanders! There's Colonel Sanders! Everywhere we'd go ...'

Some, of course, were more sceptical.

'They think,' Colonel Sanders hollers, with a sort of resonant irony, 'I'm some sort of figment of some advertising man's imagination!'

'He's not!' a Heublein executive assures me, with a quick, jolly laugh.

Howard Johnson Jr is a less flamboyant figure. No perambulating billboard he, but a New Englander, and raffiné, with an invisibly figured tie, and a triangle of white linen handkerchief peeping from a dove-grey suit of almost excessive neatness. One might take him for an economics don, say, except for the occasional remark of quite un-donnish steeliness.

The offices of the Howard Johnson chain are in the Rockefeller Plaza, just opposite the suite that houses the Belgian Embassy. There is a bland lobby, with smoky orange sofas, and a glass bowl full of Howard Johnson sweets—'samples' explains the receptionist. There are Howard Johnson brochures to read or—for the less singleminded—a pile of Reader's Digests.

'We don't make money in offices,' Howard Johnson says: 'Its just a place for the directors to come ...'

He defines the Howard Johnson aim. 'It's a food and lodging system designed to service the interstate highways in the United States of America,' he says, slowly and carefully. So far as the grub goes, Howard Johnson's is, it seems, unique.

'As you know, menus are shrinking and people who are successful have been able to come up with a limited menu, no matter whether it's at the low end of the scale or the high end.

198

McDonalds'—he instances—'does a great job serving cheap hamburgers. But there are very few people trying to produce as many products as we do. And that's part of the mystique. How do they do it in eight hundred restaurants? Our revenue' —Johnson adds, an apparent *non sequitur*—'will this year exceed the five hundred million mark ...'

It all comes down to quality control, of course. These eight hundred include both the Howard Johnson restaurants and the Motor Lodges. The Motor Lodges are larger and have that bland gridded styling which is standard *lumpen-Bauhaus*. The restaurants are much more New England. They are long and low, with a roof tiled in neon-orange. In the middle of the building, there is a sort of Palladian triangular bit, rising to a mini-spire, an obelisk. If a fairly simple-minded computer had been fed with Inigo Jones' postcards and required to churn out diners they might easily look like Howard Johnsons.

The churning-out continues. 'Our expansion programme will really be on "typicals", which is the smaller operation,' Johnson says. 'And we plan to build three or four hundred of those ... We have an evolutionary change going on in the architectural design. A gradual change into something more modern.'

In the main board-room a whole wall is aflame with various evolutionary phases. The orange roof is constant, and the real stone wall, class-in-Wimpyland, but the obelisk thing goes through abstract changes.

'We went out to California, and changed the roofline a little. This is the one we put up in Florida.' A jab of the hand. 'Then we came up with a mansard roof, leaving out the cupola, which was *revolutionary* ... and I got quite disturbed about it, and put the cupola back on.

'And then we said—let's try something completely different, and put a modern cupola on.' He points at the Howard Johnson Dream Road-House of ... 'Maybe 1980. I think we were a little ahead of ourselves ....'

What, finally, of the European Howard Johnsons? There is one already *in situ* in Amsterdam, and it is said that scouting trips have been made to, for instance, London.

Johnson is properly cautious.

'Whether or not the various aspects of our operation can be packaged and sent to Europe is a thing we're going to have to do some more research on,' he observes.

'One of the difficulties is—How can the American approach to the food business be allowed to fit in with the European scenery. And if they put restrictions on the architectural design, it might limit the potential of the site.

'One of the things that nobody's come to grips with is that, in terms of travel, the two areas are totally different. The road systems are perfectly *incomparable*. Our superhighways —And you know I'm not trying to be offensive,' he inserts, parenthetically, though with a pettish note, 'are thirty to forty years ahead of yours *at least*.

'For instance, a road going from London Airport to London is a small two-lane highway. Well, that's a *local road* in the United States. We've got a twelve-lane superhighway that's now being built to go from New York to Los Angeles. *Twelve lanes!* Three days to go three thousand miles!'

From one Howard Johnson's to another, and another, in fact. Johnson agrees, with afflatus.

'Well, the thing that services that has gotta be different from the thing that services that little road from London Airport into London, and you might be interested to know I didn't see one location out of the airport area into Downtown London where I could put a typical Howard Johnson structure because it was ... *neighbourhood*. I mean, you have the local homes,' he explains, with the faintest of sniffs. 'It was a very local-type situation. You know, the roads aren't built with the same thing in mind.'

However, and despite our lousy roads, all is not lost.

'We have a group that wants to go into France and Germany. We have another group that's been talking to us about Israel,' Howard Johnson Jr says, with optimism. 'Gee! We're looking around.'

A pale stone slab beside the road announces that you are entering the university precincts. These are about half-an-hour from the centre of Chicago in the suburb of Elk Grove, and the sign is discreet to semi-visibility between a Howard Johnson's hoarding and an eatery outside of which grazes a life-size red-and-white plastic cow. The slab reads HAMBURGER UNIVERSITY in lettering derived from Roman inscriptions and nowadays used on the title-pages of austerely academic books.

The building is smallish, and looks like a privately-funded museum of modern art. White concrete is broken into interesting shapes, and there are long windows of tinted glass. There are trees outside, and a small pool which sends bobbles of light dancing inside the lobby. The massive doors are of darkish wood and carved with innumerable miniature replicas of the golden double arch of McDonald's.

HAMBURGER UNIVERSITY, the national training ground for McDonald's carryout restaurants (I quote from one of the several available postcards) ... *is a statement of McDonald's intense interest in quality and leadership. Within these hallowed halls, McDonald's management people receive instructions on McDonald's systems and on the philosophy of McDonald's success.*

Inside the building I am introduced to the teaching staff. Robert Doran who is the Dean of Hamburger U., and Jerry Gorman, who is one of the professors. Also Clark Baldwin, who is not a university man, being a manager with the International side of McDonald's and is based in the company headquarters at McDonald's Plaza, Oakbrook.

They familiarise me with such aspects of the McDonald's saga as I have failed to pick up elsewhere. It began, really, when Ray A. Kroc, then a salesman of Multimixers, discovered an unprecedented number of these machines being used out in San Bernardino at a small diner run by Mac and Dick McDonald. They had developed a hamburger that had an almost hypnotic appeal, Kroc found, but the brothers showed no interest in starting a chain. They were happy, though, to sign the franchising rights over for a half of one per cent of the gross.

Ray Kroc opened his first McDonald's in the Chicago suburb of Des Plaines in April, 1955, and the second in September of the same year, in Fresno, California. By 1961, there were 323 outlets, and Kroc bought the brothers out for 2.7 millions.

He never looked back. McDonald's have sold their eight billionth burger and—at four million a day—are well on the way to nine. In 1970, a year in which franchises were subsiding like punctured balloons, the turnover rose by a third and currently McDonald's is doing 600 million dollarsworth of business annually through 1,800 outlets, a number itself increasing by five or six a week.

McDonald's is the seventh largest US food supplier, behind the Colonel, but ahead of any other fast-food franchise. They use more ground beef than anybody but the federal government and are the largest single syrup customer of Coca-Cola. Eight million burgers, points out their imaginative public relations department, could carpet the state of Illinois ankle-deep or—laid end to end— *'would measure 509,568 miles ... enough to reach the moon and all the way home again, or they'd form 20 and one-third ribbons around the earth at its fattest point.'*

Nor is it just as statistical fun that McDonald's are scrutinising the earth's fatter points. They have global ambitions beside which Howard Johnson seems a timid parasite of the automobile. Only the indefatigable Colonel matches their hopeful internationalism, just as only the Colonel's regiments match the McDonald's men in the devout intensity of their salesmanship.

Already the company has been operating some five years up in Canada, where it has a chain of over sixty stores. 'We are now operating in Puerto Rico ... the Virgin Islands ... Panama ... Costa Rica,' says Clark Baldwin, bouncily. 'We have two in Holland, one in Amsterdam and one in Delft ... Two in Munich ...'

Nor is the UK being forgotten—'Several groups are very interested in venturing with us,' says Stephen Barnes, president of McDonald's International—but the real go-go market is Japan where McDonald's have four outlets on Tokyo's Ginza. Here the Japanese, it seems, queue up with fanatic docility, and chomp up three thousand dollarsworth of burgers and various fixings *per day*. Splendid going, even if still running second to Colonel Sanders, who has ten Japanese stores, and plans on opening four hundred. How can one not remember Jonathan Swift's Lilliputian battle between those who liked to eat their boiled egg at the little end, and those who preferred the big? In the perfect Consumers' World the last interminable Armageddon may be between those who swear by a tub of finger-lickin' chicken and those who stand firm for the Double Mac.

A bellyful is a bellyful.   FRANÇOIS RABELAIS

Hamburger University is not the playful whim of a very rich company. It offers a training course for new batches of managerial talent. They will have paid $110/125,000 for a franchise, depending on the trimmings, and the course is free. McDonald's isn't the only fast-food chain to offer some of the trappings of the groves of Academe (There is also a Dunkin' Donuts University in Quincy, Mass.) but it is, indisputably, the fanciest. The end product is a Diploma in Hamburger-ology, with a Minor in French Fries. There have been 130 classes, and there are upwards of 5,000 Bachelors of Ham-burgerology. It is a handsome diploma, with black Gothic lettering, signed by Ray Kroc (Chairman) and Fred Turner (President), and there is no reason to suppose that the BHs find it a comical document. Rather it is, in the best academic traditions, jocular-solemn.

Classes can vary from ten to forty. The franchisees tend to be in their middling thirties, and competent. Not just any-body can get a franchise. Despite the costs, and despite the 11.5% of monthly sales that the franchisee pays to McDonalds, a strictly average McDonald's operator should make profits of fifty, sixty, seventy thousand dollars a year. *McDonald's does not issue a licence easily,* the hand-out warns. *Applicants are carefully screened and only those who look as if they have a potential for success are accepted.*

Hamburger U. is dedicated to laying the foundations of this success, by passing on the original illumination of Ray Kroc. *His then-new idea was to put the hamburger on the assembly line,* continues the missive from Cooper & Golin

Inc., *the same way Henry Ford put the Model T on the assembly line.*

This, as Kroc has noted, requires Science. Techniques are *constantly being developed and refined under laboratory-controlled conditions in McDonald's own Equipment Development Centre ...*

And, although a lot of corporations USE computers, McDonald's is one of the few outside of the computer field itself to have INVENTED one. It's a cooking computer, an electronic device which takes the guesswork out of French fries. Other inventions include a fish fry computer, a tartare sauce dispenser, a carbon dioxide alarm for a beverage dispenser and a new plastic waste receptacle.

I am shown around the Hamburger U. facilities, which are lavish. There are audio-visual aids, closed-circuit television systems, and much sophisticated paraphernalia. The course lasts nine days. A characteristic third day's schedule runs as follows.

WEDNESDAY

8:30 a.m.	Test 11
9:15	Shakes
10:15	Break
10:30	Shake Machine
11:45	Multi-Mixer
12:30 p.m.	Lunch
1:30	Carbonation Principles
2:45	Break
3:00	K-Way
4:30	Ice Machine Electives: (Kold-Draft, Whirlpool, Scotsman)
5:30	Equipment Groups

These lectures are accompanied by slides from a library of 5,000. Or by movies, roseate with well being. Jerry Gorman, young for a professor in his early thirties, flips through some titles. *Production Control* is a new one, he explains, and puts a fast-food operation into terms of a football game: 'I think it hits home pretty good with them.'

204

Here also are *The Idaho Potato Story*, and a cash-oriented film. 'It's about how people can steal from you right before your very eyes,' Gorman says. 'This *Genius and the Average Man* is a speech made by the Reverend Bob Richards. I don't know if you've ever heard of him? He was Olympic High Jump Champion. No, *pole-vaulting*. It's tremendously motivating ...'

We watch *New Dimensions*. This deals with new dimensions in store management, and stars the Ideal Manager, who has the trim, safe gleam of Sheffield cutlery, and looks a bit like Roger-Moore-as-the-Saint. In the filmlet, the manager sails splendidly over a sea of minor troubles, and ends congratulating his team.

'You were absolutely ... great today, gang! You did a good job, crew! We broke all kinds of records again. Thanks so much!'

Full frontal smile to the Class.

'Yes, I'm proud of my job. And my place of business,' the manager says. Surges of Oscar-type music. Fade-out.

This corporate afflatus is very important. On a tour of the premises I am shown the cases of goodies. Like the pens with plexiglass windows that successively flash *Quality/Service/ Cleanliness/McDonald's* when you work the plunger. Also wearables. The Golden Arches of McDonald's were originally a 3-D derivation from the initial 'M' but are now being quietly phased down, back into an ideogram where they will survive forever on ties and jacket-pockets.

In another room we find the standard McDonald's equipment. It is a cut-away, which shows the working parts, but also means that it is not capable of being used. All the actual cooking is done at the McDonald's store off down the highway. No crude cookery smells waft on campus. So unlike Dunkin' Donuts University, as one of the McDonald's professors remarks. 'It's nothing more than a *bakery*,' he says: 'It's set up just like a regular Dunkin' Donuts bakery line ...'

A Saturday lecture deals with the 'single most difficult problem that McDonald's stores have to face'. Youth. That is not to say extreme youth. Extreme youth is part of the family business that is McDonald's especial pride and joy, and consists furthermore, of enraptured fans of the surreal Commedia del Arte adventures of the red-headed clown, Ronald McDonald, in McDonaldland. (According to J. Anthony Lukas in *The New York Times Magazine* the Fourth Annual Ronald McDonald Awareness Study found that 96% of American children could identify Ronald by name, making him 'a close second to Santa Claus'.)

No, the Youth that McDonald's find worrisome are somewhat older. For a start, there is the problem of their own junior employees. *Your windowmen and outside order-takers must impress customers as being 'All-American' boys,* says a McDonald's manual. They must have neat haircuts and make adequate use of deodorants. *Personnel with bad teeth, severe skin blemishes or tattoos should not be stationed at service windows.*

So far, so good, though the Kroc hard line *vis-à-vis,* for instance, haircuts has necessarily had to be somewhat relaxed. The problem of disciplining customers is rather trickier.

'In a recent survey taken of McDonald's stores,' observes a professor, with due precision, 'it was found that 53 per cent of our stores have a teenage problem ranging from serious to very serious.' He mentions such distressing traits as sitting on each other's car fenders, 'noisy and profane language', beer drinking, vandalism in the rest rooms, the ruination of landscaping and (even) the theft of the flag, right up, or down, to heavy necking, gang fights, and—'our biggest problem'—drugs.

The fledgling managers are instructed in the preventive devices. The imposition of a time-limit in the parking lot. Floodlights to reduce the necking. And, of course, the police. A pamphlet presents the history of one textbook case; *Teenage Control—Vero Beach, Florida.*

This problem arose when the council closed down one of the local parks at 7 p.m. *This park had long been known as a teenage hang out, narcotic sanctuary, and the in place to go with no holes [sic] barred,* the pamphlet explains, graphically, and goes on to describe how the kids immediately swarmed the McDonald's. Well, McDonald's had its family image to protect, and went into action on several fronts. It printed off

An Open Letter On McDonald's Code Of Good-Neighbour Relations, in which it remarked, with a slightly agonised timbre: *It goes without saying that McDonald's of Vero Beach is vitally interested in our community ... just ask any little leaguer, Jaycee or high school band member.*

The final solution was legal. The refugees from needle park were each handed a letter. It was incongruously printed in that script known, I believe, as 'Lady' and reserved for the sort of wedding invitations that have pink deckle edges, and it ran as follows.

> *You are hereby notified that this*
> *establishment no longer desires to entertain*
> *you as its guest and you are requested to leave*
> *at once and to remain after receipt of this*
> *notice is a misdemeanour under the laws of*
> *this state, statute 509.141*
> > *The Manager,*
> > *McDonald's—Vero Beach,*
> > *Florida.*

There are tests on these subjects, and the scores are totalled. Dennis, for instance, one of the students, got 13 out of 39 possible points on Test 1 (Hamburgers, Fries, Fryers) but sank to 1 on Test 4 (Store Maintenance, Ice Machine, Teenage, Shortening, Apple pie). His Enthusiasm was rated 'Good' and his Attentiveness in class was 'Excellent'. A final comment from the faculty reads: 'We do not understand why he did not finish higher in the standing as he put forth a good effort.'

Finally, there are snappy graduation ceremonies. Cocktails, and the Dean handing out the diplomas to the new BHs, plus a few incidentals, such as the 'Archie'. This is an award to the top-of-the-class man, and consists of a McDonald's-shaped base on which rests a symbolic burger: namely a plastic sphere.

What happens to people who fail?

'We-e-ell!' Professor Gorman says, reflectively. 'There haven't *been* any real failures yet.'

We lunch down the road. Not in the McDonald's, as a

matter of fact. (McDonald's men are dedicated to selling burgers, not necessarily to eating them.)

Then back to the university, and into the main classroom. This is being given over right now to the rehearsing of a musical, a McDonald's spectacular which is to be produced in front of two thousand McDonald's conventioneers in Hawaii. The main classroom is large, in fashionable tones of beige and lambent orange. Three actresses and four actors mill around. One of them is lugging the enormous script—the proceedings are to last eight hours—while the director works on a routine with the pianist. The pianist is dark, with liquid dark eyes, suffused in humorous despondency. He isn't smoking, but a spectral cigarette depends from his lower lip. He pounds away, masterfully.

Today they are rehearsing Scene Five, Act One. This is the Customer's Song. The director gives last minute instructions. He is a Broadway veteran, with the spare, muscular grace of a dancer, and he is wearing bell bottoms and one of those tunics with a ripcord zip of the sort poularised by Bond movies.

The music strikes up, and one of the actors steps out. He has an agreeable baritone.

> *Every time I look you sell a billion more*
> *I never cease to wonder how they multiply* (he carols)
> *You've got a lot of traffic coming through your door*
> *But I hope that you remember that I'm just one guy*
> *While you watch those billions rise*
> *I hope and trust you realise*
> *Who put those billions in the air*
> *It's guys like me that got you there!*

He pauses melodiously, then sweeps into the chorus.

> *Never mind the eight billion!*
> *Just the one in my hand!*

The cast swell into a full-throated chorus.

> *Never mind the eight bill-ion*
> *Just the one in my hand!*

The actresses are petite, and sexy. Buttocks strain out of a black body-stocking which, as is the way with such garments, is ever so slightly too small. One of the actors has a lean, dark face, like a rodent of great sensitivity. Another is apparently tied together from bronzed tendons, with a worn blue denim shirt, natch, the Come-to-Marlboro-County manner. Another is older, stouter, with a faint resemblance to James Hayter playing Mr Pickwick. They have the assertive polish of professionals, and sink back on to the balls of their feet while the lead singer jounces forwards into a second verse ... a third ...

'Right! The first one is fine!' says the producer, waltzing briskly forwards: 'Remember—The second one should be quicker, so by the time you go into the last one it's really moving.'

He demonstrates. 'Never mind the eight bill-ion! Just the one in my hand!'

'Never mind the eight bill-ion!' the chorus sings, trailing away.

'Just the one in my hand,' completes an actress with a sultry trill, and giggles.

This is the first Industrial Musical (as the genre is called) that I have watched being put together, and the producer is informative. He himself is a regular performer in the legitimate theatre—'On Broadway I did *Carnival* ... *West Side Story* ... *Golden Boy* ... In *West Side Story* I was the swing boy—' but, what with nowadays showbiz being all too often no biz, he is one of the group of actors, singers, writers, musicians etc. that have built up a lucrative side-line in Industrials.

This is big business nowadays. General Motors spends a million dollars a year on Industrials, and more money is invested in live theatrical entertainment by industry than by all the Broadway backers put together. No wonder Equity's minimum rate for Industrial shows is higher than for the legitimate theatre.

'Recently I've done International Harvesters ... Celanese ... Mercury Outboard Motors,' the producer recalls. Most of these shows are one-night jamborees to instil the corporate philosophy into the salesmen, a task traditionally simplified by due helpings of female bosom and thigh. 'I've done Industrials with a budget of $60,000! $100,000! Sometimes

$200,000!' cries the producer merrily. Life holds satisfactions apart from Tonys, Grammys and Oscars.

'There are two kinds of Industrials,' he explains: 'There is the kind that we fondly call nuts-and-bolts. And that's where you get a song, and you get the cast, and you're ... rumtitumtitum ... doing a number about ... Mixmasters ...

'Whereas then you have shows which are more—*motivational*. Where you're trying to get a *gut feeling* across to the audience. A feeling of goodwill. Or complacency. Or whatever it is that you're after.'

His voice sinks with confidential sincerity. In the background, the cast snake in and out of postures, hit a note or two, riffle through the script.

'And my feeling has always been that you've got to approach it *legitimately*,' the producer says. 'In other words, if you are trying to get to a salesman, you are trying in the course of the show to explain that—*he's not alone!* And the hours that he spends on the road away from his family are not going unnoticed ...

'You have to do it right. Otherwise, he won't relate to it. If he doesn't see those moments when you're by yourself and many, many miles from town. You are having dinner by yourself, and thinking about the day, which has not been too good, and you are thinking about tomorrow, which may not be any better.' The producer's voice throbs with empathy, but now his face brightens. 'You've got to get to this guy to say—*Hey! You're gonna be okay!*

'*And there's a bunch of us up here who believe in what you are doing*. And you can't do that unless you get it to the point where it's *real*. I've done shows, and when the actors finish on stage, you'll be walking through the hotel, and the audience will come over to you and say—Hey! what district are you in? And, in some cases not realise that it's an actor at all.'

Stanislavsky rather than Brecht, in fact, with reminiscences of the Method, and more than a little work is necessary. 'Before I came to this show I had already spent days going through McDonald's stores, going through different operations, and not as somebody coming and saying—Look! I'm going to be doing a show, but going to the counter and buying my hamburger like anybody else ... looking at the manager, where he's at, what the bathroom's all about, what the parking facilities are ... and it's like the whole concept of Q.S.C. which is part of the show. Quality! Service! Cleanliness!' he enumerates.

McDonald's is a going concern, the producer says, and the message behind the musical is: 'Look, guys! You've got it going! If you don't work hard enough, you're going to lose it. You're going to blow it!

'My job is putting the show together ... You add, and you subtract, and then you balance it up ... It'll be eight hours of solid work.'

Time for another number. There are going to be six comedy numbers, one of the McDonald's professors says, and a good deal of more *serioso* material. Pep talks. Visuals. The works. The professor eyes the production hungrily, and confides that he was once attracted towards show biz himself. He wonders whether the cast shouldn't be bouncing around more, but then aren't most rehearsals like that?

The plot hinges upon the more Pickwickian actor. It is picaresque. 'He's kind of an ... ass. He comes in at the beginning and thinks he's going to buy the whole company.' Laughter. 'By the end of the show they convince him through the song-and-dance that maybe he just ought to buy a store.

'And each song, each dance-routine has a message. The theme of the convention is Success—And Then Some! *Success—A.T.S!*'

In this particular number, the Ass walks into a McDonald's store and is confronted by an actor who does a tinkly German operatic bit, explaining that he is a hamburger.

They have a jolly dialogue, filled with Achtungs and Schnells and Von Stroheim mannerisms, plus some loving detail.

'How is it by me for you huh?' inquires the hamburger, ripely Teutonic.

'Good red colour,' approves the Ass.

'Ja! Well, no filler in me, Fritz, huh?'

'So they grill you to contain your juices? So you don't

bleed out and become dry?'

'You've got it, strudel face!' exults the hamburger, from here on in to be referred to as Hamburger. *'I'm one hundred per cent pure beef!'*

An actress struts on-stage.

'Look out!' says Hamburger. 'Here comes the Frenchie!'

Rude, I feel, but music strikes up, an interesting pastiche-mélange of the *Marseillaise* and Bizet, and she reveals herself as a French fry. So crisp, she points out, and so easy.

Inevitably, Hamburger and French fry start squabbling, but quieten as they are joined by an early-'6os rock 'n' roll type who is gyrating to some sort of Bill Haley derivative, and whose opening remark is 'Huh! This is a groovy place to crash! Dig it, pops?' No reference to Vero Beach, Florida, intended, it seems. This is Milk Shake.

'You are merely for ze cheeldren!' pouts Frenchie.

'Oh, yeah! Like the kids dig me! Wow!' says Milk Shake, clicking his fingers, altogether too often, even for the coolest Shake in town. 'But I'm for everybody. *I mean ... everybody!'* Milk Shake enthuses about his flavours, and about such special treats as the St Patrick's Day green and the George Washington cherry. He's got a groovy flavour, Milk Shake points out, with further finger clicks. 'Taste me and you'll—*freak out!'*

Enter another actress, with full-blooded flurries of mood music. She represents Apple Pie. 'I mean,' she says, with a flutter of the Mae Wests, 'what's a meal without dessert?'

More squabbling, and more squabbling, until the Ass desperately calls for order, and they all gang up ... 'After all, my friends!' says Hamburger, magnificently: 'We are all one fine family of products, nicht wahr?'

'Right, baby!' agrees Apple Pie: 'and we're all in one bag!'

The number ends to the familiar strains of *Side by Side* in a choral dance. It's an earthy fable, a Mediaeval Morality playlet, but commercially styled, and with this grand Broadway finale, precision-choreographed to the last twinkle of tooth and toe—Hamburger and French Fry, Milk Shake and Apple Pie—shaking a leg in total togetherness, total identification.

'Good!' says the producer, 'Okay! I love it! *I love it!'*

❊ Hot Gospels

*In which the writer accompanies six Penthouse Pets
to their new installation in Yugoslavia.*

Penthouse is to *Playboy* as Pepsi is to Coke. Even *Playboy*, I
dare say, might well be startled at the speed with which it has
become Established. *Penthouse* is second, and tries harder.
Penthouse is lean and hungry. Even the *Penthouse* girls look
leaner and hungrier than the *Playboy* girls.

Even so, it seemed surprising that it should be *Penthouse*
that made the most definitive foray into the Eastern Bloc.
Playboy is, after all, an unimpeachably liberal magazine from
way back while *Penthouse* tends to a stern line on, for
instance, homosexuality and narcotics. Profits, though, are
something else again.

I meet the *Penthouse* shock troops at Heathrow Airport
and the commuters to Frankfurt, Brussels, Amsterdam, are
baffled. What is this? A rock opera? Here are six dolls, sitting
around the terminal in luscious inertia, and here are guys, also
... Cuban heels, bellbottoms, tapered Borgia shirts, Mafia-
Enforcer dark glasses ... the commuters clutch their Samsonite cases, and wonder.

The Penthouse Pets are gossiping. This is Pet Marian, Pet
Marianne, and Pet Lesley, Pet Helen, Pet Tina, and Pet
Angela, who is also a croupier on the side. With them are a
cadre of club executives including—in peanut butter boots
and enough navel-length chains to confound King Tut—Bob
Guccione, owner of the Penthouse Club, founder-editor of

Penthouse magazine, and soon to be operator of a leisure complex in, of all places, Yugoslavia.

Not that Yugoslavia isn't broad-minded: Marshal Tito has a Diners' Card where Fidel Castro won't even honour them. Yugoslavia, in fact, was the only possible Eastern site for an enclave devoted to the pursuit of happiness, Western-style. Our destination, is Haludovo on the beautiful barren island of Krk. Guccione set a deal up with a Yugoslav hotel chain. Under the deal, *Penthouse* will manage the complex for 21 years and remove some 75% of the profits.

'We will have 300 Pets working there,' he adds. Guccione is a New Yorker, 39, with a moody face, modishly shaggy. 'There will be Pets in the night club and Pets on the terrace ... Pets in the Casino and Pets in the restaurant.

'Right now, we are advertising for Yugoslav Pets, and looking for a Yugoslav Pet Mother. She will have to be at least 25 years old, and she will be unquestionably the highest-paid woman in Yugoslavia.

'They'd never *heard* of female execs. We're striking a big blow for Capitalism in the East ...'

On the plane I sit next to Marianne. She is reading *The Naked Lunch*, though (she says) she doesn't much care for stream-of-consciousness writing. Marianne is a blonde Glaswegian, a former teacher of speech and drama. Right now, teachers' pay being what it is, Marianne is Pet-of-the-Month. Which involves occupying the centre photographic spread in *Penthouse*.

'A Pet-of-the-Month is an aristocrat—wherever she goes,' Guccione says. Marianne has a copy of the mag. and her pictures are hazily golden, and quite becoming. She was (she confides) shy, since she had never taken her clothes off before, and won't do so again, but she is proud of the pictures as most of the girls are. Neither they nor (mostly) boy friends care much about that sort of thing nowadays, but the parents' generation are, of course, a bit different. No Pet's family it seems is stuck in a spot so remote that some wellwisher won't pass on the pics of their little girl in the altogether.

Responses vary. One girl was badly thumped by an outraged father, while another, more accommodating, dad said

—'Good! I haven't seen her naked since she was four years old.'

And Marianne's parents? Stoical, it seems. 'But my uncles', she adds, angst clouding the blue eyes, 'are vurra ... sick about it.'

Later the Pets are called up front. 'We have to put on our cozzies,' says Marianne, meaning the Penthouse costume. This is distinct from that of the Playboy Bunny though, in some respects, similar, suggesting a showgirl/waitress equipoise, a delicate balance between the thrustful and the passive. The Liberated Slave, perhaps, or Western 20th Century Geisha? Possibly, though the treatment excludes backrubs, and much besides.

The gear was designed by Guccione who derived inspiration from a French maid in a late-night movie. Summerwear comes in gingham. Great linen bows butterfly from the back, and there is a jaunty bit of lace frou-frou atop the hair. Sound engineering principles applied to the torso ensure that the bosoms protrude firm and edible as hardboiled eggs.

The nether parts, however, display more knicker than is usual in even the friendliest of French maids. The knickers are put together from see-through stuffs, so a number of layers are necessary. The effect is faintly reminiscent of a baby's nappies.

Venice, and they form up on the steps. It's the classic pose, the Starlet descending in a blaze of tooth/thigh/flashbulb, but multiplied by six. The tarmac magically swells with incredulous Italians until the Pets just have to bat an Eyelure and a tremor thrills through (it seems) the total armed strength of the State of Venezia.

The Penthouse-Adriatic is just a few minutes from Venice by air. But neither it nor the air service being (at time of writing) fully operational it takes us four hours in a bus styled like a Mack Sennett tram, the Krk ferry, and a further drive to our Grade B hotel.

We visit the new complex early next morning. It is, yes, formidable, a blanched glitter of pastry-cutter shapes like a cybernetic palazzo. The Haludovo, certainly, makes your average modern hotel look positively antique. First attraction is a Press Conference. Trays circulate with different-coloured drinks in different-shaped glasses, and perhaps a couple of dozen journalists, officials range themselves in chairs. The Pets are clumped demurely at one side in one of those marvellous impromptu groups which they seem to be able to assume at will, an instant Hollywood set-up only marred by an American entrepreneur who joins them from nowhere with a pocketful of Mickey Mouse watches.

The conference is chaired by Guccione and the Yugoslav boss of the hotel chain who—Guccione says through the interpreter—'I regard as a man with particularly dynamic vision'.

Guccione talks. Of the impossibility of selling the club without also selling Yugoslavia. About Definitive Public Relations Programmes and Direct Mail Shots. The interpreter, a bearded and sardonic man, finds most of these concepts only translatable as 'propaganda'. The Yugoslav tongue is as yet incapable of handling these nuances but this, I reflect, may well be the first private-enterprise public-relations press-conference that some of these fellows have had the privilege of attending.

Afterwards, a photo-call. Some pics around a statue in the lowered area which (the architect tells me) is to be a decorative pool. The statue is by the second-best Yugoslav sculptor, he explains, and it is a naked lady with Greco-Roman profile and thighs like hams. The Pets cluster around, smiling winsomely. Two modes of Social Realism.

Actually, Joe Toscani says, the pool isn't to be a pool at all. Inexorable logistics demand the installation there of crap tables. Joe is one of the gaming managers, an amiable bunch faced with important decisions. Security, for instance, since a weekly turnover of £100,000 is expected once that Golden Horde of tourists starts pouring in. Yugoslavs themselves are not permitted to play, but—as a local journalist puts it, delicately—no Socialist tenet prevents them from profiting from capitalist diversions.

Other facilities include the bowling alley already installed downstairs, and Sauna Baths, Mini-Golf, and 'Swinging singles bar for the solos'. Also, the Fishing Village, which is a genuine reproduction of a real Croatian fishing village. Here there is a piazza with an antique well, soon to be surrounded by boutiques. Beside the quay, a pile of netting waits to be strung to the walls.

I walk back with some of the Pets who have eluded the attentions of an enthusiastic Yugoslav photographer. We trot down to the shore for one more camera session. Sand is not a local amenity, but the grey and tortured rocks have been shaved off in areas, and the cavities filled with concrete, and smoothed down into the neatest little man-made coves imaginable.

Friday Morning, I commandeer a car with three Pets and drive off. We are looking for the 'real' Yugoslavia, and promptly find it. Laburnum, rugged stone walls, and olive trees on the switchback hills. A woman about three times older than Marshal Tito passes us on a donkey, and the girls squeal with delight. She does not reciprocate. In the town of Krk, aged Croatians appear, and are complimentary about the Pets in a variety of tongues. One of the most gnarled has, he reveals, served in the US Army. He produces a snap of himself taken, to the incredulity of Pet Marianne, in Glasgow.

Back to the Penthouse-Adriatic for the most lavish of the photo-calls. First, the bikini shots since the cozzies leave such dreadful marks. It is a brilliant day, and the girls strip to their bikinis with rapturous cries. The Pets line up on the steps of the pool, hand-in-hand. This is the whole Esther Williams number, except that the pool unfortunately is empty.

The photographers exhort the girls what to do in a babel of commands.

'Legs apart, girls,' Guccione says, a masterful gym instructor.

We run through the whole Bathing-Beauty repertoire. (A) Standing at the poolside; (B) Draped upon the steps of the pool; (C) Clutching the rail, against a nice blue horizon. The Pets are troupers. They smile, and smile, and smile, and it isn't the catalogue smile, as perfected by air hostesses and beauty queens. It's a nice raunchy showgirl smile, and, according to mood, it can light up or glaze over into utter indifference.

A special is the peasant set-up. It turns out that a great many traditional Yugoslavs have been waiting somewhere just out of sight since some gruesome hour of the morning. They are wearing the whole folk-loric bit. The males are persuaded to lift up a Pet apiece, and swirl them around; and, with more difficulty, to put them back where they found them. Folklore, ancient and modern. A petite girl lingers, prodding at Pet Marian's lingerie and pulling at her coiffure. Her name is Nevenka, and she is much impressed by the British national costume.

Later, I sit down with Guccione on a sofa, opposite a table covered with blue-prints. *Penthouse*, Guccione says, now has sales of 2,300,000, which represents an annual growth-rate of 350%. Seven years ago, he had an overdraft of £600. This year he will enjoy an annual income of two million quid.

All from boobs an buttocks, yes, but why have *Playboy* and *Penthouse* succeeded while so many others have, so to speak, gone down?

'Hefner has the same sort of background I have,' Guccione says. 'Hefner's father was a Methodist. My grandfather emigrated as a bible teacher. I was an altar-boy, and all that jazz ... What we have to overcome is our guilt feelings. We had to build in our own justification ...'

Saturday is glum, a last day, and also plagued with problems. We pack, and take off, except Pet Tina finds that she has left her cozzy so we go back and leave again. Now Casino George's bottle of mint liquor breaks in a chop of the road, and then at the ferry we find that Pet Helen's valise has bounced off the roof, a contretemps which rocks even her unsinkable temperament.

Venice Airport. Alas, our mishaps have made it impossible to snap the Pets feeding the pigeons in the Piazza San Marco. They line up for one farewell photo-call, except suddenly it's flight-time, and they are hustled off leaving the Press with a painful case of *camera interrupta*.

Milan, and more trundling through the Duty-Free shops.

218

Who wants to go and work at the Penthouse-Adriatica? Every single Pet, it turns out. And won't that barrage of bosom and cannonade of thigh and lacy knicker leave what's left of the Iron Curtain thereabouts swaying in the scented breeze like a corrugated iron fence?

London, at last, through the grungy suburbs into Mayfair, and a loyal communal raspberry as the Pets pass the Playboy Club in all its rabbity glory.

'What's that?' inquires Pet Angela.

'I don't know,' Pet Helen says, back to her bouncy self, 'but it'll never catch on!'

*In which the writer spends much time in the Imagin-
eering Department at Walt Disney Studios. He talks
to Mickey Mouse in Anaheim, and visits the Disney-
subsidised California Institute of Arts, where he is upset to find trouble in paradise. In the Walt Disney
World, Florida, he enjoys the new computerised park,
and studies the plans for EPCOT—the Experimental
Prototype Community of Tomorrow—whose rise
should amply compensate for the decline of near-by
Cape Kennedy into a cybernetic slum.*

'Billy Graham had come to see Walt Disney, and they were
sitting in the park at Disneyland, and Billy said something
like—Well, Walt, you really have a nice fantasy here!

'And that kind of hurt Walt, and he said—You know the
fantasy isn't here. This is very real ...

'This is what people really are. The fantasy is—out there,
outside the gates of Disneyland, where people have hatreds,
and people have prejudices ... It's not really real!

'And that says a lot about Walt, I think. That says a lot
about why things are the way they are at Disneyland, and
what they are going to be like in the Walt Disney World.'
　　　　　　　Transcript of conversation with Disney executive.

Smoothly glides the Monorail. This is the Monorail Mark
IV, which is to say the Walt Disney World-Alweg Monorail,
171 feet of electrified aluminium nosing through the Walt
Disney World. That's the Polynesian Hotel across there.
Artfully posed palms nod over the white Disney-made beaches
that fringe the blue Disney-made lagoon.

Across is a larger body of water, the reconstituted and rebottomed lake, bright with water-sporters and sailboats, and now we approach the Contemporary Hotel ... a monstro ziggurat, part Early Mayan, part Late Martian, and right into the heart of it we glide, the Grand Canyon Concourse, and out again to where, beckoning in the near distance, with a twinkle of turrets like rococo missiles, lies the Magic Kingdom, the Walt Disney World, Florida.

And the Magic Kingdom is—well, what can one add? Except that it offers all that Disneyland offers *Plus*. Cinderella's castle pricks the sky a good thirty feet higher than the smog-tormented California Matterhorn. The park is bigger than its parent by a fifth, and while that same comfy bestiary roam the streets—Mickey, the Mad Hatter, the Pigs, the Cats—their tremendous heads are now air-conditioned, and the streets themselves are not built from the oldfangled stuffs used in Anaheim (bricks, wood, stone) but from fibreglass, apt stuff for dreams to play with, from the Gothic capitals, moulded with Disney characters, in the castle hall to the pink, fabricated coral of the submarine ride.

The fauna and flora that menace the Jungle River Cruise appear more natural and the spectres that accost travellers on their way through the Haunted House seem more spectral. Instead of just the one Audio-Animatronic President, which is to say Abe Lincoln, walking and talking according to a science of Disney's own, there are now a full complement of thirty-six. Which is to say you also get Warren Gamaliel Harding for your money. Furthermore, Lincoln gets around to mentioning Slavery, a matter which his replica, now at Disneyland, omitted to mention.

The bears in the Country Bear Frontierland Jamboree are heftier than real grizzlies, and much more amusing. They are more active than the presidents, their size notwithstanding, but both bears and presidents have the help of a miracle tool so far denied to Disneyland: the computer.

'Walt saw that a computer could be a—fun thing,' says a Tour Guide. Indeed, yes. What has IBM got to match the Mickey Mouse Revue? This is *the first ever computer-*

programmed 'stage show', explains a leaflet. It stars no fewer than eighty-six robotic figurines, Walt Disney's much-loved characters in person. They include Disney's Br'er Rabbit, Baloo the Bear from Disney's *Jungle Book*, and the Mad Hatter/March Hare duo from Disney's *Alice in Wonderland*. (I find Lewis Carroll's possible reactions to the Electronic Alice interesting to consider. He was, after all, a mathematician.)

The show is MC'd not (disappointingly) by a robot Stokowski, but by Mickey Mouse himself. He looks a fair treat in full evening clothes with a scarlet cummerbund. It certainly seems a long way from those early cartoons in which the Varmint, as he was familiarly known, used to chew and spit baccy. A long way for everybody, Disney included, but the old touch is still there when Cinderella is standing there in her rags, the most woebegone-looking little Audio-Animatronic dummy you ever saw, until she is transformed by a glittering shower of, yes, pixie-dust.

And—in the same way as the presidential caper ends with Lincoln sinking back into reverie while a canned orchestra swells in with *The Battle Hymn of the Republic*—so the Mickey Mouse Revue closes with the Disney anthem, the Mickey Mouse Club song, something to start a tear in the eyes of Mouseketeers everywhere. The automatic doors open, and the theatre empties with a smooth uni-directional flow, and it's back into the park.

But the Magic Kingdom is just one element in the Walt Disney World, an element moreover in which its creator had showed a meagre interest, just as his interest in movies waned when he turned his energies in the 1950s on to Disneyland. The Walt Disney World occupies some forty square miles, an area as large as San Francisco, say, and almost twice as large as the independent Mediterranean state of San Marino.

Mammoth works have been done. In 1965 Disney began to drain their soggy acquisition, and dug forty miles of canals. The 450-acre Lake Buena Vista, the erstwhile Bay Lake, was thick and brown with cypress swamps. It was drained and cleaned, and there beneath the muck of ages was a bottom of lovely white sugar sand, which Disney heaped up into miles of fabricated beaches, the way that nature should have done it in the first place.

Even more formidable was the creation from scratch of the Seven Seas Lagoon. It extends over 200 acres, and eight million cubic yards of soil was excavated from the site. This mass (Disney is a paradigm of recycling) now supports the Magic Kingdom itself, thereby making possible the 'Utilidors', those unseen, subterranean corridors that service the city streets. Food and supplies move through the Utilidors on electric carts, and Disney people are on hand to maintain the cooling, the electricity and communications. Visiting engineers are much taken with Utilidors, more even than with the devices of Tomorrowland.

It's an eco-conscious place, the Vacation Kingdom of the World. Cars are quarantined in a 12,000-place car-park where nobody need see the nasty things. Transportation is as pollutant-free as the times allow. There is the needful for swimming, fishing, sailing and water-skiing. There are golf-courses, bicycle-paths and bridle tracks. There are lake cruises on 'specially themed launches' or on olde-worlde paddle steamers running on nu-world tracks.

Western addicts, unsatiated by the thrills of Thunder Mesa in the Magic Kingdom, can hang out at the Tri-Circle D Ranch. For the venturesome there are the Fort Wilderness Campgrounds. The Fort Wilderness Trail is to be found here, likewise utility hook-ups and Frontier stores.

And these are still early days, the beginnings of what Disney call Phase One. The Contemporary and Polynesian Hotels are not expected to be remotely adequate in servicing Leisureopolis. Three more are to be added in a space of a few years.

Consider the Persian Hotel. This is designed to *create the effect of visiting an exotic far eastern palace'*. The model shows a main edifice surrounded by an octagon of court-yards, and topped with baby-blue domes, like fat tears. Now that the Shah of Persia's tented palace is a desolate memory, one hopes that next time he will have the sense to call in the Disney architects. The Persian Hotel looks indestructible.

The Venetian Hotel is in the style of St Mark's Square. That is to say, more accurately, it is modelled after the white and intricate glory of the Doge's Palace, the *Palazzo Ducale*, sometimes known as the Dog & Duck, an irreverence unlikely to befall Disney's version. The superiority of modern resources is rather heavily underlined by the placing of the hotel between a double helping of campaniles. It is to be expected that they will be wired up for sound. I would suggest Vivaldi.

The Venetian theme resort will *'be strongly oriented to water activities'*, naturally, and it will feature *'an intricate system of water-ways designed to create the atmosphere of Venice'*. Details, such as the Disney gondolas, Disney-Murano glass, and—who knows?—a Disney-Harry's Bar lie, perhaps, in the future.

Finally, there is the Asian-style hotel. Certain rather tricky choices were in order here. Disney people are emphatic that it is to be mainly Thai in its appearance and cuisine. Vietnamese, Cambodian and Laotian motifs are expected to be few and far between. There are, of course, certain imponderables in politics. Whither Thailand and so on? I must assume that the Disney Worlders are alertly watching the political breeze, and—at a hint of a barney—will relocate their theme elsewhere. Would you believe New Zealand?

The Disney style is an effortless mix. The exotic lies down with the nostalgic. An imaginary past thrives in symbiosis with an imaginative future. The Wild Frontier will be cheek-by-jowl with an Industrial Park 'designed to show-case American industry at work'.

And, finally, there will be EPCOT.

EPCOT is to be the Experimental Prototype Community of Tomorrow. EPCOT was the last obsessive dream of this extraordinary man, most of whose dreams came—well, if not to life, precisely, certainly to being.

Disneyland is the prototype and Disneyland has spawned imitations: Astro World, Sea World and Magic Mountain, Marineland, Six Flags Over Texas, and such unsuccesses as Freedomland. All over Europe, moreover, there are leisure-ghettos burgeoning, inspired to a greater or lesser degree by Disney's example. Even in the Soviet Union there have been rumblings. A writer in *Literaturnaya Rossiya* praised the international carnival in Gorki Park known as Attraktsion-71. Two million Russians flocked thither, apparently, and the writer urged that a permanent installation might do the world of good in combating 'Social Problems'.

Walt Disney World is called 'The World' for short. The company is referred to as 'Disney' and Walt Disney is called 'Walt', or 'Uncle Walt' even by those who never knew him. Walt lives on. His dictates, his thoughts, his homely apophthegms are forever being quoted, usually in a warm and glutinous tone. Few new ideas have been hatched up. None so far are thought to be necessary. 'Walt left us enough ideas for ... twenty years,' a senior executive tells me, devoutly.

There are elements of hagiography rare even in Corporationland. The cartoonist David Low is quoted as describing Disney as 'the most significant figure in graphic arts since Leonardo'. Everybody who knew Walt Disney spends much time testifying to his humanity, his warmth, yet the figure that emerges from this mass of anecdotage and documentation is oddly opaque.

The comparison with Da Vinci is one in which Disney take much pleasure. It is easy to see why. The facility with which the Milanese mastered most of the arts, and his passionate inventiveness in technology, must make him seem very much a *Seicento* Walt. And neither Leonardo da Vinci nor anybody else has emulated Walt Disney in welding the Arts and Technology so inextricably together.

Nor has anybody been able to build a world so exactly in their own image. *Make the Dream Come True*, in the Disney phrase. The scrupulous inter-reaction of art and technology, life and merchandising, has produced the phenomenon of total control which has always typified Disney in both their creative and their business works. (The two can hardly be considered separately *chez* Disney.)

There has been an inner logic to the Disney progress from the beginning. First, there were the cartoons. Seven or eight minutes of laughs. Then the features, a dreamworld to enfold the audience for an hour or two.

The Disney landscape emerged into three dimensions at Anaheim, where the tourist—sorry, guest—would make his carefully plotted way for an average of $7\frac{1}{2}$ hours. With Audio-Animatronics, the cartoon creatures themselves emerged from the illusionistic dazzle of colour, light and line into the new freedom of walking, talking dummyhood.

Now the World is: Vacationland, which you may inhabit for days or weeks. And EPCOT, in which a chosen 20,000 can live forever.

Does it seem too ambitious? Too heavy a project to control with the precision that characterises Disney operations? Nothing is impossible, nothing. Brood upon the geometric conditioning of the Radial Plan.

The Radial Plan was not invented by Disney—Stonehenge is rumoured to have controlled psychic energies in this manner, and there is always Corbusier's *La Ville Radieuse* —but certainly it is Disney that has put the concept to the most startling use.

Radial Planning was pioneered out at Anaheim. As was our own, otherwise untidier, world, the Magic Kingdom was designed with but one entrance. This, of course, simplifies keeping out longhairs and assorted undesirables, but the Radial Plan exemplifies a subtler control pattern than this. Namely, if we enter and move clockwise, as nature inclined us to—we are born like screws with a right-hand thread— we can stroll up, down, up, down, and cover a maximal area, with minimal fatigue to ourselves, and maximal profit to the Kingdom.

This plan has been applied to the Theme Park in Florida, and not just the Theme Park. The satellite industrial complexes have a similar radial design as—most tightly of all —do the projections for EPCOT. It will lend the terrain an arresting look from the air. In ironic proximity to the cybernetic slums of the aero-space industry and the *triste* ramshackle iconography of Cape Kennedy here will lie the interlocking circles of this *Stupor Mundi* like the exposed works of a watch. After all, the antique Deist concept of God-as-the-Great-Clockmaker should allow Walt's World at least the spick-and-span eye-appeal of a Mickey Mouse watch.

It's a bit like a stroll through somebody's head. Walt Disney's head. There are times when the Magic Kingdom, for instance, reminds me of that kitchen-Freud entertainment in which one describes a journey. You describe the woods, castles, boats, thereby indulging in crude self-analysis for the merriment of others. But in the Magic Kingdom, the journey has already been prepared for you. The images are safe, and clean, and bright. The mirth will be your own.

Nor is this image all that esoteric. As a matter of fact Poe, that other native American fantasist has a poem *The Haunted Palace* wherein he describes a head in Gothic castle terms. With a pedantic whimsy, not unlike Walt's own, the eyes become two luminous windows and the hair is pictured as *Banners, yellow, glorious, golden,* and so on.

Now, of course, Walt has a world to play with. Consider EPCOT.

A true mythic touch attends the genesis of EPCOT.

'Walt was walking out of his seven hundred and fifty thousand dollar home in California one day,' a Disney execuive says, in those warm, respectful tones with which I am becoming familiar, 'and it was early. And they were collecting garbage.

'You know, here we leave garbage out on the kerb, and trucks come by, and pick it up, and empty the trash-can, and put it back. And Walt thought it was a—*terrible paradox* ... to have men going to the moon, and the most modern technology in the world here in America. *And to have to look at garbage!*

'So he called the fellows at WED, and he came up with the idea of EPCOT, where you have a controlled environment. And from that small thing grew this whole theory ...'

This rings very true, and the sanitary obsession is much in keeping with the Disney ethos. As a matter of fact, it has often occurred to me that there is interesting research to be done on the builders of various New Orders, New World etc. and their respective interests in hygiene. Adolf Hitler, an otherwise dissimilar figure, was once touring a city with some of the party hierarchy and is said to have pointed at the extremely clean streets, remarking, 'If what we have done here is lunacy, then lunacy becomes us!' (I must stress that the Fuhrer was a determined foe of the Mouse unlike the British Royal family and Mussolini who were by way of being fans.)

Walt's interest could be justified on simple book-keeping grounds. The Magic Kingdom, with its Custodian Hosts, and work-crews armed with knives to remove reluctant chewing-gum, is incontestably a nicer place to be in than the usual slovenly amusement park.

But a more shadowy side also seems to be involved. Richard Schickel, in his memorable *Walt Disney*, has mentioned the persistent anality of Disney imagery, the wagging bottoms in the cartoons (a tradition strictly adhered to by Audio-Animatronics) and the bizarre consummation in *Fantasia* when the pair of cherubs come together, and their lovable posteriors form a heart shape.

It was not always quite so. In the beginning, Disney was cruder, though essentially just as cute. The first cartoon shorts make much play with cows' udders and Minnie's knickers, a genre of humour which was eliminated with speed. Audio-Animatronic wildlife is devoid of udders.

Later I mentioned this to John Hench, a leading creative executive.

'Yes, I know,' he said, merely. 'I used to wonder about that myself. I wasn't part of the group then, but I did wonder about it. It was very curious to me ...

'Of course, the thing about Walt is that he wasn't trying to be something for other people. He was doing a thing that was essentially his own ...'

Yes, but what thing? As to the asexuality of the Audio-Animatronic Kingdom, Hench points out that this represents, after all, not life but theatre. True enough, but the fantasy/reality equipoise of Disney is always developing. Presumably not even EPCOT will be able to eliminate the human anus, but of one thing we can be sure, EPCOT is going to be very, very clean.

Disney's other dark drives have been documented. A sombre sense of death. An occasional touch of the horrors. There exists, or used to, a bizarre seven-minute cartoon

228

short made in 1933. In this, Mickey dreams that Pluto has been abducted by a Mad Doctor, and hauled off to an eerie castle. Mickey to the Rescue. Fanged bats swoop. The wind moans. Skeletons emerge from cupboards in unfriendly fashion. The moustachioed discredit to the AMA attempts to transplant Pluto's head on to a chicken. Mickey's shadow is cut in twain.

I go on a newspaper report. I have not seen the morsel, nor am I likely to, since it was withdrawn from the Rank film library in 1970. In just the same way, they withdrew the alarm clock which showed Mickey embracing Minnie in the 1930s.

Walt Disney was not a man to accept the dark side of fantasy. His dreams are clean dreams. There is a breakdown of the mechanism in Poe's *Haunted Palace*, as you may recall. *A hideous throng rush out forever / And laugh—but smile no more*, the piece ends.

Disney is not about to let this happen. No hideous laughs for them. Smiles, smiles forever.

Perhaps the most appropriate head of all to serve as an image for the Walt Disney World is the one that they created themselves for this purpose. This was designed by Bob Moore, who is in charge of the advertising art over in Burbank, and it appears literally everywhere, from door-mats to drain-covers. It shows the World, gridded geometrically into longitude and latitude, and adorned with Mickey Mouse ears. A planetary concept that says it all.

Control, control.

Smiles are the foundation of beauty
Edgar Rice Burroughs in *Tarzan of the Apes*

The Walt Disney World personnel are a crucial factor. *You can dream, design and build the most wonderful place in the world, but it requires people to make the dream a reality*, runs one of Walt's Thoughts. A problem, yes, but seldom for Disney. Dream people, too, can be provided.

There are 7,000 World employees or thereabouts. They have been skimmed from above 100,000 applicants, including numerous laid-off aeroscape personnel from Cape Kennedyland, and other such Non-Tomorrowlands. Alas, their skills are not necessarily in demand.

'In most cases we are looking for types of people rather than skills,' a director of employee relations tells an Orlando magazine, 'we do not think of "hiring for a job" but rather of "casting for a role" ...'

The roles are kaleidoscopic. The workers of the World are cast for jobs ranging from Tour Guide to Dining Hostess and Custodian Host (or Waitress and Street Cleaner, as they are called in more churlish milieux). The uniforms, which is to say costumes, run an exhaustive gamut of phases of movie-couture, from the Virginia-Mayo-Gothic of the damsels in King Stefan's Hall to the Darkest Africa attire, as last seen on Stewart Granger, favoured for the guides on the Jungle Cruise, from the futurismo jump-suits of the Monorail operators, who doff a shiny helmet at Courrèges *circa* 1965, to the girls with the nifty riding habits, which might just pass with the Quorn, right down to the tiny whips. Fantasyland, indeed.

The kit is different, but the smiles are the same, as—it occasionally appears—are the kids, being chosen to Disney specifications, which is to say that they are young, outgoing and personable. ('Personable' means good-looking. I shan't go so far as to suggest that a girl with fourth-degree acne, a squint, and a 'cello-shaped rump is unlikely to wind up on the job in Fantasyland, but I do feel that Ugly Lib might take a look at the situation.)

They must also be willing to work extremely hard for a pay-packet agleam as much with pixie-dust as any more prosaic currency. (The kids doing Transit out at the Burbank studio, for instance, start at about two dollars an hour.) The requisite morale is suggested by the circular which accompanies the blank application-forms for the job of Disneyland Ambassador.

The Ambassador must be a female employee, aged between 18 and 25. She must make vows of celibacy, or at least unmarriage, for a period of one year. *The position of Disneyland Ambassador will involve hard work, will be time consuming, strenuous—both mentally and physically—and must supersede personal likes and dislikes,* reads this formidable notice.

The Disney Way is impressed on junior personnel with an efficiency rare outside some of the more highly disciplined religious and political movements. Recruiting interviews have already weeded out the unsuitable. Boys may have been required to get a hair-cut.

'And we prefer girls with no experience,' says an exec.: 'We do not want girls that have worked in hotels and had five room keys handed to them every night. We would rather train our own.'

Apart from the short hair, male turn-out demands sideboards of a length not to exceed the middle of the ear and fingernail tips no more than an eighth of an inch. Also black shoes, dark socks, and 'approved' tie-clips. Apart from the evidence of rodent worship, they remind me of the lads with whom I was always being compared, to my own overwhelming disadvantage, at school.

The girls are not allowed lacquered hair, teased hair, nor even bouffant hair. Eyeshadow, eyeliner, mascara, long fingernails, 'excessive' scent and jewellery are likewise out. As to hairpieces, nail varnish and false eyelashes, they are considered closely akin to crotchless panties and silicone breasts.

The look in fact is what Disney used to refer to as 'The All-American Look'. All American being in the state it is nowadays it has now officially become the 'Disney Look'.

There are obvious parallels with the ludicrous IBM dress code, re-invoked in full austerity by Tow Watson Jr in 1971. Both businesses have a simple, primary motive, which is to give as little offence as possible to any possible paying customer. In Disney there is a deeper, secondary drive, towards a time in which all the girls look like derivatives of Sandra Dee, Carol Lynley, Annette 'Mickey Mouse girl' Funicello, wholesome cuties all; and the young men have the Pepsi-Astronaut look, which is college boy, but not so meaty as a footballer, *brighter*. It's a trip to the past, or possibly the future, but it certainly doesn't resemble any other known present.

There are some things, however, up with which even

Pepsi-Astronauts find it difficult to put. Mini-battles have raged over make-up, with tears and dismissals.

'We have been trying to make it possible for the girls to emphasise their good points,' says one of the more progressive junior executives. This, in effect, means a dab of lipstick. Eye-shadow, and so on. What are the chances?

'It's going right up to the top. They'll kick it around ...'

Getting the reactions of employees is interesting. The greater proportion by far do indeed seem to be cheery recruits to the Disney Way. 'I was told I would need a hair-cut,' says one ride operator. 'I did it right away. I needed the job.'

A few are a bit more circumspect.

'We have Orientation Phase One and Orientation Phase Two,' explains a girl from the Contemporary Hotel. 'Some people go to the University and they get oriented some more.'

Sensing a latent *je ne sais quoi*, I asked if she was looking forward to a further course.

'I guess I've been oriented *more than enough*,' she says firmly, adding on a note of caution, 'But that's just my personal opinion ...'

The university alluded to is the University of the Walt Disney World, which is the offspring of the University of Disneyland. This is in Anaheim, and it's a short term, a couple of days, in fact, during which there are eminently sensible courses in safety, guest relations, and the like, and two of indoctrination—they use the word without bashfulness —entitled *Walt Disney Traditions One* and *Walt Disney Traditions Two*.

'We hope you'll enjoy thinking our way!' runs one of the campus directives. Or, presumably, else.

Finally, diplomas are awarded. Disney is unaccountably discreet about the nature of these, but I can reveal that successful students become BMPs, or Bachelors of Mouse Power.

This is just the beginning, of course. It takes practice, practice, practice. There are constant little problems. Like the Characters in their cumbersome costumes, falling arse over tit. (The Mad Hatter did himself damage right at the opening of the Walt Disney World.)

There are dopers to watch out for and there are the mobile

hazards known (I understand) as 914s, namely girls who con-
nive themselves into the Disney territory see-through and
bra-less. Both these classes of decadents, so often one and the
same, are required to leave.

Also, there is the matter of first-naming. Everybody, but
everybody, is on First Name terms, and that's an order. This
tradition began with Walt and Roy, and has continued down
to the lowest Randy (I seem to have met fully a dozen Randys
working for Disney). And it seems ironic at first that this complex and hierarchic organisation should insist on this etiquette. I can only think of the Chinese army while rank was
abolished. The Chinese, also, I am sure knew just who was
who.

Are the boys and girls happy? Well, they applied for the
job in the first place, didn't they?

'How can you have a bad day if you see Mickey walk by and
wave at you?' bubbles a blonde: 'Or you run into Pluto ...'

An older executive explains: 'They've got a *sparkle*. And
they really don't know what they are sparkling about except
the *philosophy* ... and it's that intangible thing that you can't
put your finger on—*the Disney pixie-dust*! It's kind of the
sparkle that the people have there *rubs off* ...'

Later E. Cardon—'Card'—Walker is discussing the same for-
tunate asset. Walker is Executive Vice-President of Walt Disney Productions, and one of the two or three top men in the
company. He mentions how the president of Eastern Airlines
said, 'My goodness, how do you hire such enthusiastic people?'

Card shrugs, happily. 'It's kind of a tradition. The company
personifies something good, something of quality ... and those
kind of people seem to be attracted to us, and we to them.
And,' he adds, 'the ones that don't fit in that category don't
stay very long ...'

*   *   *

California dreaming
Is becoming a reality
  The Mamas and the Papas

Even Walt Disney needed assistance. The furtherance of project World, and its resident Utopia, was entrusted to the unusual élite creative corps which Disney had, typically, dubbed 'The Imagineers'.

Imagineering is handled at WED, and also at MAPO. WED stands for Walter Elias Disney, and houses the actual Imagineering Department, while MAPO takes care of the manufacturing. MAPO's name is derived from *Mary Poppins*.

There are about 550 Imagineers in all *which may represent the greatest concentrated collection of creative, artistic and technical talent anywhere in the world,* surmises an Imagineer copywriter. This thought tends to occur to Imagineers with some frequency. By the end, I found it almost possible to predict how long an individual had been with the organisation through this sort of parallel. The older ones felt that there hadn't been much like WED since, say the Renaissance. The younger ones might well allude to the Bauhaus. Personally, I found that the secrecy and dedicated anonymity of the whole operation put me rather in mind of a mediaeval guild.

WED and MAPO occupy adjoining buildings, compact factory size, in Glendale, a few miles from the company headquarters in Burbank. WED is an austere oblong, fronted with slim slabs of stylishly rough stone. Cypresses unfurl themselves in front, suggesting a *de luxe* mortuary.

In the lobby the secretary asks if I mind waiting for a few minutes.

'There may be some things going on they don't like people to see,' she supposes, brightly.

Disney runs a famously tight ship, and especially where WED is concerned. No Daniel Ellsberg skulks behind a Mickey Mouse mask. (Later, while examining one of the mock-up attractions I find an Imagineer peeking at my tape-recorder. 'It's a Sony,' I explain. 'I know,' he says, tersely, 'and I also know it's on.')

Anyway, I wait and wander around the good things on view in the lobby. Photographs of the Disney brothers. Some of WED's *Meisterwerke*, such as a cockatoo from the Tiki room, and maquettes of the comical ghosts in the Haunted House. On one wall is a plaque, shaped to resemble one of those scrolls that used to explain the plot in pirate movies. This was given to Walt by the 'Traditional Arts of America', in recognition of Audio-Animatronics, an art in which all the arts (explains the scroll in Gothic script) have finally found form and motion at once.

John Hench is Vice-President in Charge of Design, and certainly one of the two or three more important Imagineers on the creative side. He is a meditative man, soft-spoken, with a donnish brown tweed jacket, and a moustache much like Walt's own. He began at Disney's old Hyperion studio as a sketch artist on *Fantasia*, and was elected to the WED Board of Directors in 1966.

WED, he explains, was started in 1952.

'I guess the first I heard about it was when Walt asked me if I wanted to join a company he was thinking of setting up, ostensibly to do Disneyland. That was the first project it really got started with.'

The Disneyland scheme was treated with scepticism, not to say stoniness, by the moneymen, as they had previously been sceptical about *Snow White*.

'But Walt had this astonishing knowledge. It was more than just a hunch, it was a conviction. He *knew* ...

'And the reason you can say he knew is that in spite of all the risk there was, and all the possibilities for failure, he proceeded as if he had a crystal ball, and saw the end result. He never had those doubts everybody else had.'

'If he did, he didn't tell *us* about it,' says Marty Sklar, who is a WED writer.

'He *didn't*. He never had them,' Hench says positively, adding with the cadences that mention of Walt tends to produce hereabouts, 'If the human mind is really brought to bear—if all its powers are pulled in—Something happens! And Walt could do this.

'In fact, it was hard to keep his attention sometimes, because immediately something would happen to him, and you could see—the thing growing ... You know, his eyebrows lifted, and he got a faraway look, and he was witnessing something. He saw it in visionary terms, a visionary way ...

'He stood there, and he was a witness of something. *And it was a new thing. Unprecedented!* Sometimes he'd come in with a sketch of it. Like the time he came in with a map ... the whole plan for Walt Disney World!'

The building of Disneyland, that crucial surge of Mouse-power from two dimensions into three, was a situation where that movie training proved its worth. John Hench explains why non-Disney amusement parks are so wearisome.

'They carry over the same kind of competition that exists in the outside world. Every exhibit competes for your attention, and there's nothing more fatiguing than to have to pick up one idea and drop it, pick up another, and drop it ...

'Or you take a tour through a museum, and you go from one room to another without plan, and there's *nothing* to equal this fatigue.'

Disneyland was designed to avoid this problem of choice. A further benefit of the Radial Plan.

'What would happen in a motion picture if you didn't have any continuity of ideas between Scene One ... Scene Two ... Scene Three ... Scene Four?' points out Hench, and denies that the greater girth of the Disney World makes it less susceptible to control.

'You walk in the front gate, and this is the title. And Scene One is the Contemporary Hotel, and you ride through it on the Monorail, and Scene Two proceeds, and it becomes a little complicated, but not as much as you'd think ...'

It is only through establishing this dominant flow-pattern, says Hench, that you can communicate what you're *trying to say.*

'This is the thing that a motion picture man can run into. The things that happen, accidents and so forth, tend to contradict what *he's* saying ...'

I must look bemused, because Hench patiently clarifies further.

'This is the worst thing that can happen to a car designer. And it accounts for all the failures. It's the *contradictions* that he's introduced there without knowing ...

'One of the reasons that Walt Disney was such a great artist', he adds, simply, 'was that he avoided the contradictions.'

It's a key concept. The contradictions, in Disney terms, lie

236

between 'what boosts our survival potential and what threatens it', as Hench puts it. 'I think this is the basis of our ethics, and certainly it's the basis of our aesthetics. It is something Walt knew very well.'

'Intuitively,' suggests Marty Sklar.

'Intuitively,' John Hench agrees. 'Because really there is no system of teaching this positively. But there is a system of watching out for the negative values, and leaving those out.

'Now you take Main Street. Main Street is done with this type of attitude.' (Main Street, for that deprived minority who have never been to the Magic Kingdom, is the street through which everybody must pass.) 'Here is a period in America, and other places, where progress was a good word, and where there was an intense optimism about what we were doing with our lives, and where we were going ...

'These things are not whims of desire. They're kind of a collective dream.'

Is he alluding to the real Main Street or the Disney construct?

'I'm talking about Disney in a way, but also real Main Street,' Hench says. 'But real Main Street had many contradictions ... that *denied this optimism*. They crept in by accident. Because people didn't quite understand ...'

Accidents? Dreary buildings, Hench explains. Gloomy colours. That sort of stuff.

'So Walt's Main Street left off the contradictions. The things that deny ... the optimism. The spirit of the thing!'

One vivid exemplar of Disney's contradiction-free state is, of course, the art of Audio-Animatronics. (Man before the Fall, it occurs to me, must have been a somewhat Audio-Animatronic figure, divinely programmed.) The form has come a long way since 1945 when Walt was excited by a Buddy Ebsen robot dancing-doll, and even since the unveiling of the Walking/Talking President Lincoln at the New York World's Fair. This figure has, I mention, come under intermittent attack.

Hench has no time for such maunderings.

'Walt always said: You don't do things for critics. You do

'em for the public.

'And another thing! You do them as well as you can for everybody. Everybody who buys a ticket has the right to the best in the show. So we wouldn't use *live* animals. Or *live* fish ...

'They are just good at feeding-time, maybe. And the rest of the people see them asleep under a rock.'

'It's wrong!' Sklar concurs, 'It's wrong.'

'We made it the same performance for every boat load,' says John Hench. 'Precisely the same!'

Here are a couple of segments of the Audio-Animatronic breakdown; the Disney World Jungle River Ride. Possibly it has since been revised, but just as an example of the blend of verisimilitude and reliability that WED has in mind.

20 *Giant Butterflies*	J1-J20	– *Wing flap.*
2 *Man-Eating Plants*		– *Mouth, sound sync, head*
	J21-J22	*nod, body front and back*
		sway.
3 *War Canoes and Skulls*		– *No animation.—Moving*
		sound, both sides of river,
		moves faster than boat.
1 *Giant Python in Trees*	J23	– *Neck sway, darting tongue.*

So far, so good. There follow a number of gorillas in a tent, an upside-down jeep (*wheels spin*), and a varied assortment of Gnus, Zebras, Impalas, Giraffes, Vultures, Crocodiles, and Lions, which include *3 Female Lions Eating*. Nothing Audio-Animatronic, of course. Verisimilitude can go only so far.

Passing several Native Dancers, Drummers and so on, we approach the 'Cambodian Ruins', which are furnished as follows.

1 *Tiger*	J118	– *Head nod, neck up and*
		down, jaw opens, sound
		sync, body sway, eyes light
		and blink on/off.
2 *Cobra Guards (Coiled*		

around pole)	J119-J120	–	*Neck sway, tongue darts out.*
7 *King Cobras*	J121-J127	–	*Neck sway, tongue darts out.*
2 *Large Spiders*	J128-J129	–	*Web moves*
6 *Monkeys*	J130-J131	–	*1 Mother and 1 Baby on back—Pelvis, front legs bend, tail. Baby—free animation, body bounce, tail.*
	J132	–	*1 w crown—head nod, arms forward, elbow bend, tail, head nod.*
	J133	–	*1 Sitting w/jug on head— jug moves, tail.*
	J134	–	*1 Head down in jug—fanny up and down, tail.*
	J135	–	*1 In jug baby monkey— head nod, head turn, bells jingle.*

And so, past the Elephant Pool, and to the landing stage. The last goody on the Jungle Ride, incidentally, is *Native Salesman Sam* (*Arm forward, elbow bend, eye blink*), and here perhaps the verisimilitude sags. The thought of even the subtlest Audio-Animatronic salesman competing with the real ones at the Disney World is going altogether too far.

Tampering with magic is traditionally risky. The communal processing through which an idea emerges from the head and on to the drawing-boards, off the drawing-boards and into the street, is the magic of WED. Luckily it is also organised to a T.

Consider the Model Shop. This is reached through a central chamber which houses some of the more massive projections of World, a twenty-five foot square tableau of the terrain itself, that kind of thing. Outside the Model Shop a white-smocked girl is colouring some fibreglass Gothic corbels. Behind her is a shelf-full of Polynesian Gods *école de Trader Vic*.

This is characteristic of the variety demanded of the WED sculptors. I am shown around by the principal sculptor, Blaine

Gibson. He is lean and mild, with an almost clerical air, and he has been with Disney for thirty years. Harry Holt, who is working on a mouse in the corner, has been here thirty-five, working first on *Snow White*. This is normal around WED, and it is a company joke that people with less than ten years service are more or less new boys.

I thread my way among the implements and artefacts. A box of skulls intended for the Haunted House and a grislier case of loose, pink hands. A sheet of possible ways of drawing the dollar sign (909 are given). A shelf of presidential heads, including a Truman, hairless and unrecognisable, and an unmistakable LBJ. Spares in case somebody bungs a coco-nut in Liberty Hall?

The work on view covers a spectrum of realism and fantasy. There is nothing magical about the presidents, nor about the crouching American Indians. Perhaps the black hair is a bit on the coarse side and the MAPO-applied skin a shade too red, but they were modelled from ethnic photographs, and look it.

The animal characters, of course, are pure cartoon. At indeterminate stages in between is a Caribbean pirate, and the ghost from the Haunted House, all weirdo naturalism, hyperthyroid, and with eyes like mismatched boiled eggs.

WED sculpture is put to a variety of uses. There is décor for 'The Attractions'. Here, for instance, is some Cambodian statuary, which will adorn the Jungle River Cruise at that section where it glides discreetly from Africa into South-East Asia. This statuary has the proper look, enigmatically voluptuary and 'antiqued', which is to say that soda was added to the mould, lending it a stippled, weatherbeaten effect.

'Maybe Angkor Wat would turn out to be ... kinda anticlimactic?' suggests an Imagineer later, jovially.

There is no material which the WED sculptors seem incapable of metamorphosing. Harry Holt, for instance, is perfecting a sequence of designs into which some of the Disney World trees are to be trained. These topiary *jeux d'esprit* include the Reluctant Dragon, a whale, an elk, and an elephant balancing on its head upon a ball.

Right now, he is working on a concept which even he agrees

is ambitious. The bush will be in the shape of a mouse standing on a wedge of very holey Gruyère cheese.

These *œuvres* have been dreamed up or approved by the creative planners, such as John Hench, and many of the figures are finally to be animated. The sculptures will be cast in plaster, and will be rendered by MAPO into fibreglass, but by no means will they pass right out of the sculptor's ken. Deviations of skin thickness can destroy a carefully wrought likeness as can mechanical botches like awkwardly set eyes. Nothing is ever finished, nothing is incapable of improvement.

MAPO is a 65,000 square foot building with two floors, immediately adjoining WED. I am taken around it by Roger Broggie Sr whose career before joining Disney included doing the special effects on Chaplin's mordant *Modern Times*.

We walk through lines where dummies are in various stages of assembly. Segments of fibreglass carcass are being fitted up with mechanical innards. It's like a robotic Emergency Ward. Broggie takes me across to where a young man with a trim beard is tinkering with a head.

This is in a perspex cube. The young Imagineer shows me how the controls are worked that would set off the facial movements, if it had yet been fitted up with a face. In fact, it is stripped to the basic working components. These include the eyeballs The iris is blue, and the eyes are convincingly red-veined, to the point of hangover in fact, since they are real glass eyes, the product of the American Optical Company.

There are also teeth, which are pure white, emerging from gums like pink candy, and rather dainty, which counteracts the head's slightly simian look, as of an automated chimpanzee.

What about the eyelids? I ask.

The Imagineer touches the controls, and they flip into place. They have as yet no skin, and are brazen. They look a bit like monster toe-clippings, and they give the head a sleepily knowing look, as if, like Walter Pater's Mona Lisa, this is *'the head upon which all "the ends of the world are come", and the eyelids are a little weary ...'*

The cost of the head is, maybe, ten thousand dollars, or

maybe fifteen, the Imagineer thinks, and it contains 180 working parts.

The Model Shop furnishes that inimitable Disney Style. MAPO puts in the works. But it is, for instance, Bill Justice who gets the figures to do whatever it is they do.

'I'm one of the animators ... programers, whatever,' he explains. Like most of the cadre of WED animators, he started as an animator of cartoons. Amongst the Audio-Animatronic *œuvres* to which he has turned his skills are the Hall of Presidents and the Mickey Mouse Revue.

The figures come in degrees of complexity. 'We ask MAPO to put in certain functions. The flowers that sing along with Alice in the Mickey Mouse theatre were fairly simple. They would tilt from side to side, like this'—he demonstrates—'and their mouths would open ...

'But Mickey Mouse is the most complicated figure we've ever had. Even beyond Lincoln. He has thirty-seven functions, and Lincoln had thirty-two. The key figure in the Pirate Ride had seventeen, and the Bears ... I think the most complicated of those has got twenty-four ...'

Justice explains the controls, and how there are three main functions of the head—Head Turn, Head Nod, and Tilt— and how you can get almost any desired facial movement or grimace from the combination of those three.

He shows me some sheets of drawings and notations showing the functions of the presidents. They look a bit like Muybridge's famous photo-series of (say) a horse galloping, though undeniably less vivacious.

Here, for instance, is George Washington's picture-script. It contains a block of notations, like logarithm tables, and some small sketches of the founding father, in a Seated Position, standing with Hands Behind Back, and making a Gesture to Lincoln, no doubt friendly. JFK seems much less sprightly, being restricted to putting his right hand behind his back, and his left somewhere over his midriff. 'Those hand positions didn't work,' confesses Justice. 'He looked like a store dummy!'

There are problems in working with 3-D figures. Both problems and limitations. Al Bertino, another animator/programmer, was unsuccessful with one of his Country Bears, the Shaker. The Shaker was never got to do a really uninhibited Shake. Equally, President Lincoln can't tug properly at his lapels. Any movement close to the body poses difficulties. If the limb is held away from the body it can look unrealistic, but if it's held close in, within weeks you will find holes being rubbed in coats and skin torn off hands.

In more imaginative areas, too, the robotics cause limitations from which the movies were free. Bill Justice fetches down an old cartoon still. It shows Mickey screaming, his mouth a stupendous black O.

'If we wanted Mickey to yell, we would just open his mouth to ... this extreme. And this would give a lot of sparkle, and life.'

The AA Mickey Mouse lacks this capacity ... 'It looks stilted, and it's extremely dissatisfactory to some of the animators ... With the Bears we were pleased, because we were able to get real wide mouth animation that made them look more ... *cartoony* than, for instance, Lincoln's mouth.'

The virtues of the system far outrun its occasional shortcomings, though. Think how well the models perform compared with ordinary actors, Bill Justice points out.

'I've seen actors when they're better at times that they are at other times. But these figures perform the same way every time!

'They're reliable, and they don't belong to unions, and they don't go on strike and they don't want more money.

'And they have a lot of things going for them.

'Of course', Justice adds, grinning, 'they've got their limitations too ...'

Nothing, one feels, that time, money and WED impetus can't solve. When will it be possible to program an Audio-Animatronic model so that it is indistinguishable from the real thing?

'Oh, we've done that. For some of the pictures at the studio ...

'We had a racoon, and an owl, and a couple of blue jays that would talk to people ...'

As to more comical verisimilitude, Justice indicates the designs for one of the Country Bears. 'This bear comes across *beautifully*. We've seen him on film, and he's in perfect sync ... and he *acts*, and his eyes are sparkly, and there you are examining *big close-ups*, and he comes over very well ...

'Do you know that story they had in the paper about a month ago?' he asks, with a chuckle. 'About this little boy who went to Disneyland, and first he saw the Pirates, and then he saw the General Electricity Show, and he asked his mommy —Are those people real?

'And she said—No they're not real.

'And then he went to see Mr Lincoln, and came out, and said—Is he real?

'She says, No, he's not real ...

'He says—*Momma, am I real?*'

Bill Justice rumbles with approving mirth.

Here and there, slotted into the WED demesne, full-scale Disney Attractions are being worked on, in model, or projection, or full-size assemblage. Bob Sewall, who shows me the Western River Ride, was blessed with an ideal Disney background, what with working for fifteen years in natural history museums, but actually starting as an *artist*.

'Everyone around here is an artist of one sort or another. I started building a programme terrain for these animal dioramas, the artificial grass, and all that sort of thing ...'

Sewall was given leave of absence from the museum to work on some of the Disney animal pictures, *The Living Desert, The Vanishing Prairie et al.* I mention that some critics, while rightly praising the detail, have objected to anthropomorphic touches. I recall some vigorous insectile activities being scored with Square Dance music, for instance.

Bob Sewall makes no bones that purists might well object. Disney's biz is entertainment, he says, inarguably. It's the same with the rides in the Magic Kingdom.

'It's a *concentrated form* of nature. In other words, you could spend days and days and days, and never see situations like that, but we string together all the experiences you might see in a lifetime into one thing.'

244

The Western River Ride's treatment of nature is deliberately somewhat on the broad side. Coyotes and cattle singing in time with the cow-pokes around a fire in the Wilderness represent a greater liberty with ethological patterns than anything in *The Living Desert*, but this is, essentially, a comedy ride. It is still in the form of a miniature display, but will probably be gracing the Disney World within two or three years.

The Eastern Airlines exhibit is much closer to realisation (as I write), being at the stage of full-scale mock-up. It is demonstrated by another art director, Claud Coates, who is tall, and craggily diffident, rather in the manner of the late Gary Cooper. He has been with the firm thirty-six years—'since *Snow White*'.

Even in its unprepared condition, the exhibit packs quite a punch. The trip starts with a wait in some sort of terminal lounge. In the day of the jumbos this part of the experience, at least, will be fully authentic. This is reinforced when one of those seductive simulated voices is heard. It's the sort of voice—a Muzak condition of the larynx—that one hears in the better class of air terminal and which (I am told) issues instructions to pilots in the new series of F111s, and it is telling us about the pleasures ahead.

The pleasures ahead turn out to be a bowdlerised Grand Tour of Mexico, the Caribbean, and such parts of the United States as, unsurprisingly, are serviced by Eastern Airlines.

As in the Monsanto Ride, out at Anaheim, the tourist gets into a car on a moving belt, and is subjected to a montage of film, music and special effects. Now he is in Mexico beneath an Aztec moon, and now Mariachi music strikes up and ethnic dancers are flashing their white teeth at us. In approved Mc-Luhanesque style verbal messages are beamed at us amongst the dazzle of visuals. *Olé!*, for example, *Bravo!*, and *Saludos Amigos!* As I recall, *Caramba!* is omitted.

Now we are in a seascape, gay with watersports—'like fishing. It's gagged up, you know. The fish gets longer'—and now the Islands ... Grand Bahama, with all those gorgeous white uniforms and epaulettes, and now Mardi Gras ... New Orleans, alive with jazz ...

'It's a sort of ... *glamourised* version of what they will eventually see,' explains Claud Coates.

'*To travel hopefully is better than to arrive*', as Robert Louis Stevenson, originator of Disney's *Treasure Island* wrote, not being prescient enough to see that it's probably better not to go at all.

Archaeologists will be able to establish three main periods of Audio-Animatronics (to date). The Tape Period, the Camshaft Period, and—most recently—the coming of the Computer.

The computerisation of the figures is still limited to the Disney World, and it is the province of Dave Snyder. We meet in the WED Computer Centre, which differs from almost all other computer centres through which I have made my way in that it is extremely clean. In most such installations (I allude to the more creatively inclined ones), clumps and coils of intestinal tubing protrude here and there, as if temporarily left by a schizoid telephone engineer. Billion-dollar number-crunchers accumulate coffee-rings, and interfaces appear to be held together by somebody's hairclip. Not so the Disney system. This resembles an IBM sales-room, down even to the corporate touch of a Mickey Mouse clock.

There were, Snyder says, a few psychological problems about computerising the World. Some of the older animators that had started, say, three decades before in the movies became extremely nervous.

'There was a state of Computer Fear,' Snyder says. He has a look of dogged intelligence, rather like a young George C. Scott, and wears a snazzy pink shirt, with side-burns way below his ears. Unusual garb in Disney circles, but much is forgiven computer freaks. They have claimed the privileges previously accorded to artists.

The Computer Fear was allayed through explanations. David Snyder wrote a pamphlet called DACS FACTS *or A Mickey Mouse Guide Through The Snow*. The system is called DACS because, in a world of acronyms, this stands for *Digital Animation Control System*.

It was rapidly given an alternative reading of *Disney Audio-Animatronic Control System*. Similarly, the actual hardware —though here and there a plate reads Honeywell, or whatever—is crisply labelled *Walt Disney World*.

Snyder explains the niceties of DACS. His entire computer operation, Snyder says, costs, say, a million dollars, whereas some of the individual shows, Audio-Animatronics and all, can cost as much as five million.

We walk across the great WED building, to the Moon Ride.

The facsimile of the Cape Kennedy Space Centre is in a partitioned-off area. Black hangings preserve it from prying eyes. It is a cluttered and memorable scene. Facing us are the banks of artificial computers, while the real ones are to one side. The artificial ones are in brighter colours, and lights wink bewitchingly, if meaninglessly, on and off. Orange/green/cherry-red.

The Audio-Animatronic NASA personnel sit at their consoles in various attitudes. Their heads are still hairless, and— since no make-up has yet been applied—their skins are obviously too thick and pink. They have a third-degree burn sort of look. On the more incomplete figures, the skin joins are clearly visible up the neck and across the cranium.

As we watch, two men in white coats are soldering the skin joins together. This process is called 'buttering'. The skin on the hands is properly pored and wrinkled, since the hands were, after all, cast from live models, but it has the slightly exaggerated texture of a hand left too long in the bath.

The uncompleted chests and torsos are of transparent plastic, thickish like the fake breast-plates across in the Model Shop. The gears and working parts can be seen inside. The expression on the faces is, as always, unnerving. Uncanny is, I think, the dictionary word. Implacably alert at their interminable make-believe tasks.

Everything is controlled from a central console. Beside it are the computer instruction sheets, striped blue and white, and defining the set-up's capabilities in binary notations and in English. There are thirty-two separate possible functions. REVERSE FOOT SKIP, read the instructions, or RIGHT EYEBROW.

247

Snyder invites me to have a go. I attempt to programme 'Larry' who sits on the Extreme Left. I push one button which makes him twist, then another. He jerks his neck. Ambitiously, I play several buttons, Harpo Marx style, and Larry goes into convulsions, shaking his right hand violently, as though trying to dislodge an unpleasing substance, and jerking his neck so hard that the still unbuttered skin flaps crazily.

One of the engineers comes over, a shade suspiciously. He has a Marine crop and a short-sleeved green shirt. Also the inevitable Mickey Mouse watch, though being a technician this isn't the gold model, but a cheaper model with a sort of tank-track wristlet.

Snyder reassures him, and tells me that I have now programmed Larry. He can repeat those motions any time. I say not to bother.

'Mr Morrow', who talks to the audience, stands facing us. In the fairly primitive Moon Ride out at Anaheim, 'Mr Morrow' stands way out in front, with a serious NASA face, talking to the audience ... but exchanging friendly ripostes with a girl dressed in orange. The girl is our guide, and is real.

In Florida, Mr Morrow will stand surrounded by his glittering computers. And, of course, again unlike his Magic Kingdom counterpart, he will himself be computerised. The ripostes with the Disney staff, though, will no doubt continue. It is this frolicking amongst the realities that makes Disney what it is.

One of the Imagineers speaks of the philosophy of WED and MAPO, the cohesiveness. 'A lot of fine artists that we tried to use here haven't been able to work in a *team*, and that's what we definitely had to do. We have to be able to take criticism from each other, as well as from the Boss. My own opinion of the work that I've done is that Walt got more out of me than I thought I was capable of doing, and as a team than I think we were capable of doing separately ...

'It's definitely a team effort, *and if you don't belong to the team, you don't belong here at all!*'

Well, yes, but who is the boss right now? Who has replaced, or can replace, Walt Disney?

'No one ... I mean, there's probably twenty people doing it. But, so far as the creative people go, I think we have to be more or less our own critics ... and do it just like we were planning to show it to Walt the next day.'

Is it possible to maintain the magic while being run from the, shall we say, more commercial end of the business?

'Well, I think that's slipping away a little bit, I'm sorry to say.' (Sombrely.) 'There is an element of maybe trying to ... cash in. Maybe a little more than they should ...

'For instance, the merchandising end. Every little sketch that anyone ever made, it's on a T-shirt, or it's on a pen, or on a post-card, or ... you know, it's just everywhere.

'It's been going on at Disneyland ever since Disneyland opened. But I've never seen such an extreme case of it as at the Disney World. It's really *saturated* with it.'

Wouldn't Walt have permitted it to this degree?

'No, I don't think so. I certainly don't think so ...'

The Imagineer considers and adds that on the other hand there are young kids that have never seen the original movies. As far as they are concerned, Mickey Mouse is a picture on a shirt, a character in the Park.

'So, up to a point, I suppose it's the merchandising and publicity that are still keeping the characters alive.'

*　　　*　　　*

A life-size imitation horse is standing on a building hard by the Walt Disney Studio in the Burbank suburb of Los Angeles. The Disneyfication of landscape proceeds apace, and it is ironical that the Disney presence in Burbank is discreet to the point of bashfulness.

No sign suggests that this is the focal point for the manifold Disney enterprises, the control centre for such subsidiaries as the Buena Vista Distribution Company, which handles the movies in the United States, and Buena Vista International; the Walt Disney and the Wonderland Music Companies; WED and MAPO; Disneyland and the World; the Celebrity Sports Centre of Denver, and the embattled Mineral King.

Walt Disney himself once hit the roof when one of his artists loyally suggested that the water-tower might be ornamented with Mickey Mouse ears.

No mandarin scruples lay behind this. Walt, the artist explains, didn't want the studio to be pestered by disappointed would-be visitors who might, anyway, be more profitably occupied on the rides of Anaheim.

Such callers as do gain access must be passed by security, and given a card. This is blue and white, and specifies my errand, besides clearing the company against any claims I might make for damages sustained on the premises. A design on the card shows Mickey making a welcoming gesture.

I am taken on a tour by a youth with a candid smile and a Mickey Mouse pinned on his tie. It is gold, and not statutory equipment but an item from his own collection. We turn off Mickey Mouse Boulevard into Dopey Drive, moving in and out of various screening-rooms and such. The lawns have a springy textured look, like Astroturf, and there are some ever-so-slightly cutesy signs like SPECIAL EFX. Walt just *hated* the sterile studio look, explains my guide.

Into a main building. Corridors are filled with show-cases of Disney relics. The guide explains their significance *serioso*. Here be images. Walt in an early group with Roy, their respective wives, and a sister. Early days this. Walt wears a light-coloured trilby and a checkered woollen sweater. Roy is jacketless, with a watch-chain on his waistcoat.

We move on to the 'cels', or single frames, from some of the studio greats. *Snow White* in '37, *Pinocchio* '39, *Fantasia* '40. Magic realism. Disney people of all ranks pass us in the corridors. They hail my guide cheerily, by his first name, as protocol insists, and give me that careful measuring look.

We move across to the backlot, where one of the four soundstages is still in use. Disney have been happily unaffected by the doom patterns elsewhere in the industry. No wonder *Reader's Digest* has announced that it is dealing itself into the wholesome movie game.

On the set, there is a balloon. Reyner Banham has pointed out how obsessed Disney—true natives of California—are with mobility, but oddly preferring modes past or yet to come.

Balloons are very Disney. This one carries two actors (male) and a boy actor with a blond *Village of the Damned* bob. They are swaying, thanks to the combined efforts of a wind-machine and a stage-hand who is moving the basket from underneath.

One of the adults puts his hand comfortingly on the lad's shoulder. A friend has expired, or possibly an animal. The boy's face crumples momentarily, but firms up with resolution. It is a scene that seldom fails to move me.

In these troublous times—1971, to be precise—no fewer than five features were released; *The Wild Country*, *The Barefoot Executive*, *The Million Dollar Duck*, *Scandalous John*, and *Bedknobs & Broomsticks*.

Only one of these has proved disappointing: *Scandalous John*. E. Cardon—'Card'—Walker, Chief Operating Officer of Walt Disney Productions, feels that this may well have to do with the word 'Scandalous'. Just not Disney.

Walker is one of the most influential of the junta of executives that now control Disney operations. His powers are probably only second to those of Donn Tatum. These operations are at once complex and sublimely simple. There is something disarming about the glee with which Disney contemplate their endlessly recycling self-supportive money-making machine.

In February 1958, *The Wall Street Journal* produced a study entitled 'DISNEY'S LAND: *dream, diversify—and never miss an angle*'. This was accompanied by a chart resembling an elaborate printed electronic-circuit or conceivably an Armageddon battle plan, which portrayed the intricate way in which the Disney interests variously feed off and succour each other.

Disney found this totally delightful to the point of making the chart over, and up-dating it. A current version chortles that Disney certainly has dreamed, diversified, and missed very few angles indeed. Arrowed lines show who is benefiting from whom. Mickey, Donald, Goofy hurtle here and there to lend this awesome scheme the 'Disney touch'.

Just to indicate the *modus operandi*, a few random examples.

251

WALT DISNEY STUDIO *Motion Pictures*, which is positioned centrally, feeds material to *Comic Strips*, which feeds reprint material to *Publications*, which promotes *Disneyland*, besides plugging films and stars for *Walt Disney Studio*, which does film-plugs on *Disneyland*, which trains manpower for *Celebrity Sports Centre* and *Mineral King*, while Disneyland's peninsular outcrop (I refer to the chart drawing), the *Magic Kingdom Club*, communicates directly with customers on behalf of *Publications*, which provides material for 'Storyteller' albums for *Music*, which promotes premiums for tie-ins for *Merchandising Licensing*, which exploits films for the *Walt Disney Studio*, which creates and produces *Industrial Films*, besides providing shows for *TV*. Am I making myself perfectly clear?

Card Walker who helps oversee this pixie-powered dynamo is himself a man of drive abounding. Sitting with one foot curled beneath him he expounds the Disney technique.

Every seven years sees another Disney generation, Card Walker says. 'The films that Walt made—like *Snow White*, and *Bambi*, and *Cinderella*, and *Pinocchio*, and *Alice*, and so on, we continually reissue them. *Nobody*'s made any pictures as good, or certainly not any better. And each new generation sees them!

'*Snow White*'s been out five times now, and last time out, domestic alone, it did five million dollars. So it's substantial . . .

'The thing that pleased me the other day, we took *The Living Desert* that came out in 1950 and *The Vanishing Prairie* of 1951, and we've combined 'em into a double feature. They both won Academy Awards in their day, but they are very . . . *pertinent* today. They still hold up.'

Snow White has amassed $27 million to date, a sum just topped by *The Love Bug* with 28. But both of these are Mickey Mouse compared with *Mary Poppins*, which has grossed $44 million.

In 1970 the studio realised $21.7 million in profits, and every year, in a dream-cycle of financial ecology, there is more waiting to be re-released. *Mary Poppins* for instance will be just about due, so to speak, in time for the studio's fiftieth anniversary in mid-1973. Certainly celluloid represents a diminishing slice of the Disney cake, but—as Card Walker demands—where's another studio turning in that sort of profits? The Disney library comprises some 22 animated features, 68 live action features, 7 true-life adventures, and well over 500 shorts. And the shorts themselves are now being chomped up into a new TV show, *The Mouse Factory*, which will itself be added to the tele-hoard of (for instance) 78 *Zorro* shows and above three hundred hours of *Mickey Mouse Club*.

The man who has made some of the biggest Disney successes is Bill Walsh. Walsh is the director of *Davy Crockett, King of the Wild Frontier, The Absent-Minded Professor, Son of Flubber, That Darn Cat, Mary Poppins, The Love Bug*, and recently *Bedknobs & Broomsticks*. His combined box-office grosses are well in excess of $163 million, which (as he is too polite to underline) is rather more than many snootier directors *combined*.

Walsh is dapper, with an apricot shirt open at the neck, and a loose silk tie, a rare Hollywood touch. He started writing gags for the Mickey Mouse comics, but was soon cross-posted to the movies, and worked on *Robin Hood* in England —'We were there before it was chic'—putting together an exploitation picture.

'It's been a tradition round here to milk what we can out of exploitation,' he says, unnecessarily. Indeed, one of these movies, the promo for 20,000 *Leagues Under the Sea* won an Emmy, an unusual accolade for a commercial.

These were critical days for the studio. There had been ups and downs in the later '30s and the war was a boon for Disney, a certified WASP producer. Soon most of the facilities were turned over to propaganda movies. And after the war Disney was increasingly driven out of the cartoon short business by such uppity pests as Bugs Bunny. The last Mickey Mouse cartoon *per se*, and the close of a distinguished twenty-four-year career, came in 1952. This had been curiously prefigured. When BBC television closed down at noon on 1 September, 1939, the last sentence to be heard was Mickey Mouse saying —in the burlesqued manner of Greta Garbo—*Ah tank ah go home*.

Disney turned his attention to full-length features, live

action (and, of course, Disneyland), and never looked back. The reason being, Bill Walsh explains, 'The Disney Audience.'

'The kids from about seven to twelve, that's the hard core of the Disney audience. With their mums, and their grandparents, and their doting aunts ...'

Occasionally this audience may be expanded—as with *The Love Bug*, a great hit with the sandal set, Walsh says—but there are risks *vis-à-vis* the doting aunts. In *Bon Voyage* there was one scene in which Fred McMurray plus boy meet a prostitute in the Champs Elysées. 'There was nothing offensive in it ... nothing deleterious. But—we got a few squawks!'

Care pays off. Walsh produces the list of *All-Time Box Office Champs*, as codified by *Variety* newspaper. These are the motion pictures that have raked in above four million dollars, and it looks like a Disney trade ad, including 40% of all Disney features. *Mary Poppins* is at number eight, *The Love Bug* at twenty-six, *Snow White* at thirty-nine, and thickly they cluster ever more thickly. *Fantasia* finally made the list, not to mention such lesser-known examples of the studio *opus* as *Babes in Toyland, Monkey's Uncle* and *Summer Magic*.

The list of champs, Walsh however points out, contains but few examples of the movie genre that 'looks as though it's shot in a pay toilet ...

'You kind of lose track of things when you go to cocktail parties and see what the Swinging Scene is ... The modern film that swings, with all forms of depravity and all, they really don't turn up in this thing!' He indicates the chart, with justifiable satisfaction. 'We must address ourselves to this occasionally ...'

The Disney success, moreover, has come quite without the undesirable trimmings considered necessary by the one-time majors. Disney has no star system, to speak of. It has proved impractical to emulate that earliest generation of movie-moguls and do without stars altogether, though that system has worked pretty well across at WED. Audiences require stars, but the Disney stars are not star-stars. *Prima donna* behaviour is not encouraged. And nobody, but nobody, has ever had a piece of the action. Nor are Harold Robbinsesque sums expended on the story.

'They don't let us buy ... expensive stage-plays, or best-sellers, or anything. So we make things out of chicken-wire and sealing-wax. It does place a certain premium on ingenuity.' Not to mention out-of-copyright material.

Walt arrived at material through a process of intuition and consultation, often fairly random. 'He'd talk to the janitor ... the gardener ... anybody he bumped into in the men's room. He'd get a *feel* that way.'

The same continues, though largely at higher echelons.

'We kind of get together like bees rubbing our wings together' buzzes Bill Walsh, comfortably.

Animated cartoons is how it all started. The job with the Kansas City Film Ad Company turning out one-minute ads in 1919. The association with Ub Iwerks, whose purely creative flair provided an element without which Walt's more entre-preneurial creativity might easily have gone in other directions. Laugh-O-Gram, Walt's hodgepodge of jokes and information, which was run at the local movie-house. *Alice in Cartoonland*, in which a live girl—a prophetic technique—was integrated with a cartoon background. *Oswald the Rabbit*, the more sophisticated series which Walt evolved in 1927. He was then twenty-six, and he was shucked out of the rights by his distributor.

Later in life, Walt Disney was to lose interest in the cartoon side of the business. Schickel records the lugubrious scene of Walt glimpsed not merely trying to draw Mickey well enough to satisfy requests, but even trying to master his copyrighted signature.

But the animation continues, though on fewer engines than of yore. The Animation Director is Wolfgang— 'Woolie'— Reitherman, a tall, mild man, more handsomely networked with crinkles than a cigarette-commercial cowboy. He is wearing a sleeveless blue shirt and smoking a yellowy cigar.

Reitherman is working at a sequence on his desk. This is

to be *The Adventures of Robin Hood and His Merry Men*, a full-length version of that British epic, which has already been so thoroughly Disneyfied that not even the most folk-loric can object that the parts are to be played by cartoon animals.

Following this, another Winnie-the-Pooh number is slated. This will feature Tigger to an extent never contemplated by A. A. Milne. As of this moment, Reitherman assures me, there seems little likelihood that Disney will be further tackling Tolkien. *The Lord of the Rings* is notoriously complex, not to mention poetical, and at times even gloomy. It is true that these factors didn't prevent the studio from transmogrifying the Arthurian Cycle, but that was at least *funny*.

Reitherman shakes his head, puzzled. Professor Tolkien poses problems. 'Young people are quite crazy about it ... but, I don't know how to say it, it just doesn't seem to afford the kind of *humour* we can do.'

Animated features are not something to be entered on to lightly. They require three years of work apiece nowadays, a considerably lengthier gestation that was required in the old days. But in the old days (Reitherman explains), there would be thirty animators working on something like *Pinocchio*, or *Fantasia*.

'Counting the so-called junior animators, many more. And then the follow-up artists, who were assistant animators, were in a ratio of two-to-one ...'

And now?

Reitherman speaks slowly, almost reluctantly.

'We have around six first-rate animators. Very, very good, and for our purposes the best in the world, and they still enjoy it, and are still keen about it.

'And maybe four junior animators. It runs around ten ...'

It takes a full three years for Disney to finish an animation feature now, though the improvement in technique makes a direct man-for-man equation with *Pinocchio*, say, impossible. There was, for one thing, the advent of Xerox.

The process was economically inevitable, if not exactly desirable. When Mickey shook hands with Stokowski it was almost a gesture of farewell.

'What it's done', Reitherman says 'is that we go with lines that have to be done in Xerox, where before we used to have an—infinite number of lines. I think there is less subtlety in the rendering of the characters. There's got to be. I don't know whether it's noticeable ...

'If you start looking at the form itself, I think you would notice that it's not as good as the old way. We did a *Sleeping Beauty* here years ago ... the most expensive picture we ever made, and I think the most *beautiful* picture we ever made.

'But, by concentration on the beauty—it's kind of a gentle picture all the way through—and to audiences generally it doesn't play as well as *1001 Dalmatians*. We felt that the beauty of the backgrounds would add a great deal, which they did. But not enough ...

'Of course, *Snow White* is to me still one of the great ones we've done ... the simplicity of the characters, and the backgrounds are so simple, with all that warm sepia. There wasn't any attempt to get flashy.

'*Snow White* had many things wrong in terms of animation. And yet the total impact is better than anything we ever put on the screen. She looks like a girl, she's naïve. *Sleeping Beauty* became more sophisticated. The voice, and everything ...'

Woolie Reitherman considers animation—Xerox or no Xerox. 'It's one of the great new art-forms. No question about it ...'

The animated features may, or may not, be on the wane, but the iconography is as omnipresent as ever. As the spores of pixie-dust work their way into the cerebrum the whole Burbank studio seems at times to have been metamorphosed into an animated movie. Employees and executives with their bounce, and sudden smiles, can seem, briefly, like Prince Charming and Goofy, Cinderella and Daisy Duck boringly transformed. Gold Mickey Mouse watches flash on the wrists of Card Walker, John Hench, Jack Lindquist, Woolie Reitherman, while Mickey timepieces of inferior value adorn other wrists at other levels. Awards and memorabilia abound.

257

Reitherman has a small gold chair from the Directors' Club of America. Bill Walsh had a wallful of award nominations. In senior offices, there will be plaques awarded after ten years service—'The tencennial' in Disneytalk—or maybe a signed photo of Walt. There will be Disney ashtrays, Disney visuals, bronze statuettes of Disney characters. The overall effect is simultaneously votive and businesslike, like the Curia of the Vatican.

Bob Moore has a pronounced influence upon Disney imagery. Bob Moore is one of the creators of Disney's advertising art. Upon his office wall is one of the psychedelic posters for *Fantasia*. 'We're trying to capitalise on the fact that the picture is Today,' he says.

Mickey Mouse is one of Bob Moore's responsibilities. Mickey has developed over the years, of course. His nose is shorter now. He is more compact all over, in fact, and resembles the Character in the Park rather more than the protagonist of the cartoons.

Ironically, it is the original Mickey Mouse that is preferred for those zillion T-shirts.

Moore shows me the Mickey Mouse model-sheets, a new wheeze to eliminate distortions to which foreign comic-book artists are prone.

'They don't realise . . . They make a mistake, and the mistake keeps getting worse and worse. You know, the artistic personality starts altering things a little.' (On the islands of Greece, I recall, all comics are called Mickey Mouse.) Moore pushes across the Mickey specifications. These seem to cover almost any probable stress or tolerance of the Mouse form, like aeroplane studies.

'This is the pattern. This is the way Mickey Mouse is to be drawn. Period.'

It was Bob Moore who was responsible for the Walt Disney World logo, that mouse-eared globe itself. It seems somehow apt that it should have been achieved by the advertising department.

'It is used on just about everything. I think it's a perfect symbol. It's on everything that I know of. Down to the sewer caps in the street!' Bob Moore says.

258

People are looking for illusions, they don't want the world's realities
Morris Lapidus, designer of the Fontainebleau, Miami.

Lunch is usually in the Coral Room, which is, in fact, brownish, and majestic with Disney Awards. A plaque from the British Film Academy, for instance, the Grand Prix Technique, and an award for Americanism. The Coral Room is where the upper echelons eat. Also such bankers or business executives as may have affairs to transact in Burbank, and even the lead actors from whichever picture the studio is making, though stars are hardly a Disney studio thing.

Today, Roy Disney was eating with a knot of colleagues. His chief accountant, and Donn Tatum, and Mel, the overall boss of WED. Disney had a sharp blue jacket, a slim black tie, and a ruddy tan.

Roy E. Disney, his son and Walt's nephew, is eating in a corner with another group. Roy E. Disney is a producer, with a particular interest in animal movies. A couple of other producers are eating by themselves, Bill Walsh and Bill Anderson, identical in their Malibu chic of expensively casual beige jackets, tieless shirts, and moccasins.

Conversation is general. There is the annual Miss Disneyland election upcoming out at Anaheim. Roy O. Disney is fixing up cheap flights, to Florida, for Disney employees. I personally am intrigued by the idea of flying back to Florida in the executive jet, an ageing Gulfstream, Mickey Mouse 234.

Roy Disney quizzes me amiably about my comings and goings. 'You certainly do seem very interested in us,' he says, and it is said with the genuinely Disney folksy wonderment, but also a certain carefulness.

I am not invited to the election of Miss Disneyland nor to fly on Mickey Mouse.

Merchandising and promotion are based on Burbank, and it goes without saying that they absorb some of Disney's fiercer energies. The Disney characters were first merchandised in 1932 and have been in the public eye, not to mention in their hands and on their backs, increasingly ever since. The same cannot be said for Hopalong Cassidy, say, or Batman.

A show-room displays a little from the colourful crop of gee-gaws, mainly from the Mickey Mouse watch and Snow White record player end of the trade. 'We've got 12,000 companies under licence around the world,' says a zealot from the Character Merchandising Division, 'and about 5,000 different items on the market.'

The items include (I quote at random) Play Wallets and Money Sets from the Chemtoy Corporation; Disneykins, wind-up and friction toys from Louis Marx & Co.; talking 'patter' pillows from Mattel Inc., a near Anaheim neighbour, and home of the Ken & Barbie dolls; Yo-Yos and pre-seeded roll-out flower and vegetable gardens from Union Wadding.

This is just plain licensing for a flat fee, say 10% of the profit, and straightforward enough, compared to the complexities of promotion. In 1964, for example, a colour ad in *Life* announced a ten-week promotion. Three thousand supermarkets during this period were expected to give away eight million games based on Walt's movie, *The Sword in the Stone*.

In 1967, the seventh re-release of *Snow White and the Seven Dwarfs* was launched with more tie-ins than most Hollywood *premières*. Procter & Gamble's Clorox spent $325,000 on a *Snow White* oriented campaign. Standard Brands offered Snow White games on six-packs of Royal gelatin, and Colgate-Palmolive distributed half a million Snow White and Dopey Soakys. Nabisco did a yet more enticing job on their Wheat and Rice Honeys.

Each package will be dominated by a Snow White and the Seven Dwarfs identification, reported *Advertising Age,* and continued to say they would contain *two moulded plastic two-inch high walking dwarfs. There is a possible total collection of seven dwarfs plus a dwarf cottage.*

And later that year two more pictures were to be released by the tireless Mouse Factory, a striking duo, *The Gnome-Mobile* and *Jungle Book*. The first—authentically Disney in its mix of whimsy and engineering—was to benefit from a $250,000 Del Monte fruit drinks promotion and also from the effects of four and a half million people discovering gnomes in their packets of potato chips.

Jungle Book (I quote *Advertising Age* once more) already had tie-ins set up with Kimberly-Clark and, again, with Nabisco, and with Kimberly-Clark.

Kleenex box bottoms ... will offer a self-liquidating 'Jungle Book' premium, possibly a plush toy Kleenex dispenser modelled after a character from the movie. Kleenex were also to lash out with sets of 'Jungle Jewels', six of Rudyard Kipling's, um, Walt Disney's characters, reproduced as pins and charms, with bracelet to match.

But the movie spin-off is piffling compared with the Magic Real Estate. Here, no angle has been missed. There is, for a start, the massive trade in souvenirs. Stroll around the Magic Kingdom in the Disney World from Olde Worlde Antiques in Liberty Square to the contemporary gifts in the Space Port, Tomorrowland. In Fantasyland you can buy toys from Tinkerbell and magic tricks from Merlin, while across in Adventureland there is a veritable bazaar with Mid-East brass in the Magic Carpet, novelty hats from Tropic Toppers, and Polynesian or African kitsch from, respectively, the Tiki Tropic Shop or the Traders of Timbuktu.

And this is just the icing on a most substantial cake. The Walt Disney World, like the Magic Kingdom before it, is the infinitely saleable dream. 'There is no corporation in the world that wouldn't love to be associated with our family appeal, our ... wholesomeness. I've got to say it, wholesomeness,' says Jack Lindquist, the Director of Marketing.

Those profiting from the Good Fairy Seal of Approval include Eastern Airlines who have acquired the ten-year right to call themselves *The official air-line of Walt Disney World* at a fee of ten million dollars. Yes, I said ten million dollars, but this is a trifle compared with the sixty to eighty millions that US Steel is shelling out on building the first two of the Disney World hotels. I hope some of that pixie-dust rubs off on you, J. Pierpoint Morgan, wherever you are.

Other beneficiaries of the wholesomeness include Coca-

Cola, who have sponsored the restaurant on Tomorrowland Terrace, and are dispensing Coke on Main Street; Borden Inc., who have a *fin-de-siècle* ice-cream parlour in the same key location; Monsanto, who sponsor the Circle-Vision spectacular *America the Beautiful*; Elgin, official manufacturer of the Mickey Mouse watch, who sell the same on Main Street; Hallmark; Hertz, who have become the Walt Disney World *'official rent a car company'* and took a full-page ad showing Mickey, Goofy, Donald Duck, Pinocchio *et al.* to celebrate the fact.

Frito-Lay and Pepsi-Cola are joint sponsors of the Mile-Long Bar, Pecos Bill's Café in Frontierland, and, zippeedee-doodah, the Country Bear Jamboree; the J. M. Smucker Company will mail-order jams and jellies by way of the Market House; and Florida Citrus, representing a somewhat depressed industry, are none-the-less spending three million dollars to promote a Sunshine Pavilion. Oh, yes, and Kal-Kan took a full-page in *Life* to announce its impressive status as *Official pet food in Walt Disney World*. Bring your pets, it implores. One is relieved to hear that they are sponsoring *'a unique pet motel at the entrance to the Magic Kingdom'*.

And companies are still clamouring for access, though less wholesome firms regard the hard-nosed bargains that Disney can strike with envy. It costs a participating firm—'an advertising associate'—between seventy-five and two hundred thousand dollars just to use the Disney name and characters. If it wants a location to promote itself or sell goods, it will cost forty thousand a year. As long as it shares with other penny-pinchers, that is, because private quarters can set a company back a hundred grand. Nor does this include construction costs which may run to thirty-five thou in a shared building. Strictly Mickey Mouse compared with costs for a private pavilion which might be a quarter million.

Now the money starts rolling in, right?

Wrong. No firm that he knows of, Lindquist says, has actually made a profit from selling goods in the Magic Kingdom. Not *cash* profits, anyhow. The profits, he emphasises, are the advertising and the intangibles ... that wholesomeness again, in fact.

US Steel, for instance, has no immediate way of recouping on all that petty cash which went into putting up the Contemporary and the Polynesian hotels. There is just the warm glow of a job well done. And done extremely visibly.

Nor will all the firms willing to hand over the lolly actually be allowed to do so. Disney made their early mistakes—there was an emporium on Main Street early on where one could buy *brassières*. Not Disney at all, I was told. It had to go.

Finally, there have been a few joyless firms that have found one can be screwed just too far for the sake of wholesomeness and family appeal. TWA, for example, once had its name in the Anaheim Moon Rocket, which was an attraction (one might remember) long before they wasted all that money on the real ones. Anyway, Trans-World paid fifty thousand dollars a year for this privilege for five years. Then they, so to speak, blasted off. 'I think Disney wanted to up the ante a little bit,' recalls a Trans-Worlder.

The most recent hoo-ha concerned Eastman Kodak. Eastman Kodak had been in Anaheim for many years, but are now absent from both locales. Not a matter to wipe the grin off Mickey's face. GAF promptly stepped in, and became *The official film of Disneyland and the Walt Disney World* over a three-year period for just one million dollars. Happy snaps, GAF.

The Disney attitude to publicity, as opposed to promotion, tends to be guarded. Ideally, they would like to originate all Disney material themselves, much as they do with such well-crafted bubbliness in their own domains.

We outside are not quite ready yet for that degree of rationalisation. Media assistance is necessary, but the media are watched. Alan Whicker, for instance, was required to cease and desist before completing his Yorkshire TV film as planned. Observers had detected traces of irony, and nothing curdles Disney's milk of human kindness more speedily than irony does.

Despite its lack of control, and aside from the odd displeasing episode, Disney publicity must be literally unparalleled in its quantity and persistence. What other firm launching a new business venture can expect competition from the world Press to blazon it on their covers? The advertising budget for the Disney World was nil—zero—but who needs a budget when a television network is going to run an hour-and-a-half of promotional programming, and is paying handsomely for the privilege?

Disney is instant copy. Premiers and movie-stars are photographed being introduced to Mickey, Pluto and Snow White, and starlets flaunt them on T-shirts. Western society at large seems on the verge of metamorphosing into a Disney costume party. A picture in the *Daily Mail* shows an undercover New York policeman artfully disguised in a Mickey Mouse T-shirt and Miss World's rock singer husband is thrown out of a Knightsbridge hotel for wearing the same. A London magnate is alleged to have attended his last annual general meeting, to the surprise of his share-holders, wearing a Mickey Mouse mask.

Further afield as among the CIA-trained 'Secret Army' of Meo tribesmen in Laos.

Meo warrior No. 1 is General Vang Pao, reported the *Daily Express* in 1971. *He liked to impress his troops by strutting about in a Zorro suit given to him during a visit to Disneyland.*

Disney imagery is now so deeply embedded in the global psyche that the results are often unpredictable. In the US Army, Mickey Mouse suggests phoney whereas in Harlem—extremely inappropriately, I would have thought—a Mickey Mouse means a white. London Cockneys, disrespectful fellows always, use Mickey Mouse to signify the female crotch while Donald Duck has been a popular addition to rhyming slang, usually as 'a Good Donald'.

It is doubtful if this is the kind of dissemination that the Disney folks most enjoy, so to speak, but if you sell a line of products, you can hardly complain if people buy.

It is also homage, of a sort. The miscreant who took Bing Crosby's *Going My Way* Oscar from the Crosby museum, Gonzaga University, Washington, and replaced it with a three-inch Mickey statuette might have acted flippantly, but

264

the other dastard who hoisted a 300-pound cement sculpture of Pluto from a Maryland gift-shop just had to be a fan.

The formidable Disney backlash can also be taken as an inverted tribute. As an overseas phenomenon, it crops up now and again. British librarians complain that Disney has processed *Alice in Wonderland* or whatever. A city official in Sao Paulo, Brazil, felt that Mickey's standing amongst the kids had hampered a campaign to exterminate rats.

Chile was (inevitably) the scene of a yet more ferocious attack, arising from a 1971 best-seller, *How To Read Donald Duck*, which analysed the comic characters as a 'threat to Chilean reality' and 'class enemies of the Chilean people'. Donald's grasping uncle, Scrooge McDuck was seen as peculiarly inimical, especially for an episode in which he swindled the Abominable Snowman by trading 'Genghis Khan's crown of gold and precious stones' for a cheap watch.

It was even hinted that there are more than 'casual reasons' why Donald's nephews seem to have no parents.

Donald's reaction can well be imagined. A Disney spokesman contented himself with saying: 'Disney characters are pure fun and are intended that way. We do not deal in social commentary or political commentary.'

They are a mite less placid about the backlash back home.

This is largely a matter of Disney's relationship with—to use a boring grab-bag word for an elusive and changeable reality—the Youth Culture. This relationship has always been low on pixie-dust.

Right at the beginning, this didn't seem to matter so much. Not even that first and memorable act of *lèse-majesté*, a double-page cartoon published in *The Realist* 1957, which showed the Disney menagerie, centring on Snow White, and which was executed with such impeccable Disney style that it took a double-take or two before you realised they were all having it off, joyfully, and explicitly.

The cartoon was, of course, an implicit protest about the Disney sexlessness, from the nipple-free mermaids in *Anaheim* to the lady Centaurs with their mimsy bikinis in *Fantasia*.

'The background was that Disney died,' says Paul Krassner,

editor of *The Realist*, then and now, 'so I took some LSD to celebrate ... and there was a Peace March somewhere near Christmas in New York, and—I was wearing gloves. That's it, it was very cold, and I said I feel like Mickey Mouse...

'And I started improvising about Disney, how I didn't think he was really dead. Because you used to see him sometimes with Goofy at his side ... he mixed his own personality in with the characters and he became one. So he didn't die...

'And then I thought—What's going to happen to all the characters if Walt is dead? They would have some kind of binge, like at a Roman orgy, doing all the things they weren't permitted to do by him while he was alive.

'That was the concept of it, and I told it to this artist, Wally Woods ... and he executed the drawing ... then I published it in the magazine, and a lot of people refused to sell it. And there were complaints from the Post Office, but I won out at those levels, because it wasn't obscene within the Supreme Court's definition of obscenity.'

The Disney people were not, at this stage, into image-denting lawsuits. Krassner's problems, ironically, were plagiaristic rivals.

'The original art-work was stolen, and a lot of pirate poster people put out copies of it. And they never asked for permission, and they never gave me royalties. So'—he concludes with relish—'it is their bad karma that is now bringing lawsuits on them.'

Because relations were to worsen, after something of a false dawn.

Throughout the '60s, Disneyland had been firmly out-of-bounds to persons with long hair, no shoes, 'unorthodox' clothes, and what have you, but as this grooming itself became orthodox for an increasing slice of the market, Disney was driven to re-think. The ban was slowly relaxed.

This inching towards tolerance was reflected in the merchandising. *Fantasia* had unexpectedly become something of a hit with the Underground, being commended on all sides as eminently suitable viewing while on an acid trip, or prefer-

266

ably mescalin. (The 'Dance of the Mushrooms' became a dramatic highlight to a degree unintended, I think, by Walt.) And the Disney promo men seem not ungrateful for this new audience, which was wooed with quasi-psychedelic ads.

But Disney peace-making was rudely rebuffed. On August 6th 1971, to be exact.

This was declared National Yippie Day by certain local underground papers. Three hundred youths gathered to celebrate it at Cinderella's Castle. They followed the Disneyland Band down Main Street, cheering for Charlie Manson and Ho Chi Minh. The Law dispersed them, but they re-formed and annexed Tom Sawyer's Island where they smoked dope, and ran up the Viet Cong flag.

Eighteen were arrested by closing time, and the Dress Code was reintroduced, more severely than ever.

Outside the Magic Kingdom, things are less susceptible to control. Krassner's successors include the T-shirts that show the lovable rodent with an elongated nose, with the legend 'Mickey Rat', and one graphic poster on which Mickey, Donald and Goofy are getting wiped out smoking a hookah. Krassner quotes a columnist for the Houston *Chronicle* who proposes a 'sort of first-aid kit for any children who stumble on the wrong cartoons. If a little one asks you why Mickey Mouse is holding a hypodermic needle to his arm, simply say he is giving himself a tetanus-diphtheria booster before school starts ...

'As for the Seven Dwarfs, uh, reaching out for Snow White, you might say that she had been out getting groceries and they were welcoming her back with open arms.'

It would take some really fast talking to explain away, for instance the San Francisco comic-book, *Mickey Mouse meets the Air Pirates,* a parody in which Jiminy Cricket appears as a pimp, Donald Duck as a panhandling Peeping Tom, and Minnie—bereft of her polkadot knickers—is carried off to be fed to the young of a giant bird.

The artists' motives are mixed. One of them is Dan O'Neill, a quirkily brilliant cartoonist, more widely known for the strip, *Odds Bodikins.*

'Disney is a language,' he claims, passionately, and he speaks of those days when the movies were doing pretty dire business, and the studio was partly dependent on its comic-strips. A time (O'Neill says) which they now prefer to forget.

He is, he feels, striking a blow for that neglected part of the Disney tradition ... 'Their cartoonists are terrible now. The work is terrible. They lost all those people because of politics. And the younger cartoonists just get turned off by Disney ...

'We wanted them to sue,' he adds, and the wish was certainly granted. Disney finally decided that the underground just wouldn't go away if they ignored it long enough. A half-million-dollar suit has been pressed by the studio.

It is time (they feel) that Mickey was protected from appearing in a 'lewd, drug-addictive manner'.

One other genre of exploitation is worth a mention. Disney, no less than Coca-Cola, has suffered the attentions of artists and the urban intelligentsia. These are not always vindictive, and are indeed frequently respectful.

Ernest Trova is just one artist with a Mickey Mouse collection. (This is a bullish market, as a May auction of 220 items of Disneyana at the Los Angeles branch of Sotheby's Parke-Bernet proved. A London dealer paid a hundred quid for *an early and fine Mickey Mouse wrist-watch* dating from 1933. One of the lower prices was £19 for a couple of wrist-watch bands together with a belt buckle *decorated with Mickey in his classical pose, circa 1935*. Rather less classic was the alarm-clock on sale, which was banned by Disney in the same period. It showed Mickey and Minnie *in a passionate embrace*.)

Donald Duck has also come in for due homage. Frank Zappa includes the querulous fowl in *200 Motels*, and Eduardo Paolozzi some time ago, but with a shrewd prefiguration of things to come, produced Donald Duck in a programmed version.

These attentions are unwelcome none-the-less. There was a brief period in Disney's earlier career when Walt appeared as a Folk Hero Artist and there was some flirtation with the intellectuals, but *Fantasia*, his high cultural fling, bombed, which dismayed *him*. And then Walt Disney emerged during the War years (to the great profit of his studio, which did a great turnover in propaganda movies) as Hollywood's Super-WASP. And that dismayed *them*. Reconciliations have been few and brief.

One such reconciliation was brought about in the later '60s by the Los Angeles County Museum of Art. Maurice Tuchman of that body was running a terrific art and technology project which consisted, essentially, in getting specific artists into symbiotic relation with specific corporations, and seeing what happened. R. B. Kitaj worked with Lockheed, Rauschenberg with Teledyne, and Tony Smith constructed a cardboard cave with the assistance of the Container Corporation.

Disney were approached, and at first refused, giving as a material reason '*the highly confidential nature of much of our work here at WED*'.

Strings were pulled. Disney capitulated, though specifying strict contractual rights of withdrawal if the artist's work proved not to their liking. At which stage Tuchman hooked Claes Oldenburg.

The collaboration was protracted, hilarious and doomed. It is described in some detail in Tuchman's book on the entire programme. '*The name of my piece for Disney, Maurice, will be "Leaves of Grass"*,' Oldenburg is quoted as writing. '*Disneyland must have its Whitman section full of homosexual streetcar conductors.*' No wonder his association with the Magic Realists of WED was an abortive one.

The incident still rankles, evidently. John Hench discusses Earth Art, Non-Art, and similar intellectual games with some acidity, even proposing an aesthetic experiment of his own. 'Now, of course, with computers and with statistics, it's easy to prove what's art and what isn't art.

'Maybe, if an object, or a painting, or a device moves so many people statistically, it becomes automatic that it qualifies for art?'

Maybe, and that would probably see Claes Oldenburg out. His project, incidentally, was, as Hench describes it, 'a large ice-bag that had convulsions and moved in some kind of rhythmic way'. Disney was unmoved by the convulsive ice-bag, and pressed the artist to attempt an alternative project, the Fanana, an electric fan which turned to a 3-D banana.

Oldenburg took his ice-bag to GeminiGEL instead and, what's more, erected a Mouse sculpture in the courtyard of the modern Art Museum, New York. It was called the Geometric Mouse, but it certainly looked reminiscent of you-know-who.

'He transposed the round forms of Mickey into square forms,' Hench says, sadly. 'Of course, this wasn't Mickey. This was a translation of the *idea* of Mickey, but a violation of everything that Mickey is.

'I mean, Mickey is again one of those intuitive approaches to a figure, done with simple round forms, which are very friendly ...

'No one's ever had any problems with round forms. We have ten million years of association with women's breasts and babies' behinds and soft clouds and so forth ...

'So our survival is not threatened by Mickey as it was by Felix the Cat, for instance, which was full of sharp angles, and dangerous.' And the durability of the Mickey image lies here, John Hench feels, in this 'extraordinary intuitive collection of round forms'.

The logo of the Walt Disney World is, of course, even rounder. Whether it will be as durable remains to be seen.

Scene in the Magic Kingdom, Anaheim.
Child: I saw Mickey ... 'n Goofy ... 'n Dumbo ... 'n the
  Little Pigs ... and ... and ...
Adult (helpfully): Didn't you see Snow White?
Child Oh, yes. I saw *her* ... But she wasn't real.

A mouse with a fibreglass head was real. A girl with a wig was not.

The Walt Disney World is to furnish prototypes for all of us. But the Magic Kingdom, Anaheim, was the prototype for the Walt Disney World. Votive visits were called for. The drive down the Santa Ana freeway is barely enlivened by the opportunity to visit such Disneyesque phenomena as

270

Knott's Berry Farm and the Japanese Village, and then the Matterhorn aloof, impossible ahead, and one is among the unenchanting slurb outside Disneyland. To Disney's intense annoyance, the annual take of these rapacious suburbs many times exceeds the hard-gotten gains of Disneyland, a mistake they vowed not to make again. Nor have they, nor have they.

Since the 1954 opening, one hundred million tourists have been through Disneyland. The average length of their stay is seven-and-a-half hours, apparently, and their expenditure is six dollars and ninety-some cents. How many of them have adhered to that clockwise programming there is no way to tell.

I am taken around by Tour Hostesses. Fantasyland. The Monsanto ride. Great Moments with Mr Lincoln. It is a refresher course and comparative research at once, and the girls quiz me wistfully about the World. Will those flaccid Floridans prove as deft in administering the pixie-dust? As a dedicated Californian, I also wonder, because Californians certainly can *smile*.

'Sometimes I find myself at school ... just *smiling at every-body*,' says Barbara, my tour guide. 'And they all look at me like ... you know, Uhh-Huh!.' She mimes their incredulity.

One day I am taken to lunch in the 33 Club. This is rather special, in all senses of the word. Only Walt's private apartment over the Disneyland Fire Station had the same mystique. The 33 Club is for the private entertainment of members, for the most part executives with those corporations shelling out such substantial sums for the privilege of backing a Disneyland ride.

My hostess presses an electric buzzer beside a discreetly unmarked door in the New Orleans Street, and whispers into it, strictly Speakeasy-style. We wait a moment or so while the populace mills past chewing candyfloss to the pink-plonk of old-time music, and are admitted into a lobby. There is a hostess in a veritable frou-frou of black and white lace. It's not quite Frederick's of Hollywood, but it's unexpected for Disneyland.

We ascend in a wrought-iron lift to a suite with all the

appurtenances of upper-class clubbery; marble and gilt, veneered rich woods, a floral display of accurately tinted plastic, and an antique-style harpsichord played at intervals for the VIPs by a girl named Joyce.

The style is Gallic, over-all, with those tempting lacy waitresses just an inch-or-so of thrust short of Playboy Club demands, and an exemplary menu, and—Oh, yes. An oasis! —the only alcohol to be had in Disneyland. One might, in fact, almost forget that one was in the Magic Kingdom at all. But for the heads of deer and stuffed miscellaneous wild-life on the walls, that is.

These (the girl explains) are going in due course to be programmed by the Audio-Animatronics workshop. A complex mechanism will enable them to pick up conversations, and accost the clubmen with vaguely relevant remarks.

Which shouldn't hurt the booze turnover one bit.

Back in the Park, I meet some of the Characters. Pinocchio, first. Pinocchio is new to this role, having previously played most of the Seven Dwarfs. The Characters do about twenty minutes in costume and forty out, because it gets devilish hot.

'The worst are the two mice ... I've been in both of them, and they're really hot. Like 130 ... 140 ...'

'Don't you have air conditioners in there?' asks the girl, twinkling dewily.

They have them out in Florida, Pinocchio says, but he isn't so sure about them.

'The guys that tried them out here *got colds*. They caught cold from them ... taking it off, and putting it on ...'

MickeyMouse is taking a breather round the corner. He is in his dinky costume, but holds his head in one arm. He is a 'Small Person' as they phrase it delicately in the United States, and irrepressibly jolly. The sun strikes sparks off his Mickey Mouse watch.

'That's the fifty dollar one. It's got the date and the calendar,' he says, chirpily. '*Sure* I've got the Mickey Mouse watch. *I'm Mickey Mouse!*'

And apart from being Mickey Mouse?

'Paul Castle ... but I'm not allowed to say that, see!' he

adds with a hectic laugh, like walnuts cracking.

Why not?

'Because I'm—*Mickey Mouse!* But you're not supposed to know that, see?'

Why not? I ask, again.

'That's what THEY say.' (heavy emphasis) 'I'm not allowed to use my name or anything. It depends on your clearance. What clearance do you have?'

Pretty good, I believe.

'Well, if you can use my name ... *They* don't like me to identify myself,' (again that ominous Edward Lear *They*) 'but I *like* to. So that people know there is ... somebody in there. Anybody who's an adult knows that's not a real character walking around by himself ...'

Again that great, hectic laugh. 'It's not a *real* mouse, you know!'

Paul Castle's career commenced in ice-skating.

'Twenty years professionally. I skated with Sonja Henie in *Holiday On Ice* in Europe for two years ... Rome ... Copenhagen ... I played Wembley for two weeks the Summer of '55. I was known as "The Mighty Mite—Paul Castle. The Smallest Skater in the World".

'And I did all these Animal Characters, see? I've been doing Animal Characters almost thirty years,' Castle says, proudly: 'Teddy bears ... monkeys ... any animal you can think of ... French poodles ...

'And then I did the Disney Characters on Ice for Ice-Capades. Right here in Hollywood at the Pan-Pacific Auditorium. We used to have the sound-track from the movie right over the loudspeaker system. And we used to act out the parts on the ice, which was all pantomime, you see.

'I was doing *Snow White and the Seven Dwarfs* ... I was Dopey, the littlest of the dwarfs, and I used to run around and get kissed by Snow White all the time ...

'That was *fun*! And Walt Disney saw me skating. And that's how I got the connections ...'

Thus followed ten years of Mickey Mouse. A role not to be taken lightly.

273

'It's like all the Characters. They try to pretty well portray the characters from the movies. We've seen a lot of movies. They show us films, and all that kind of stuff, you see . . .

'Mickey just walks normally. He's just a real little cocky guy who walks around like I do! You know, not just cocky, *sprightly*. Happy-go-lucky, and always smiling. A smiling face! I'm a happy mouse, you know, basically . . .'

Happy, even despite the oven heat. 'It's a lot hotter than skating in Ice Shows, I'll tell you that! Because there are so many . . . *thousands* of people around you, right at close range. They grab hold of you, and pull on you, and so forth, you know. But it's really good to see the little kids, individual little faces and all that kind of stuff . . .'

What age do the kids begin to wonder? I begin, and he answers before it's out of my mouth.

'Five or six! Right now the kids—American kids especially —they see everything on television, so even at five or six'—he mimes—'*We know you're in there!*

'And they want to take you apart, and who's in there? And look in my eye, and all this crap . . . The two- or three-year-olds are still mystified. You get the five-year-olds—about my size. You get to be five, you're this big'—spoken factually, perkily even—'and they know just about *everything*. They're not afraid of Frankenstein's Monster and all that stuff, you know . . .'

What does Mickey do under this sort of inquisition?

'Well, I *talk* to those kids . . . I talk with a higher-pitched voice.

'*Hi kids! How are yer!*' he says. The Mickey Voice is a rapid and dissonant squeak, which sounds like a 33 album being played at 45.

'Well, I'll put my head on!' Castle says, with one more staccato laugh; he does so, and reverts to Mickey.

'*Hi, kids! How are yer! . . . Hi, kids! How are yer . . . Hullo! Hi there!*' he says, in rapid sequence, making those Mickey gestures of welcome, an open palm wave, that evergreen sign that a man (or Mouse) comes in peace.

Nor does Mickey just get to meet the kids. 'I've shaken hands with presidents and famous people from all over the

274

world. Haile Selassie, for example. And the Prime Minister of Italy ...

'He's just a prime minister,' he adds.

'And the Russian cosmonauts,' says the girl.

'And the cosmonauts. Right. They were dressed up in space suits ...'

The proudest moment in Paul Castle's life, though, relates to neither president nor star-man. 'I would say the most memorable day in my life', he says seriously, 'was with Walt Disney himself as Grand Marshal in the Rose Bowl Parade ... in 1966, the year that he died ...'

He pauses, and I ask: Does he identify closely when he is wearing the costume?

'Oh, yes ... I feel I'm Mickey Mouse! In fact I get upset when anybody else does it!' As, for instance, now in Florida. 'They sent my substitute to make me mad. Actually they sent *Minnie* down there ...' He laughs, hectically, but adds, 'It upsets me.

'Because I've been it for ten years, and I was the first little one that they had. They always had big characters. They had this great, big old head.' He makes a face. 'Like a—pig head.

'This is a small head ... for a small Mickey Mouse. It's been my life's work, you see,' Paul Castle adds, simply: 'And it was like this job was made for me, and I was made for this job.'

The Disneyland Band, milling around us, begins to tune up. It's time for another parade.

What (finally) does Mickey Mouse mean?

'I think he's a symbol ... I think he's the greatest symbol ... *He's the symbol of Walt Disney.*' Paul Castle replaces his head and, half-relapsing into the Mouse's skittered consonants, says *'Goodbye! Have a jolly time now!'* before striding jauntily into the Park in a swirl of music.

I return to Los Angeles with somebody from Guest Relations. We discuss the occasional problems that beset the Magic Kingdom. Few serious. Hassles over lost children (they often turn up at home). Safety (a tip-top record). Union problems (The Teamsters have unsuccessfully tried to unionise the Disney girls).

The odd drugged guest, who is escorted sharply to the gate by one of the security officers, the man from Guest Relations says.

How many of these are there?

'Twenty-five to fifty ...'

Are they in uniform?

'Some are,' he says, obliquely, adding: 'But we call it costume.'

Costume. Disneyland is a Magic Kingdom indeed.

There can be few, I imagine, who will not marvel at the sophistication of computer technology devoted to the Country Bear Jamboree, the roomful of electronic Presidents, the Mickey Mouse Revue. But there are in the Cybernetic City uses for data-processing machinery which go far beyond such *coups de théâtre* as these. The colossal (if sometimes unfortunate) Radio Corporation of America was involved in depth-computerising the Florida dreamscape just about from the beginning.

'I think it was recognised by RCA very early—in fact, back in '68—that Disney World, which was a project that started out in the swamps of Florida, would wind up as a ... *huge city,*' says an RCA man, warmly. He is a Vice-President, and this is his office in Rockefeller Plaza. It is richly furnished with coloured Disney charts, Disney maps, and abstruse RCA projections.

'RCA took the position that the electronic equipment was absolutely vital in tying the whole place together,' the VP says: 'We proposed to Disney to take a Total Systems Approach ... It offered an opportunity, um, really to try out an Integrated Electronics Approach.'

The capitals are underlined with little taps of a glottal hammer. 'We believe this is very applicable, not only to projects like Disney, but, you know, we're building huge new cities ... They've been built from the ground up, they have homes, schools, but as far as the electronic systems are concerned, they were sort of ... *grafted,* piecemeal. The thing I'm trying to say to you is that probably the most important thing about Disney is that the electronic systems were planned from the very beginning, and really had a major influence on the whole project ...'

Neither RCA nor any other information-systems giant, such as you-know-who, had ever had such a golden opportunity.

'This really came out of our government/military experience,' explains the RCA man: 'We have huge systems. Let me give you an example—BMEWS, which is the Ballistic Missile Early Warning System. RCA was a prime contractor, and the fellow who worked up these concepts for Disney had long been associated with the BMEWS system. He was one of the Systems Engineers, who did a lot of the creative thinking ...

'So this was truly a first in applying this type of thinking to *a community*, or to any kind of large non-defence project.'

Systems-wise, this is a situation that has been much assisted by the very unusual powers that Disney managed to extract from the Florida state legislature in exchange for their shot in the arm to the languid (if not declining) economy.

'There's an interesting issue here. Disney got, in fact, extra-territoriality within the state of Florida. So that basically Disney World operates as a county. Now I don't know if you know what that means, but counties have certain *legislative* authority that relates to the installation of sewers, utilities, electric power, right-of-ways. For that matter, telephone service, because that is franchised in the United States on a territorial basis, and they arranged for a joint venture with the Florida telephone company.

'So one of the critical things is that if some of the new cities that are going up are going to exercise the same freedom of choice and forward-looking planning, it means that they will have to be successful in achieving some type of extra-territoriality. For instance'—he marvels at the simplicity of it all—'Disney has *police authority* within the confines of their property. They have their own police! Their own stand-by power plants!

'They have a great deal of freedom, you see. If you attempted to do this in a skyscraper, or a series of skyscrapers, on the Island of Manhattan, you'd run into many problems.

Some of them would be trivial—red tape—and some would be significant in terms of what you can and cannot do.'

Happily, he turns from the obstructive shortcomings of the older cities to the expanding possibilities of the new. Some of the computer goodies are not dissimilar from those being developed elsewhere, not always with complete success. Reservations, instant billing, and such.

What is the single biggest innovation?

'I think the first and foremost is the Automatic Monitoring and Control System,' the Vice-President says, with a discreet glow: 'This gives Disney at one centre and many other places the ability to monitor, and be aware of, really ... the total status, everything that goes on within the confines of the park, in so far as it is measurable.'

The system is explained as follows. There are outlying computers, known as 'Sentries', and then there is the operational centre, where activities at certain critical points of the Disney domain are under permanent review on a great many computer video-terminals. There are also the main computers.

'It contains seven quite small computers. Technically, they would be known as mini-computers, and this has a very interesting history. RCA has a division up in Massachusetts, and for many, many years they've had a very attractive business with the Military to build automatic test and check-out monitoring systems for such things as missiles, or even tanks with jet-engines. We use the systems to check on the state of readiness etcetera etcetera.

'So these are quite small computers that are hooked up literally to thousands and thousands of individual sensors in the park. And this is really the—*heart of it*.'

Sensors?

'They take many different forms. For instance, a people-counter would be a photo-electric eye where a person walks through a light-beam and interrupts it. But really any possible control device you've ever seen would feed one way or another into the system ... so the computer is programmed to interpret that, and display it as a meaningful bit of information.'

What, I inquire with heartfelt interest, are the possibilities for the remoter future?

278

Well, of course, the monitoring is capable of greater sophistication.

(Yes.)

And there is the colour TV.

This is nothing special right now. Each hotel room has a colour TV set, and air-time is not restricted to the ordinary channels, but some air-time is available (rather predictably) for programming originated by Walt Disney Inc.

'That has tremendous implications,' says the man from RCA: 'If they go forward—as they plan—with the experimental community of tomorrow. Because, from there you can go to having adult education. Training for jobs, if you will ...'

It will be possible to use your sets to get some information, even.

'With some limitations, of course. The limitations being that you couldn't call—the Library of Congress. You could only call for certain types of information. You know, the programmes that are available ...'

All the tides of Disneyist Historic Inevitability appear to be moving towards EPCOT. It seems the destined fulfilment of the Integrated-Electronic City.

'I think what you're going to see in the outside world', says the RCA man finally gathering up his charts, 'is that more and more projects of this kind will be planned around the electronics system ...'

'The emphasis in our implementation would be in futuristic forward-looking things,' says the RCA Vice-President, forcefully: 'Prototyping the Community of Tomorrow ...'

I am beginning to feel that this—Walt Disney's last magnificent obsession—is what the Disney World is, or will be, or was, all about. The World with Mouse's Ears can carry more readings than one. Mickey's jolly face (produced to rather tight model-sheet specs, perhaps, but unarguably a face) has been replaced by Planet Earth, but not an Earth, contrasty with sea and land, but gridded with latitude and longitude. An abstract or, better, a philosophical concept, though I am getting a bit shy of the word 'concept' nowadays.

EPCOT awaits us with the welcoming shimmer, the absolute logical beauty, of a Platonic Idea.

There have been a few times when the dream didn't work out quite on schedule. There is, for one, Mineral King. This is a winter-sports resort which Disney has for some years been planning to construct in California, mid-way between San Francisco and Los Angeles.

'Walt felt that skiers are probably the most abused people in the world as far as facilities go,' explains an Imagineer. What Disney intends to lavish on this deprived group is a $35 million development, groomed to service 12,000 visitors daily. There will be snack bars, buffeterias, a teen centre, a splendid hotel complex, and well, what would you expect? —an 'Alpine Village'. There will also, naturally, be all the impedimenta of ski-lifts and such.

This would require some 300 acres, while a further 13,000 acres will be affected by the ski facilities. What (at time of writing) is causing a bit of a furore is the location of the proposed funspot. Namely, the Mineral King Wildlife Refuge, a national reserve in one of the last untouched parts of the Sierra Valley, and bordered on three sides by the Sequoia National Park.

It will be necessary to build a new 26-mile road across this park, with the probable loss of about forty-five giant redwoods. Stuart Udall, LBJ's Secretary of the Interior, refused to grant a permit for this. Governor Reagan put pressure on Johnson, and in 1967 Udall issued the permit.

Surveys continued, but so did the protests. My facts are mainly derived from an article by Roger Rapoport, published in *Ramparts*, November 1971. The cover shows Mickey Mouse, with Walt's face, spading up the forest, while Bambi and Thumper watch, disconsolate.

In 1955, Walt Disney received a citation from the Sierra Club for his wild-life movies. *Disney is like a sun ripening the grain for the wilderness advocates to harvest,* wrote the Sierra Club president Dr Ernest S. Griffith, emotionally. *We need Disney, an army of Disneys, to tell the world what we have found, what we are fighting for, the glory of creation with the bloom on it, the splendour that men can continue to explore and enjoy as long as they respect all that is alive, protect beauty and cherish the equal rights of future generations in this precious planet.*

Well, the Sierra Club got its Disney, in fact its army of Disneys, and they are not as happy about it as they might be. In July, 1969, the Sierra Club obtained an injunction against the scheme. It is considered in conservationist circles a confrontation as important in its way as the Trans-Alaska pipeline. A sign of things to come.

Oh, Mickey, Mickey.

The oilmen seem quietly confident about the pipeline, and it would be untrue to suggest that I found despondency *chez* Disney about Mineral King.

'I think there's no question that the Mineral King development became embroiled in, and frustrated by, the very rapid growth of a concern for the environment,' says Donn Tatum, Chairman of the Board and President of Walt Disney Productions: 'Which, of course, a lot of organisations took advantage of in terms of recruiting membership, funds ...

'And certainly in some of the aspects of that sweep of public opinion there have been elements of hysteria. Mineral King became a kind of *Cause Célèbre* in protecting the environment.'

A scapegoat?

'I think it became more of a ... rallying cry for the more extreme elements in the protectionist movement,' explains Donn Tatum.

At time of writing, the case continues. One way or another, Bambi and Thumper can rest in peace.

*   *   *

Walt Disney had one further dream. Something else he wished to bequeath before moving on—as he expresses it in a loop of film—to 'greener pastures'. He had put together the greatest funfair in the world. Well-matured plans were afoot to do the same for the ski resort; the all-in vacation resort; the city.

Disney's further target of improvement was the community of artists itself. A college wherein older masters would teach the gifted young, and not by precept, but—as Walt himself learnt—by practice. A substantial sum of money was hived off

281

from Walt's estate for the realisation of this project which was, and is, named the California Institute of Arts.

The name of the college was soon shortened to Cal Arts. For one thing, the acronym CIA was in use already, but more importantly Cal Arts was to (is to) stand in perfect balance with Cal Tech, which is one of the two or three most distinguished colleges of science and technology in the world.

Cal Tech boasts five Nobel Prize winners. Walt Disney, on the other hand, accumulated five Emmys and thirty-two Academy Awards. It seemed like a fair match.

Cal Arts was later to be known, with academic irreverence, as the Magic Mausoleum, the Mousoleum, and Walt's Tomb.

The story of Cal Arts is—as most Disney stories tend to be described—the story of a dream. It is, in fact, the story of several conflicting dreams, Disney's and others'. And if it is a story of conflict to the point of *angst,* this seems perhaps inevitable. Cal Arts was the only major project in which Disney ever became involved where the turning of the dream into reality necessarily involved relying on people not trained in Disney ways and groomed to Disney ends. That way anarchy lies (lay).

There are phases of the dream.

First there was the Hollywood Bowl dream. It is so called because Walt Disney originally proposed building the community in the vicinity of this Los Angeles landmark. The basis of the college was to be provided by folding in two institutions which Disney had long held in esteem, the Los Angeles Conservatory of Music and the Chouinard Art School. Both of these—especially the Chouinard—had a history of co-operation with Disney studios, which had proved both agreeable and fertile.

Many drawings exist showing Cal Arts as it might have been.

'It was mapped out as a City of the Seven Arts,' says a designer, with some excitement. 'The main street would be made of buildings that were two-thirds scale of all the famous buildings in the world. You'd have a Japanese temple, and a Greek temple, and a Gothic cathedral, and they would be designed by the officers of the school ...

282

'And students would work like under the great masters.

'Yehudi Menuhin in one wing ... Andrew Wyeth in another ...'

And—as always with Walt Disney—an element of sound Kansas practicality enters into it: the scheme behind the dream. His sound experience with building up the Imagineering Department was not far from his mind.

'A lot of us have been ... *trained* since we came to Disney,' explains an animator: 'Like a school, almost. We taught each other.

'But Walt felt he needed Cal Arts to continue the advancement of animation, and picture-making, and music. He felt he would be able to pick the cream of the crop out of there, and use them ... to advance our own industry so to speak.'

If EPCOT was the Ideal City, for Disney Personnel, tourists and the world, the California Institute of Arts was to be intercommunion between Old and New Imagineers. In effect, a WED nursery.

Nor was this Disney's only adaptation of his own know-how, as the young designers explain.

'People were supposed to come around and take a look ...'

'From balconies ...'

'And little parapets.'

'It would be like Disneyland. People could pay to take tours through, and see working artists ...'

'Painting ...'

A drawing does indeed exist showing a gentleman in a smock working at an easel while a little girl watches him, holding a balloon. It was not, the designers suggest, that Walt actually expected Cal Arts to pay its way. It was just the principle of the thing. Walt felt that the public had the right to take a look. The designers, anti-elitist by inclination, are quite taken with the idea.

Some of the Seven Arts themselves projected at this time arouse less enthusiasm; the animation, the ceramics, modelling and chamber music. 'They're very sophisticated in technology, and they thought they could simply take people, and train them better than they had ever been trained before.

'And it simply got out of hand.'

283

A judgment with which the animator at WED had agreed. 'We are very disappointed,' he had concluded, sombrely. 'It's gotten almost completely out of control.'

In the years immediately prior to Disney's death, work on Cal Arts continued apace. There was expert advice and assistance. The dream of the City of the Seven Arts shone as brightly as ever, but there was some change in the details. There is, for example, no estimate of tourist appeal included in CALIFORNIA INSTITUTE OF ARTS: NEED AND CONCEPT, which was commissioned by Walt from ERA. There are elements of tragic irony in that the report was presented to RETLAW on December 7, 1966, the year of Walt Disney's death.

ERA, by the way, is the Economic Research Associates, a Los Angeles-based company, which has done a good deal of work for Disney—they spent three years doing feasibility studies on the World, for instance—besides working on non-Disney, but Disneyesque, projects. These include the Magic Mountain, relatively close to Cal Arts, and a theme park under consideration near Paris, Harrison 'Buzz' Price, a bluff, but shrewd, businessman and 'frustrated musician', is president of ERA and chairman of the board of trustees of Cal Arts. RETLAW—Walter spelt backwards—is a Disney company, in fact. The brochure tells it like it might have been.

'There is nothing more powerful,' said Victor Hugo, 'than an idea whose time has come.' The California Institute of Arts is such an idea, it rumbles at one stage. In the space of a few pages there are allusions to Michelangelo, Sir Herbert Read, Joseph Conrad, George Bernard Shaw, Einstein and John D. Rockefeller 3rd.

It is an idea unique in the annals of the arts, and Cal Arts campus will be unlike any other since Aristotle's Peripatetic school in 4th Century Athens. On a beautiful 38-acre campus a half hour from the great entertainment, communications, and cultural centres of Los Angeles, Cal Arts will create, like the Peripatetic, 'a society devoted to the cult of the Muses'.

So far, so fantastic.

There is, however, one other trend to the presentation, though Aristotelian rather than Platonic. A 'prominent art donor and museum trustee' is quoted thusly.

Art is no longer the exclusive province of mugwumps in New England studios, Bohemian painters in Greenwich Village, professors of English at Ivy League universities, or scions of old families gracing the boards of civic symphonies and art museums. The great American middle class of the mid-twentieth century has arrived on the scene in full strength and ready for action.

The architect's drawings harmonise these concepts. The buildings are shown bisected. There is an art gallery, and what looks like a fashion show. There is painting in approved fashion from the nude. Elsewhere a string orchestra play in tuxedos. A costume play is being performed on a traditional proscenium stage.

A brochure called *Cal Arts Progress* likewise stems from this early period. It celebrates the grant of land to the students by a gift from Walt Disney Productions. The grant, incidentally, came hardly a moment too soon, since Cal Arts had been set up on a temporary basis in Burbank itself, cheek by jowl with the Disney studio.

Cheek by jowl is right. Students and staff meandered through Burbank in the glory of radical chic, torn-off levis, shoeless, long hair; just the sort of attire calculated to have one thrown out of Anaheim.

No doubt it was felt that a breath of country air would somehow inculcate Cal Arts with the Disney ethos. Certainly the surroundings, as shown in *Cal Arts Progress*, seem propitious. This new home is in Newhall, which lies thirty-five miles north of Los Angeles, close to the new town of Valencia. The site itself is an old Disney property, the Golden Oak Ranch, in Placerita Canyon.

It has a history. There was an insignificant gold-strike in the mid-19th century, then somewhat more paying activities in the 20th. *Since the purchase by Disney Productions, the picturesque ranch has hosted the famous Zorro galloping through the hills on his horse Tornado, Old Yeller baying across the meadows, Sancho the Homing Steer, Mr Stubbs, the chimpanzee whose antics have made millions laugh ...*

Progress heralds that campus-that-is-to-be with Disneyesque relish. Walt is seen in deep discussion with Edith Head and Nelson Riddle, distinguished alumni, respectively, of Cal Arts' two progenitors, the Chouinard Art School and the Los Angeles Conservatory of Music. Edith Head is long-time Hollywood costume designer and Riddle is Frank Sinatra's musical director. He suggests to Walt that students might enjoy coming and watching him rehearse.

Elsewhere, typical Cal Arts students are shown exploring Zorro's former demesne. One girl, demure in a two-piece suit is described as a co-ed using 'sketch pad to capture the beauty of the new campus site'. A young man with a marine hair-cut and rimless specs is doing the necessary to a violin, while a couple of others with crew-cuts and white chinos are sitting in a tree, possibly one of those Golden Oaks.

In vibrant colour, on the back, *Fashion design students pose for illustrator in clothes of their own creation.* The girls have well-coiffed hair and evening gowns.

It is the campus that never happened.

This might be described as the Golden Oaks or Zorro Dream Phase, and all boded well at the opening. The architect is Thornton Ladd, an elegant modernist who likewise built the Pasadena Art Museum, with which Cal Arts shares that luxuriant austerity appropriate to the arts. It's a goodish distance from Walt's primal vision of a Main Street wherein the Parthenon might snuggle next to the Taj, and Angkor would jostle Chartres, but no doubt better fitted to its job.

WED artists had their work on view at the opening, and the Imagineers were invited to attend, at twenty-five bucks a head. A president was acquired, one Robert Corrigan, elegant founder of the *Tulane Drama Review*, which the Disneys may, or may not, have read. Corrigan was examined by the Chouinard, and given positive vetting. Corrigan acquired Herbert Blau, fresh from a slightly unhappy experience with the Lincoln Repertory Theatre. Blau brought in Mel Powell, sometime associate of Benny Goodman, and a man of expertise in global music.

Fair seemed the breeze. The promise of the ERA brochure seemed trembling on the brink. *'One need only reflect on the intellectual and artistic climate that existed in ancient Athens and Rome, in Renaissance Florence and Elizabethan London, in turn-of-the-century Vienna and 19th and 20th Century Paris to be reminded of how profusely the sparks of creativity fly when, like crossed wires, artists of all skills and men of protean imagination are jostled together in one place.'* Or at the Imagineering Dept, Glendale, as ERA are too genteel to point out. *'It will be a primary aim at the new campus of Cal Arts to breed this kind of climate.'*

Well, the wires crossed and the sparks flew. Firstly, the *éminences grises* of the Chouinard were axed. Chucked. Cut adrift. New staff were acquired. Allan Kapprow, pioneer of the Happening. Maurice Stein, hot from Brandeis, and author of, for instance, *Blueprint for a Counter-Education*. Ravi Shankar.

At this stage, one might reflect, an alternative dream blossomed.

Cal Arts—the Experimental Playground.

'Everyone was naïve. Both sides,' says a young staff member: 'We heard there was going to be a Community of the Arts, and ... some thought that meant some kind of *commune*. Or a collection of brilliant artists. Nobody envisioned it the way the Disneys did ...'

The facilities are unparalleled. Cal Arts is theoretically not yet complete, but it is sizeable enough for its hundreds of students, and it is splendidly equipped with sophisticated dance studios, music practice rooms, movie cutting rooms, darkrooms, and so on, not to mention a wealth of video, sonic and other media hardware fit to make a student at the Royal College, London, sob into his tea.

'It is really extraordinary,' Kapprow says. 'I don't think you'll find that kind of plant and physical equipment anywhere in the world.'

What uses those media were being put to was something else again. Skin-crawling stories began to filter around Burbank. Underground movies. Naked ladies in the college magazine. Not to mention the usual Three Horsemen of the Young Apocalypse; Dope, Sex and Revolution.

Well, there is no profit in analysing the causes of an inevitable conflagration. It cannot be said that the Cal Arts faculty were invariably sensitive.

The counsel and fatherly help of the Imagineers was seldom sought. No illustrator was taken on. No animator was hired, until this created a ruction, and an animator *was* hired. Namely, Jules Engel, not a favourite down Burbank way, since he was one of the UPA artists (Mr Magoo *et al.*) who helped destroy The Disney domination of the short cartoon field back in the '50s. The school, moreover, was described not as Animation but Film Graphics.

Moviemaking did indeed begin to thrive, but it owed little to *Mary Poppins*. 'In the first year a *tremendous* number of underground pornographic movies surfaced,' recalls one of those fresh-faced Cal Arts co-eds. 'And there was an episode of silk-screening a ... *ménage à trois* sort of having at it on the walls of the buildings.

'That was a student protest, and silk-screened directly on to the walls. It was quite artistic.'

The trustees soldiered on, or some of them. There had been lengthy attempts to get Mr Elliot Handler on the Board. Mr Handler was an old crony of Walt's. He owns the Mattel toy complex which lies within easy reach of the Magic Kingdom, Anaheim.

Certainly, Mattel would seem to be an ideal choice for some sort of participation. They are perhaps best known for Barbie, eleven and a half inches of nubile blonde dollhood, with her extensive wardrobe, and perfection of bosom, calf and thigh. (Better-than-perfection. Unlike Baby Tender Love, another Mattel creation, Barbie does not wet.) Where Mattel have been given insufficient recognition is for their developing technique. Nowadays Barbie has such live-action accessories as a dressing room which *'allows a child to actually plug in action accessories—a two-way lighted vanity mirror and working hair dryer'*.

Nor it this all. Consider the Rock Flowers, Lilac, the brunette, Rosemary, the darlingest black, and Heather, who is blonde and looks like a teensy Gloria Steinem. Each Rock Flower fits on to her own hit record—*'Spin the record 'n' watch her twirl. Far out fashion fun with a new dimension—*

288

music!' It isn't quite Lincoln, but Mattel are plainly on their way. And, in view of their recent merger with Ringling Bros. —Barnum & Bailey Combined Shows, Inc. not just post-pubescent-dollwise. Mr Handler would obviously have been something of an addition to the Board of Cal Arts trustees.

Anyway, Handler arrived on campus one day, and was obviously completely freaked.

'They were looking like, you know, students do,' says one of the professors, fondly. Not Elliot Handler's favourite look. (For an insight into this, examine Barbie's boy-friend, Ken who has the clean appeal of a surfer turned insurance exec.)

Mr Handler aparently went as far towards a compromise as anybody could reasonably expect, suggesting that the design group have a 'project' re-decorating some wrought-iron play equipment, which was among the assets of a company that Mattel had acquired.

The Design Group didn't quite get enthused about the prospect, but said how about they set up a Research Unit on children's playthings?

Elliot Handler left. 'He seemed a bit offended,' the professor says mildly.

The crucial point here is one that bothered most of the trustees. They couldn't see any *practical use* for what the school was doing. There were 'very, very hairy meetings' between the trustees and the staff. The trustees did include a few mediators. Like Jerry Wexler, from Atlantic. But it was Disney money, and it was the Disneys who counted. 'Bank-roll is clout. All the rest is bullshit,' remarks another of the Cal Arts faculty members.

Already it was being felt that if Walt could return, he would close the place down in five minutes flat, but graver matters were impending.

There was the great Anarchist experiment, for one. This was pioneered by Maurice Stein, who desired to start a Total Anarchist school. The deal was that he would resign the dean-ship, and everything would be decided by communal consent. This might be seen as an extension, or perhaps ironical coun-terpoint, to Disney with that incessant, mandatory first-nam-ing, but in fact Disney didn't like the idea at all.

No.

Money began to play a not inconsiderable part in the increasing resentment. The annual Cal Arts deficit is something like $1.2 millions, and costs appeared to be rampaging. The Modular Theatre cost $1,600,000 of itself. This was a brainchild of Blau, and a notable theatre designer, Jules Fisher. The Modular Theatre is a neutral grey space, gridded all over. It is a bit like being in the core of a four-dimensional crossword puzzle, a similarity heightened by the fact that just about each square rises, lowers or disappears, or something.

The floor-squares rise hydraulically, for instance, except not during performance they don't. Fire regulations invoked after the theatre had been built insist that they remain as boringly *in situ* as, say, the backcloths of the Old Vic, if not more so. Oh, well.

Much as the Disneys hate to see good money disappear, other developments proved yet more harassing. There was the occasion on which a faculty member removed all clothing during a meeting with the trustees, conventional enough behaviour, banal even, on any other campus, but rather too exotic for the Disneys.

Symbols lurked. The iceberg that had been awaiting the *Titanic* turned out to be an attempt to install Herbert Marcuse as a professor. *Herbert Marcuse.* Surprisingly, the *eminence grise* even got so far as a visit to the campus. 'He was such a ... nice, warm old man,' says another faculty member, recording also that Marcuse would keep referring back to Picasso, say, and Matisse. The Old Masters. Revolutionary stuff.

The Disneys knew little of Marcuse, but what they did know was quite, quite enough. It is doubtful if it included niceness or warmth. That was the *casus belli*. The last goddam straw.

'The guy who tried to bring him in was a tough revolutionary from Brandeis,' says Buss Sawyer, with resignation rather than rage. 'And Brandeis is very liberal *anyway*!

'And he wanted to bring in Marcuse, and a bunch of people like that, and lead the world in telling where the revolution's going, and how does it relate to art! Well, Christ Almighty, this was not our bag!'

On another occasion he put it more practically. 'As long as eighty-five per cent of the money in this place is Disney money, the family will feel free to discuss the school's future with anybody it chooses.'

Allen Kapprow concurs.

'Mr Disney is quite right in saying that if they wish to have a say in the operating of the institution, they'd better kick in as many millions as he does. It's plain, simple business. Why should he pay for something he doesn't like? In fact, it's *ethics*.'

The Disneys not only didn't like it. Almost immediately they tried to sell it, attempting, with some secrecy, to unload their wild white elephant, firstly on the University of Southern California, secondly on the Pepperdine College. Neither of these places of learning liked the look of those deficits.

Disney moved. Stein, the Brandeis revolutionary, had already been fired by Blau. Now Blau, too, resigned. Corrigan remains, until the expiry of his contract a couple of years from now. Disney watcheth, and all, as I write, is peace.

The question, of course, is—How could Cal Arts ever have worked? Even ignoring such extras as the Marcuse episode, a modern California campus is not a place where the Disney Ethos is accorded the same respect that it is elsewhere. I paid a visit to Cal Arts in the wake of the storm, but even now there is minimal Disney iconography to be seen. The bookstore dispenses the habitual campus fare of paperback classics, *Malcolm X Speaks*, Hobbitry, *The Psychedelic Review*, and all manner of brainstretchers dealing with upcoming crises in Ecology, Narcosis, and Femlib; but Mickey Mouse? Forget it, unless you can count some Moscoso fancies in *Zap*.

Scrutinise the courses. 'There is, you know, complete cross-discipline,' says Don Levy, a teacher with the film school, himself a physicist and director of such films as the enigmatic *Herostratus*. The cross-discipline is a Disney concept in its way, and based on the infinite adaptability of the Imagineers. At Cal Arts it would rather mean that a student could glide from Chinese Sutra Meditation to Subotnick's course in Advanced Electronic Music and then, maybe, across to Levy on film.

'The students that I've got are mostly into very experimental parts of cinema,' Don Levy says: 'Since I'm into multimedia, and bio-synthesis, and so on.'

Kapprow's class is called 'Happenings as Programmed Activity'.

'We did one recently called "Calendar" in which my class —which is a class in this kind of thing, which is somewhere all over, and yet not specified as art ...

'We came to a part of the valley near the school, it's a very lovely area, grassy, and quite wild. We brought with us, let's see, eighteen pieces of green sod, squares of *green turf,* and eighteen pieces of square *dry* turf ... they were multiples of six. We tripled the six ...

'And first they tried to find an area where they could plant the green sod so it was *invisible.*

'And then we found a place where it was a little drier, and planted the green sod there ...' And so on, and so, Kapprow and his group moved through the valley with colour-sharpened eyes planting their sods in progressively drier areas. Until?

'Until the sixth move, when the contrast was maximum ... very dry, with this square of green ...'

At which point, Kapprow explains, it was 'as if the Season had started to change', and they began to move in reverse with the dry sods. Not retracing their steps, necessarily.

'It was done by mutual decision. As long as the parameters of the main were followed. And there were sometimes disagreements,' Kapprow records, with relish. An entirely satisfactory event, in fact, though I don't know what Bambi would have made of it. Or Burbank.

There is much respect for Disney at Cal Arts. For the expertise manifested by a drawing spotted by one designer, which had 'a gazebo-type affair, and it had an inscription: *Build so as to fall apart as if hit by a truck!'* The designer marvels. 'That's all they had to write. There's somebody there who can just figure that out!' Such a person is evidently not to be found in Valencia.

292

The Walt Disney mind also comes in for approval.

'If Disney failed as a *business*, people could really start thinking what it was all about.' As they do about the conventional *avant-garde*, in fact. 'But because it's a smash hit nobody bothers!

'I suspect that at some point there was an extraordinary and rather dangerous level of fantasy in Walt Disney ... which he managed in a miraculous fashion to smooth over into acceptable archetypes. If you look at some of the earlier works, the fantasy that emerges is less the placid ... rapacious beasts, pianos gobbling up fingers ... incredible ... *I think that's a part of Disney that could have been tapped.*'

Maybe, maybe, but it is there for the tapping no longer, and an autumnal pessimism lingers over Cal Arts. The members of the faculty (some of them) seem to feel that Disney was so accustomed to artists with a low level of ego-gratification, that it will never really be at home with more egocentric creatures.

'The good people will slowly leave,' they suggest. It will become precisely the conventional liberal arts college that it was specificially not to be. Or the Disney courses will be introduced as originally programmed, Animation, and Ceramics, and Fashion Design. Cal Arts will, in fact, become a truly Disney University as in Walt's dream. Could one imagine such a thing?

'Yes. You can. (Firmly)

'In *Southern California* you can ...' adds another designer.

Harrison 'Buzz' Price, chairman of the trustees, is more encouraging. He is a forthright man, and competent. On the wall there is a painting of his son composed, no doubt illegally, of the American flag.

'Disney was a fundamentalist, but he was also an innovator,' Price says. True, there is little visible Disney diffusion up at Cal Arts. 'But I think we'll get to it. It'll have to be worked on. And the people that have a career involvement in Walt Disney will have to become active out there. Either in a teaching way or some participation. And that's understood ...'

He talks, with a touch of grimness, about re-structuring.

'From a practical point of view, forces that are imbued with what Walter wanted to do'—Price is the only man I have ever met who refers to Disney as Walter—'do control ... They do control,' he repeats.

In the Disneyland Hotel, I talk to Tommy Walker. The Disneyland Hotel stands only a few hundred yards from the Park. It is, however, owned not by Disney but by Jack Wrather, and it was because of such alien operations siphoning off so much of the green stuff around the Magic Kingdom that Walt Disney was moved to acquire such a wide terrain in Florida, and used to fly hither and thither under an assumed name, leaving the aircraft as little as possible.

Tommy Walker (whose Texaco entertainment we have seen) is former director of entertainments for Walt Disney. It was Tommy who produced the Mickey Mouse Club shows, and it was Tommy who initiated one important advance by bringing Mickey Mouse to life.

'They were Walt's characters,' Tommy says, 'but it was my idea to have them walking around in costume ...'

Tommy Walker is a little concerned. He has no doubts about the viability of the Florida World but Disney will miss (he feels) the flair and guiding hand of Walt. 'Walt would oversee every little thing ... right down to the story-boards.'

Without this overall control? He purses his lips.

Nor is there an absence of speculation around WED itself. And most of the doubts centre on EPCOT.

Even with Walt in charge of realising his dream, it would have taken ... 'oh, years and years and years'.

With Walt Disney gone, some feel, it may well take forever.

The Walt Disney World vice-president with one of the most specific EPCOT responsibilities is Major-General William Potter. Potter is compact, with wavy grey hair, a deep tan, and the air of preternatural gusto that distinguishes some politicians. He is, as a matter of fact, a sometime governor of the Panama Canal zone. He is an engineer and first got close to Walt while helping run the New York World's Fair.

I meet him in his Florida office, which is as compact as the

294

General, and hung with a battle-array of Preliminary Master Plans. He is checking a talk he is giving about EPCOT with one of the public relations staff whose job it is—Potter says in an aside—to prevent him from actually saying anything much.

'This is just notes. Take a look. That's going to be the ... gravamen of my approach.'

The PRO reads. He seems well content.

'It's innocuous in other words,' Potter says to us both, jovially, then settles down, and begins to discuss the philosophy and the coming about of EPCOT.

'Walt was not interested in building a new Disneyland. He wasn't! He'd done it. He was not a repeater. His whole concept revolved around EPCOT ...

'The amusement area he just drew a circle around! He worked on scrim—you know what I mean, tissue paper—made sketches, and the architect knew what he was doing, and put them in the plans.

'And when Walt died, we had the one way over to the left'—the General indicates a sizeable chart—'That's the Seventh Preliminary Master Plan, and that's what we're doing. Right in the middle of it, that's EPCOT ... that spidery-looking affair.'

Why did he just draw a circle around the Magic Kingdom?

'That his people *knew* how to do,' the General says, just a bit dismissively. 'He had all the expertise in the world for building that sort of thing ...'

EPCOT was to be fashioned to a new and more grandiose vision.

'The thing that was in Walt's mind was the fact that our cities are developed by entrepreneurs. And the cities once had a governable size, and the people *knew* each other. Even in New York at one time or another.'

No more, no more. The General goes into a passionate analysis of urban wrongdoing, right down to the lack of cultural facilities in the San Fernando Valley.

'Now Walt's whole feeling about life was that the family was the thing that made America great, and in England, in France, the family *as an entity*. And the way we developed caused the family to disperse ... because we don't have any city law, national law, or anything like that to control the standards of development, we divide the family ...'

Hence EPCOT.

'Walt philosophised that EPCOT could be a ... core community. That in its core—and the core is about fifty acres—there would not only be the shops, and the big hotel, but there would be the theatre, and all these things handy, and connected by easy transportation. They would be exciting to use, rather than dull and dirty.

'And he visualised that there be a size to this thing, just off the top of his head, a hundred thousand people, which is a self-governable thing. You would know people in that area!

'The one that we plan'—another forceful jab towards the chartage—'would have a size maybe of twenty thousand people, but with a core for a hundred thousand people. And the other eighty would be tourists.'

He pauses, evidently lost in what must, by now, be a fairly familiar dream. 'And when the city got to be a hundred thousand then we go to the English law which says—That's all the bigger it gets! Now a city depends on industry and, of course, the industry we wanted here'—There are occasional slides into the past tense in discussions of EPCOT which I find disconcerting—'would be sophisticated industries. Like computer centres, research laboratories, sophisticated production of little black boxes, and all that sort of stuff ...

'That's our legacy! That drawing over there,' says General Potter, devoutly. 'Now we've got five years of developing that amusement area. And all the time we're doing that, we're doing our EPCOT research.

'EPCOT doesn't depend on just building a town. Anybody can build a town. It's the philosophy Walt had of ... utilising new systems, materials, things, programmes, and all that. Which are in the back rooms of the research laboratories of our big industries ...

'And after about six months Walt said: You get on your horse and go around the country. And I visited a hundred industries, all the way from food-packing industries to ... oh, almost all of them that would have a research capacity.' He particularises: 'IBM ... AT & T ... US Steel ... Dupont ...

Bell Laboratories ... Honeywell ... Allied Chemical ...

'When I first started out, I said, Walt, how am I going to get in? And he said—Tell them I sent you! And I wrote to all these industries saying what we were going to do, and I would like to come and talk to them, to see what the hell they ... and I never got turned down once ...'

The General describes visits to (unnamed) super secret labs, the signing of secrecy oaths. Everywhere the wand of Tinkerbell waved, and the door opened. The Disney name relates to 'a certain kind of activity ... a clean activity, a family activity'. In the corporate world, a Disney association is the Good Fairy Seal of Approval.

The brainstorming has borne a fruity harvest.

The General tosses around with facility concepts like the Cashless Society, apparently on the Disney agenda just as soon as the accountants can get it figured out. There is, also, AVAC.

I had, coincidentally, just studied a brochure on AVAC. With some interest since it seemed to relate straight back to Walt's original inspired perception on the Bel Air road.

GIANT VACUUM WILL HELP KEEP THE MAGIC IN THE MAGIC KINGDOM, read the panegyric for a garbage disposal system, which was discovered by Disney in Sweden, and which was developed in the States under licence by the Envirogenics Company, a division of Aerojet-General.

'We worked with them, and we are spending three-quarters of a million dollars on the thing,' says General Potter, with offhand pride. Essentially, the system works thus. There will be fifteen AVAC stations. The solid wastes will be vacuum-sucked down acoustically insulated pipes to a central station, where they will be compacted, and taken off for incineration. The system is already working full blast in the Contemporary Hotel. The garbage moves silently, underground, at sixty-five miles per hour. There is no earthly reason why one should be confronted with the disagreeable stuff ever again.

And then again, there is the linear motor.

'In England you have a very fine research programme on a linear motor. We found a firm here that has a patent on a linear motor, and we are doing a big prototype on it. Eventually it will be here. It will be the first installation in the world ...

'You can go a thousand miles with a linear motor, and more. And you can *compute* it. You get into a car, and nobody has to pay any attention. You push a button if you want to go off at the next interchange, and the computer puts you off at the next interchange.'

And one final area ripe for technological breakthroughs will be the actual construction of EPCOT. Amongst the other quasi-feudal privileges that Disney extracted from Florida was the power to implement their own building-codes. 'We are the only private company that has that,' says the General, maniloquently. We spent a quarter of a million dollars on a set of Blue Books back there that's the most advanced building code in the country!'

Building codes are those statutes relating to the safety of buildings, permissible materials, and so on. They tend to be enforced by bureaucratic, not to say downright unhelpful, officials. 'Their tendency is to turn things down. But we'll say —Okay! Now you can't use this in a big building, but you can use it in a small building over here ...

'Building codes are developed by two classes of people—labour unions and politicians. Now there's no city in Florida that permits modularised room construction. The labour union doesn't like that because you're turning something out of a factory instead of employing people on the site.

'But in a factory, you can watch every guy. You've got a long assembly line. It's just like producing automobiles ...'

Disney's concern for spreading the pixie-dust has always rather bleakly excluded the labour unions. It should come as no surprise that the Disney hotel rooms rolled off a 'unique assembly line' designed by a gleeful US Steel.

Nor is this all. Modes of education have also been explored by the Imagineers in concert, apparently, with a high-ranking fellow from the Ford Foundation. Two factors have been taken into account.

'Little Johnny', firstly. Little Johnny, General Potter instances, is good in mathematics, moderate in history, average in English. And so on.

298

Secondly, there are all those ill-timed vacations. 'It's habitual for factories to take vacations when the kids are out of school. That may be just exactly the time when that factory is getting its biggest number of orders!

'February and March is when factories get the fewest orders, so that maybe should be the time that people should go on vacation. But they can't do it, because Little Johnny's in school.

'Under the new system the factory would say everybody should go on vacation in February and March—half each month,' the General explains, briskly. 'Little Johnny gets a computer card from his school—which says he's here, here, here, here—and he comes down here to Disney World for three weeks to a month, and he goes into our school.

'And when he goes into mathematics, he's with people that have the same reading in mathematics. When he's done—he takes the computer card back home!'

General Potter beams at the simplicity of it all, but then broods a bit over the difficulty of transforming *mores*, keeping people at large up with the Disney system.

'Mom and Poppa have gotta get used to it,' he says.

I take a final look at the drawings of EPCOT. The starfish spread of it all, the slim immaculate tower, somewhat like a jumbo air-terminal.

'Other people in the United States might demand the same quality of life that we have here,' the General says, seriously: 'They'll say—Why can't *you* do it the way that Walt did?'

Is there not, I ask tentatively, the possibility that EPCOT might be altogether too futurised, computerised, er, *modern*?

The General and the public-relations man look at each other, and break into positively pantomime grimaces.

'Oh my God, no! It's based on—*family*,' says the PR man.

'You're going to have some of the same Disney *façades*,' General Potter emphasises, making brisk salami-slicing gestures in the EPCOT direction. 'Walt visualised a ... Swiss section ... a German section ... a Chinese section! I mean with *façades*. *Fun!*'

* * *

Interlude: Journey into Space, and Back.
*... vast megalithic cities of the elder world, around whose
dark towers and labyrinthine nether vaults lingers an aura of
pre-human fear and necromancy ...*

H. P. Lovecraft

It seems entirely appropriate that I am driven to NASA-land
and the Cape from the Walt Disney World. It is a flat scrub-
land, but with an arid beauty. We pass the Gulf Oil ranch,
and Martin Marietta, the aerospace firm who are building the
Disney monorail system though, of course, to the Imagineer's
specifications. 'They are also involved with the Cape. They
worked on the Titan series. They are *very* versatile,' Anita
Rettig says. Anita Rettig is now importantly concerned with
promotions at the World, but used to handle public relations
around Cocoa Beach which is hard by the Cape and became a
boom town, a gimcrack Vegas, while the Space Programme
was at its splendid zenith.

She explains how her own translation came about. 'We had
a Moonwalk Festival every year,' she explains. 'It went about
three-and-a-half miles ... through Cocoa Beach and Cape
Canaveral. It commemorates the first man to walk on the
moon, the Apollo Eleven launch.

'This was the second annual Moonwalk Festival, and we had
a big parade, and so they called me and asked if I could get
Mickey Mouse.

'So I inquired, and we got Mickey,' Anita Rettig says, joyously. She is blonde, attractive, in her early thirties, and is
sounding near-mystical.

'I had the pleasure of riding with him, and our Walt Disney
World ambassador in the parade. And as we were coming
down A1A, little old ladies were saying—Oh! There's Mickey
Mouse! And the kids were saying'—she is mimicking the various accents perfectly—'Mummy! There's Mickey! ... And
the hippies were saying—Hi! Mickey Baby!

'But there was a thing ... inside me I will never forget.
The *faces* of all those people ... all different walks of life, all
different backgrounds, all different philosophies ... some with
a lot, some with none. But all identifying with a *mouse*.

'You know, that's an incredible thing to watch ... and this word "Mickey Mouse"!

'And we had Mrs Deavis, who was Dr Deavis's wife, the director of the Space Centre, sitting in the VIP stands, and we had seven or eight ambassadors here watching the parade, and all in foreign languages saying, you know—Mickey ... Mickey Mouse!

'You know that's an incredible thing to watch. And this word "Mickey Mouse"! They were in a parade with *the astronauts* and yet Mickey Mouse was the thing I heard more than —There's Ed Mitchell! Or there's Jim Lovell! It was just a fantastic thing, and that was *my first real connection.*' Anita Rettig's voice sinks to near-hoarseness. There are some experiences almost too deep for words. Then she speaks out, ardently. '*And that's what the pixie-dust is all about!*' she says.

Later experiences in this same day merely rubbed the dust in. There was, for instance, the astronaut luncheon.

'It was at George's Restaurant down here in Cape Canaveral. That was during the Apollo Fifteen Launch ... There were twelve of us, and, you know, people were very excited about the Moonwalk, and the whole thing. And it was Mickey Mouse in the parade that did it!

'There were most of the local chamber people, and the Mayor and so forth. And the astronauts, and we had Jim Lovell's wife, and his five-year-old little boy.

'Everyone was seated, and we kept Mickey in the backroom, and brought him out ... and he did the little soft-shoe shuffle and he did the thing with his hands that he does. Of course, he doesn't talk, but his hands said—I love you and Hello!

'And I cried! I'm thirty years old, but it was that kind of thing ...' And the astronauts? 'They were just delighted. They were—*just delighted.* He shook hands with them both, and they said, Are you going to eat lunch? And he shook his head No, and they said, Are you going to have a bite of cheese? And he sniffed ... He's just, you know, *precious.*

'That's what he is,' Anita, says with a note of discovery: 'He's precious. And no one in this world will ever want to misuse him. And that's why you will find

Disney being so very, very cautious about that logo.'

As to the Space Programme itself, it is catastrophically low on pixie-dust. Conversations among the *cognoscenti* rumble bitterly with cut-back. Physicists driving cabs, and aerospace-engineers applying to run the rides at the Disney World. Even the astronauts, maybe especially the astronauts, are not un-affected.

'Some of them hope to get jobs on Skylab, but after Seventeen no one will go to the moon again,' surmises Anita: 'The next thing is Mars ...

'Several of them are leaving the programme. It's a criminal waste.' She speaks with the tetchy passion of a Cheshire colonel deploring the disappearance of a further regiment of Hussars. 'You know, the Space Programme hasn't been sold so that your average folk, Little America, can identify with it ...

'When NASA sends out Press releases they tell you how many pounds of fuel, how much steel, all the technical things, which you and I and most people don't understand ... and the scientists are very excited, and they can't understand why we don't know what they are talking about!

'And yet *Walt Disney* has seen things through the eyes of the Space Programme. Things like Teflon saucepans, and telephones that have a television set so you can see who you are talking to ... Many things that were invented because of the Space Programme, and have never been related to the average household.

'Walt Disney took them. Walt Disney took modern tech-nology, and ... humanised it for Little America better than anybody I've ever heard of.

'There are *great parallels* between the Walt Disney World and the Space Programme. EPCOT with its ecology, and its sanitation programme, and its controlled environment. The controlled environment is because of the Space Programme!'

Anita Rettig runs through some of the other revolutionary uses to which Disney have put the new technology, the modular construction of the Contemporary Hotel and so forth, but the important comparison between the Space Pro-gramme and the burgeoning of Disney is (she stresses) a more mystical one.

'I think of the excitement, and I compare it to a launch so many times. The launching of the sociological philosophy of Walt Disney, and the launching of the ... *intangible* things that the programme brings. The closeness of the world, the people.

'For instance, during the trouble of Apollo Thirteen, the whole world prayed for this one man, and it became a—oneness, a *feeling*. And I think that Walt Disney has a feeling like this. Of a cleanliness, a wholesomeness, and the American way. But'—she concludes, sombrely—'I don't think the Space Programme has as much to offer.

'Maybe. Maybe if there had been a little bit of ... Mickey Mouse on one of the rockets, that everybody could identify with. And a Disney programme about—how the satellites can now tell us whether there is a crop failure in one area, or whether the beetles have taken over the wheat ...

'I think perhaps that had we had a Walt Disney the Space Programme would never have been cut back.'

Maybe, indeed, but a cut-back there has been. Cocoa Beach has a sad, ramshackle air nowadays. Bars have gaudy celestial motifs that somehow seem less related to the pure cold passions of science than to the imagery on an occultist's stall in a run-down carnival. There is Rock-and-Roll in the Satellite Motel, barbecue at the Polaris and a swimming-pool in the Sea Missile Motel.

I am studying at the Ramada Inn. There is a stall selling the equivalent of pilgrims' brooches. Medallions of *high-relief silver plated bronze in custom plastic holders* to celebrate Apollo flights 7 to 14 depict the respective modules and astronauts. Likewise Tie Bars, Tie Tacs, rhodium-plated Charm Bracelets, Brooches, Necklaces. (*Truly a memorable space age token of esteem.*)

In the restaurant a singer in a suit, white tie and authentic Beatles cut, Moptop period, is singing *Yesterday*. There is no sign of the morose and short-haired engineers who create reasonable hell in Cocoa Beach as the launches approach, but bring good business. One astronaut, Commander King, is drinking alone, quietly at the bar.

Next day I go out to the Space Centre. My credentials are

checked briskly and politely. It's a piece of cake compared with effecting entrance to most corporations, but then it was fixed up by Disney.

My guide is a NASA Press man. He is verging on middle age, and soft-spoken. We pass through the lobby, and into the main Vehicle Assembly Building which is huge beyond expectations, even with the foreknowledge that it is the third biggest building in the world. It is also oddly desolate. Hard-hatted personnel get in and out of lifts occasionally muttering at each other with a brusqueness which suggests pressure of work less than introspection. From the top, we can see the segments of rockets, bigger than church-towers, but scaled down to the size of Lady chapels.

Through the computer rooms. Control, familiar from TV and the movies, those creamy chambers where during a launch the scientists will be ranged at their instrumented dashboards like kids at schoolroom desks. The Mission Control audio-animatronic mock-up being built for the Disney World is, I feel after a look around, a very fair stab at the unearthly feel of things. Except the Disney version will, of course, be working non-stop while most of the terminals at the Cape are not in use right now, and are draped with translucent covers, like furniture during spring-cleaning or a recent corpse.

On my way back to the airport, we stop, and he shows me an item of iconography from happier days in NASA-land, the announcement of the birth of a son in 1969, some weeks after Astronauts Armstrong and Aldrin became the first men on the moon, and walked the Sea of Tranquillity.

The son is referred to as an Astronaut. His payload statistics are given, and likewise the launch team. On the cover there is that greatest of lunar photographs, in which the module is reflected in the visor of an oncoming space-suit.

'Already, he points to rockets,' the NASA man says: 'He can walk outside and see an unmanned launch as routinely as another youngster might see a sporting event.

'Skylab is scheduled for 1980 ... Mars is just around the corner. Maybe, the '90s ... My boy is truly a child of the Space Age.'

The Space Age? My guide speaks of the cut-backs in a

gentle sing-song, but with the in-the-bone despondency of a farmer discussing a searing drought. 'It isn't the American Way. The government condones it,' he says.

He has himself taken a massive pay cut to remain at the Cape, and anyway he can always return to teaching or, maybe, freelance writing.

'But I'm lucky compared to some. A technician who might have specialised in ... launch-pad equipment. Just that,' he hypothesises.

Well, there are always the rides at the Walt Disney World. And there is always the Experimental Prototype Community of Tomorrow.

Phantasy abandoned by reason produces monsters: united with reason she is the mother of the arts and the source of their marvels.

GOYA

Some of the most precisely developed diagrams and models of EPCOT are in Marvin Davis's offices in the Imagineering Department, still a continent's width away. They share space with exhaustive documentation. Studies on Economic Feasibility, bulky works dealing with water resources, folders on transportation and mental health facilities, back-numbers of the *Architectural Record* and *Progressive Architecture* analysing such non-Tinkerbell notions as 'Life Support Systems for a Dying Planet'.

Marvin Davis has the fine, austere look of a rather old-fashioned diplomat. He graduated in architecture, at the University of Southern California, becoming an art director in the movies. He helped, for example, in the building of Atlanta for *Gone With The Wind*.

Then Disney. Marvin—'Marv'—Davis was one of the first two people recruited to work on Disneyland. His first project was the master plan, for which he made 160 separate groupings. Now EPCOT and the Walt Disney World.

Right now, Marv Davis is into plans for a new ride. A simulated diving-bell. 'This would probably be within the

305

next five years ... We have to think five years or so ahead.

'People would supposedly go into this diving-bell. And the people on shore'—these are the shores of Disney-bottomed Bay Lake—'would see this diving bell submerge. And they would think that these people are going down in our lake ...

'Actually, by a devious method we herd them into a theatre ... a circlevision theatre, and we would open up the screen, and they would see bubbles going by, and then you would go into an undersea show, shot with a 360-degree camera.

'The inspiration for this was seeing some of those Jacques Cousteau shows, where he's had these gorgeous underwater things. Coral gardens, and stuff like that.'

It is Commander Cousteau's gloomy view, by the way, that all those gorgeous underwater things are likely to be extinct in twenty years unless marine pollution is dramatically checked. It certainly seems on the cards that one of the last available ways of enjoying the life of the depths will be in the Disney diving-bell.

Marv Davis takes me next door. 'This is the room in which most of the master planning was done.' It is War-Room style, with an urgent display of maps, blueprints, aerial photographs and projection screens, and I find it obscurely troubling, until I recognise the sense of *déjà vu*. Isn't this the self-same setting in which Walt stands in that much-viewed film where he waxes visionary about the World and EPCOT? Yes, indeed. Except that, apparently, it proved impractical to shoot here so a mock-up was erected over the studio.

Back to Marv Davis's own office, and to EPCOT. With General Potter in charge of the practicalities, the MAPO side of things in a sense. Marv Davis is effectively EPCOTs leading Imagineer.

Despite its polished futurismo, he says, EPCOT will be as human as anything that Disney has done. 'Let me show you,' Davis says, gathering together some transparencies and charts. These are more complex and detailed than anything I have yet seen. The flat plan is radial, with spokes springing out from the centre, and connected by ringways, rippling out from the centre to the circumference. It looks like a section of geometrically grained tree.

Apart from the main road and Monorail track which neatly bisects the circle, the spokes are WED-ways, which is to say moving pedestrian walkways. This Master Plan owes everything to Walt Disney himself.

'We would be sitting around. And conversation would be a matter of everybody contributing what they could think of ...'

'And then Walt would often take the drawings that I had done, and work them over—*literally*, with these little drawings he would do—For instance, he came in one morning with this circulation of traffic worked out on a paper napkin ...'

Marv pauses, almost in reverie, then points at the outer ring.

'This is all residential. The houses are all set on the green where there are no automobiles. Just carts, and bicycles, and strolling, and things ...' He indicates four figure-of-eight layouts, girdled with greenery, that break up the residential massif. 'That would be the golf-courses, and playgrounds, and pools. The road is on the outside. You see, you can't get away from the automobile yet. But there wouldn't be any where the houses are *facing*.'

Between the residential area and the centre lies the Green Belt—'and in the Green Belt would be the churches and schools'—and so, inexorably, into the centre itself, neatly marked on the dream diagram as AIR CONDITIONED COMMERCIAL CENTRE. This maintains the radial pattern. The 3-D models show flattish outskirts and a fluted skyscraper dominating the whole of EPCOT with a touch of Flash Gordon bravura, but more functional. It bears, in fact, a disconcerting resemblance to the London Hilton, but topped with a needle spire, like an aerial sting.

The outermost ring of the centre would be devoted, largely, to the needs of the residents. Dentists and doctors, Davis instances, theatres and office-buildings, with high-density apartment buildings facing out on to the green.

The central structure is designed to be thirty-five stories high, with a lobby soaring up for eighteen floors, internally, in a lower tower, and the ground floor being a sort of trans-

307

portation nexus, just as in the Contemporary Hotel, but more so.

'The proposal first was just to build this as one of the original hotels. Then later on we'd be building the balance of it ...'

But the heart of EPCOT is probably that inner circle which lies between the Transportation Lobby and the business district. These are the International Shopping and Dining Arcades, and they are to be a spectacular development of Mainstream-Disney, a rich injection of fantasy to pump life into this whole clockwork Utopia.

'Branching out from there,' says Marv Davis, jabbing a finger dead centre, 'would be these radiating ... international shopping areas, in which we would have a block—and these would literally be a city block. I believe about fifteen hundred feet across—Italian buildings, English buildings ... Spanish ... Chinese ...

'In other words, the décor, the food, the costumes, would all be relative to the country of which you are trying to display the merchandise.

'And this would become the *intimate part* here. Because the structure is designed to be a fifty-foot high enclosure—*roofed-in*, and lit by radiating panels in the ceiling. So you have a total, over-all glow ... and we could control the lights.

'We can make it go from night to day, and—you see, in this height, you can actually build *streets*, and get the intimate ... personal and human qualities ...'

Would the streets be life-size?

'Yes. Life-size,' Davis says. 'It would be comparable to Main Street.'

These plans are, of course, by no means definitive. 'It will take at least six years before we get to a stage that will be approaching the final solution,' Davis says, and the EPCOT team will more or less parallel the one that created the Disney World, although involving the Imagineers in certain new disciplines. Sociology, for one.

'Walt had great hopes of using this community as a model form for treating the Teenage Problem: And his idea was to devise a system by which youths would judge their peers

... monitoring their own behaviour.'

Disney-trained youth shows a real capacity for this, it seems, and the wide powers granted to the Walt Disney World are perfectly geared to this sort of experimentation. A point well taken by the Governor of Florida on one visit. 'The governor was saying we have everything but the name of who the king is going to be!' Marv Davis says, with a booming laugh.

These powers are essential. Consider, for instance, the length of time it normally takes for technic improvements to reach the consumer.

'What these labs are working on is at least five years away from the public. Because once they've perfected anything in Research & Development, then they've got to market-test it, and run it through all forms of ... experiments and tests to see that it's all right, with a lapse of five years probably between the time it was created and when the public gets it.

'Walt wanted to eliminate that, and actually take it right off the Research & Development boards, and put it into EPCOT ... and let people that are *living* there be the ones that are market-testing it right there ...'

This is, of course, the twenty thousand EPCOT residents?

'That's the nucleus, yes. A comfortable living area for twenty thousand people ...'

Employees?

Marvin Davis nods assent, vigorously. 'Employees of the World. It is supposed to be a *working* community. And Walt's thought was that in order to maintain the—original philosophy of keeping this an experimental prototype, it would have to be something that was pretty much controlled by the company.

'In order to do that, if you have a boarding community there ... This is something we never really discuss very much publicly ... In order to have the control that is necessary there, you would just about eliminate the possibility of having a *voting* community.

'Because the minute they start voting, then you lose control, and that's the end of the possibility of experimental development!'

'Because if we wanted, for instance, to change a whole

block. And maybe General Electric, or Westinghouse, would come in and—completely refurbish all these houses with a particular environment or advanced way of living. *Then we've got to be able to do that!*

'And as long as it is all leased out, no property sold to anybody, then that control can be maintained. And that's the only way you can do it. *Walt knew!*' Davis adds, with a spurt of intensity: 'He planned for this to be a prototype ...'

A prototype for other communities presumably?

'Yes, that was the thought. He would experiment with all the advanced ... comforts of life, and new creative ideas in making life more pleasant in every way.

'And then passing this on to the world!' Marvin Davis pauses, and delicately begins to collect up the EPCOT papers. 'Whoever wants to take advantage of it,' he says.

*　　*　　*

Walt Disney is dead, but Walt Disney's World lives on. Inevitably, even Walt Disney's death has became metamorphosed into fantasy. There is the recurrent rumour that Disney, a late enthusiast for the science of cryogenics, now rests tranquilly in a container of liquid nitrogen at a temperature of 196°C. And when one considers both Disney's morose distaste for death and his lifelong passion for making over new technologies to his own uses, well, the rumour assumes at least a poetic justice.

If that should be so then Walt is not dead, but sleepeth. Like King Arthur, he will return when his Kingdom needs him; though I would think that the British monarch's failure to stir at the Disney version of *The Sword in the Stone* might lose him some credibility on this score.

Anyway, no disaster appears to threaten the Disney Imperium. There are those who wonder whether the magic can survive the merchandising, but the Disney path is strewn with sceptics, and Mickey marches on. The skies are technicolour in the Disney World, and everywhere it's smiles, smiles. Business is a dream. And, of course, vice versa. Everything, but everything, is under control.